The Birth of Dionysia

THE BIRTH OF DIONYSIA

Out of the New Dithyramb

by

James Chester

James Chester Publishing

Published in the United States by James Chester Publishing, Boston Massachusetts
All inquiries may be made at https://www.JamesChester.org

Library of Congress Control Number: 2020915920

Front cover image by Gerard Dou, Astronomer by Candlelight c. 1665. Digital image courtesy of the Getty's Open Content Program. Book design by James Chester.

ISBN: 978-1-7350167-2-6 (Paperback)

Second edition September 2020

Printed in the United States of America

FOR THE COLLEGE STUDENT

"The gates of hell are open night and day; Smooth the descent, and easy is the way: But to return, and view the cheerful skies, In this the task and mighty labor lies.

—Virgil, *Virgil's Aeneid*

... I had undertaken something which could not have been done by everybody: I went down into the deepest depths; I tunneled to the very bottom.... [Now] *I have come back, and — I have escaped.*

—Friedrich Nietzsche, *Daybreak*

Who would have guessed that the way out of the abyss was to descend into it more deeply? Apparently, just one person, who then went on to teach us everything he learned with the creation of the first dithyrambic tragedy — *Thus Spoke Zarathustra.*

Table of Contents

Preface

The difference between the first and second edition of *The Birth of Dionysia* is mostly the references, all of which have been replaced with translations that are now in the public domain, with only a very few exceptions. Obviously, some translations are better than others, but, for the purpose of my work, which is to reiterate or re-articulate Nietzsche's ideas in words that I hope are a little easier to understand, I deem the public domain sources sufficiently reliable — with the exception of *Thus Spoke Zarathustra*. For whatever reason, the translator, Thomas Common, chose to use Old English. Given the difficulty imposed by the reading of dithyrambic music, I believe Mr. Common's use of Old English makes the reading that much more difficult, which is not helpful.

To fix this problem, I thought the easiest thing, since the translation was already in the public domain, was just to re-word the translation and change *only* the Old English to Modern English. *Then I got an idea.*

I have been reading dithyrambic music for fifty years. I was the first to learn how to read it, having taught myself, and I was the first to learn how to practice it, having successfully completed the drama, which took me a lifetime. And I have written enough theory about dithyrambic music, as you will read in this book, to demonstrate that I am, in fact, proficient in dithyrambic music. With that proficiency, I know full well exactly what inner circumstances of the will to power that the metaphorical gestures in the dithyrambs point to. Accordingly, in this second edition, I made a decision to rewrite some of the music, for no other reason than to make it easier to render — because, frankly, in some instances, Nietzsche made it impossible to render, with the idea being that it should be difficult. Indeed, some of that difficulty is necessary, insofar as extensive introspection is required to find the states of being — and of becoming — that are depicted. And any difficulty created for that purpose must be preserved, which I have struggled meticulously to do. But I believe there are some instances wherein a different metaphor would be more spot-on. Therefore, in those instances, I have rewritten the music. But by and large, I would say in 98 percent of the cases, I deferred to Nietzsche and changed nothing, only the Old English, with the exception of the names of the dithyrambs, which I have taken full liberty to change, or to add.

For instance, the third dithyramb (not starting with Zarathustra's Prologue, is variably translated as "Of the Afterworldsmen" by R.J. Hollingdale, "Backworldsmen" by Thomas Common, "Of the Hinterworldly" by Adrian Del Caro, "Of the Afterworldly" by Walter Kaufmann, and "On Believers in a World Behind." By Graham Parkes. Knowing precisely what the dithyramb is about, I can tell you that the best English translation is the one containing the word "After," which in Greek goes to "Meta," and which, with the German "weltlern," goes to "Meta-worldly." This dithyramb is about "The Tendency to Seek Comfort in the Metaphysical World," which is a tendency that can be found in all of us and which exerts a profoundly negative influence on the will to power.

I have renamed some of the dithyrambs, when I was able to rename them, in order to show the pupil what, in fact, the dithyramb is about, and to give him or her a jump start on the rendition. I have eliminated the need at least to render the titles, which takes nothing away from the all-important renditions of the dithyrambs themselves, and gives the pupil a running start. I believe it will be helpful to have a starting point, to have a general idea about where to begin to look for a rendition of the numerous aphorisms that follow in each dithyramb.

In another instance, in the dithyramb entitled "The Wanderer," at some point Zarathustra says that he must descend deeper than he has ever ascended. Grammatically, the reader would expect to read I must descend "deeper than I have ever descended," which is how both Hollingdale and Kaufmann translated it. But the literal translation reads "I have to go deeper than I ever climbed (or ascended)," and that makes no sense at all — unless you have lived through the dithyramb. If you have lived through the dithyramb, it makes more sense that Zarathustra says 'I must descend deeper than I have ever ascended," not "climbed," and certainly not "descended." In instances such as these, I have made the correction. Again, the only way you could ever make that differentiation is to have lived through the circumstance wherein the actor finds himself needing to descend deeper into his subconscious, knowing that, if he succeeds, then he will find the springboard on which he may ascend higher than he has ever ascended before into the supra-conscious. Thus, he must descend deeper than he has ever ascended before.

Given my early education in the reading of dithyrambic music and the many years I spent living through it. I think any rewrites I do to Nietzsche's dithyrambic music can be trusted.

And I hope they will be. They are only meant to help you, to make it just a little easier for you.

Acknowledgements

Nietzsche, F. Wilhelm., Common, T. (1917). Thus Spake Zarathustra. New York: Modern Library.

On Moods. Translated by Graham Parkes, *The Journal of Nietzsche Studies: Mood, Music, and the Subject*. Autumn ed., vol. 2, Penn State University Press, 1991, pp. 5-10. Copyright © 1991 Penn State University Press. This article is used by permission of The Pennsylvania State University Press.

Introduction

> When on one occasion Dr. Heinrich von Stein honestly complained that he could not understand a word of my *Zarathustra,* I said to him that this was just as it should be: to have understood six sentences in that book— **that is to say, to have lived them**— raises a man to a higher level among mortals than "modern" men can attain.[1] (emphasis added)

In the above quote, Nietzsche qualifies an understanding of *Thus Spoke Zarathustra* with an experience of *Thus Spoke Zarathustra.* And by experience, he means a dramatic, proactive, and very lengthy experience, not merely a passive or momentary spectator experience and certainly not a typical reading experience. He means the reader must become an actor within the drama. Insofar as there is not one other book on the planet that requires such an experience in order to achieve an understanding, the above statement might easily pass unnoticed — as incomprehensible. In fact, *Thus Spoke Zarathustra* is a new art form called dithyrambic drama. And, as we are about to see, a reading of *Thus Spoke Zarathustra* requires an education in *how* to read a dithyramb, which I am about to provide, *and* an education in how to *practice* dithyrambic drama, which I will also provide. In any case, according to Nietzsche's own statement, as above, an understanding of *Thus Spoke Zarathustra* requires an experience, sentence by sentence. Nietzsche also said "Take, for instance, my *Zarathustra*; I allow no one to pass muster as knowing that book, unless every single word therein has at some time wrought in him a profound wound, and at some time exercised on him a profound enchantment...."[2] I am making just such a claim that I understand *'Zarathustra*, and I base that claim on five decades of experience. I think it would help the reader to give me their ear more willingly if they knew my history with *Thus Spoke Zarathustra*, which I will now provide you.

The first time I picked up one of Nietzsche's books, I was seventeen years old, in 1969. The book was *The Birth of Tragedy*, and I could not carry a thought between just two sentences. That was the end of Nietzsche for me.

The next year, I was perusing my school library, and I came across the classical Greek philosophers: Socrates, Aristotle, and Plato. Incredibly, I understood what they wrote. When they spoke of time and beauty and form, I found those concepts within my reach. And, when they added those concepts together with other concepts, I understood the conclusions they drew.

With this, I knew immediately that I was a philosopher. And I knew that I would spend my entire life in philosophy. I knew that right then and there in that library.

But I did not want anyone to know that I was a philosopher. I wanted this secret world all to myself. I did not want to share it with anyone, at least not for a while, and I did not want anyone to know that I had entered into this world. But I also thought it would not be possible to share this world with anyone, except the philosophers themselves who walked me through it. I was certain I would never find anyone with whom I could share what I had suddenly discovered

Upon discovering the Greeks, I became especially enchanted with dialectic, as the Socratics engaged frequently in dialectic. But, in the back of my mind, I thought there was something sophomoric about dialectic, something very shallow, so I did not fully embrace it.

I also learned from the Greeks about being virtuous and reasonable and how the two together would bring me happiness, which was the most important thing in life, or so they taught and so I believed. I learned about moral values being the most estimable values. I learned that it was very important to know myself, that there was good in certainty, and that it was also important to understand as much about life as I could achieve, that it was not good to let things happen inside of me without also understanding precisely what was happening, to bring everything into my consciousness. And most curiously, I learned about the ancient fascination with the mystery of tragedy, specifically the question of people's enjoyment in tragedy and how it was possible to derive pleasure in the horrific destruction of magnificent individuality. I read Aristotle's answer to this question and learned that the pleasure derived from the catharsis of pity and terror, according to Aristotle.

At about the same time, I discovered morality and moral values. While I generally learned about the existence of morality as a system of values from reading Greek philosophers, and though I also learned some moral values from my more general reading, my moral values came mostly from within me. For instance, I learned "art for the sake of art" from reading, but I learned "banish all suffering" from within myself. Some of my highest morals came from within me, and my morals were sufficient to cause me to act, which I found very exhilarating in the face of adversity. Then, one day, I discovered righteousness, and, for me, that made morality and my moral values profoundly more forthcoming and more efficacious.

The next year, while perusing a bookstore, I came upon Nietzsche's book, the Will to Power. And I discovered a completely different mode of philosophical thought: intuition, as opposed to dialectic or logic. Nietzsche's way of thinking was intuitive, in the style of Heraclitus, and it was also very practical.

For instance, in the Will to Power, he wrote about the biology of the drive to knowledge. Biology! And knowledge? And he spoke of the origin of reason and logic. Its origin. He also postulated that there was no such thing as cause and effect. People with whom I shared these ideas, specifically the illusion of cause and effect, dismissed the notion out of hand as ridiculous. I, on the other hand, was fascinated with the possibility of it being possible. Here was a way of looking at the world very differently than the way the Socratics had looked at it. But most importantly, here was another world, a whole and complete world: the inner world of man. And Nietzsche was going to walk me through it. The Socratics had introduced me to philosophy, but Nietzsche introduced me to a whole world, the inner world of man, and his writing suggested to me that he might be able to uncover its genesis, a possibility that I found just extraordinary. Given that potential, I wholeheartedly devoted myself to his study. And with that, my passion for philosophy quickly grew into a patient and enduring love. And, with regard to Nietzsche, that love would play a very important role in my study because Nietzsche's writing was extremely difficult to understand. I'll come back to that later.

At around the same time, in the spring of 1972, when I was twenty years old, I had a profoundly transformative experience: I discovered Self. This epiphany came (in one moment) after I had spent three years in talking therapy after having been injured in a crime of kidnapping when I was a child.

For me, the discovery of Self was profoundly empowering. It was like placing a mighty sun amidst a chaotic swirl of planets: it brought everything into its orbit and kept them there. The Self brought order unto the chaos within me. Suddenly, there was a perspective through which emotion became both interpretable and manageable. I wanted desperately to preserve it, but it would take me a very long time to learn how to do that.

And it would be Nietzsche's Thus Spoke Zarathustra that would teach me the journey because reading the book leads the reader to his Self — and his demons, which is a claim no other book can make. Thus, the need to find one's Self plays very significantly into a successful undertaking of the book, which, as we will shortly see, is actually a drama, but a drama in the sense of doing not play-acting. As for the kidnapping incident, that, too, would play very significantly into an undertaking of Thus Spoke Zarathustra. Consider what Nietzsche himself said about the type of reader he sought.

> Should my experience—the history of an illness and a convalescence, for it resulted in a convalescence—be only my personal experience? and merely just my "Human, All-too-human"? Today I would fain believe the reverse, for I am becoming more and more confident that my books of travel were

> not penned for my sole benefit, as appeared for a time to be the case. May I, after six years of growing assurance, send them once more on a journey for an experiment?—**May I commend them particularly to the ears and hearts of those who are afflicted with some sort of a "past,"** and have enough intellect left to suffer even intellectually from their past? But above all would I commend them to you whose burden is heaviest, you choice spirits, most encompassed with perils, most intellectual, most courageous, who must be the conscience of the modern soul and as such be versed in its science: in whom is concentrated all of disease, poison or danger that can exist today: whose lot decrees that you must be more sick than any individual because you are not "mere individuals": whose consolation it is to know and, ah! to walk the path to a new health, a health of to-morrow and the day after: you men of destiny, triumphant, conquerors of time, the healthiest and the strongest, you good Europeans![3] (emphasis added)

I would focus your attention on the statement "May I venture to commend [my books] especially to the hearts and ears of those burdened with any kind of 'past' and have sufficient spirit left still to suffer from the spirit of their past too?" For the sake of clarity, I would reiterate that statement to say that he commends his books, and especially Thus Spoke Zarathustra, to someone who not only has a past but was also the victim of a crime, someone with "the hardest fate," "whose lot it is to be sicker than any other kind of individual."

On these two points, a robust need to find one's Self and possessing a horrific past, I qualified most propitiously for an undertaking of Nietzsche's drama.

Exactly at around the same time of my monumental epiphany, I had discovered Nietzsche's Thus Spoke Zarathustra. But, after reading it studiously for some time, it mostly made no sense, except for a few passages. Somehow, by a stroke of luck, the passage in the Vision and the Riddle about the dead man choking on a snake struck me as a metaphor for the suffering Self. And the subsequent passage about the dead man biting off the head of the snake and rising up as if through some resurrection struck me as a metaphor for some way of ending the suffering of Self. This made me think that Nietzsche was telling me that, if I could find my way to my deepest Self, deeply enough to relive whatever was causing my torment, and then summon some instinct that was indicated by "the biting off of the head of the snake," then I personally could end my suffering, which was a hope I had pursued since I was a small boy. Given the extent of the suffering I was enduring, which was severe, that was a possibility I was willing to go to the ends of the earth to achieve. There was nothing I was not willing to attempt to end my suffering.

Then in June of 1972, when I suddenly discovered Self, or rather a much more profound Self, I tried what I thought might be the instinct he meant by "biting off its head." Every time I felt humiliation, which is something I felt all the time, suddenly and inexplicably, then I turned away from it, denying it a place in my soul. Quite incredibly, one day I suddenly felt this upheaval within me, as if something was trying to exit me, like an exorcism. Unfortunately, I did not trust myself sufficiently to allow the discharge and I blocked it. But I found it extraordinary that it nearly happened and that Nietzsche's book had so accurately depicted it, as in the dithyramb entitled Of the Vision and the Riddle:

> Meanwhile the shepherd bit down as my shout advised him; he bit with a good bite! Far away he spat the head of the snake – and he leaped to his feet. –
>
> No longer shepherd, no longer human – a transformed, illuminated, laughing being! [4]

This book was no story, I thought. This book was an instruction manual.

Eventually, the profoundly deep sense of Self I had discovered so suddenly then faded on me just as quickly. But now I knew this book would help me to find it again. And I knew this book would also help me to transform it, to end my suffering. And one day that summer, as I stood at the corner of Main and Grove Streets in the town of Melrose, I vowed that I would spend my entire life reading Thus Spoke Zarathustra and practicing everything it taught, until I had learned everything and succeeded in saving my Self. It was a solemn vow I made in that moment, and, as I write this nearly five decades later, I can even tell you in which direction I was looking: west, toward Main Street.

The next revelation came just a month or so later, the day of the Vendome Hotel fire in Boston. I was lying in bed at my apartment on Dartmouth Street, and I was studying the same passage in the Vision and the Riddle. I was focusing on the passage about the moon going over a house, and about a dwarf jumping from Zarathustra's shoulder to the ground at exactly the same spot where a gateway stood, and about a dog suddenly appearing in the night and becoming frightened of the moon. And I asked myself, why would Nietzsche expend so much effort to painstakingly create an accurate representation of a specific inner circumstance of Self and suffering in metaphor and then revert to literal storytelling. And my answer was yet another epiphany: *he didn't*. He wrote all of Thus Spoke Zarathustra in metaphor. These symbolic representations were highly intricate, detailed, and verisimilar depictions of will that were meant to be embodied, acted out with one's own will. None of the text was meant to be taken literally. And with that, I entered into a secret world within a secret world. This was why Nietzsche dedicated 'Zarathustra "To All and None." He had built a wall around his instruction manual. And that wall prevented any individual ego from entering and defiling it. But if you got inside, which required first shedding your own ego, what you found was an accurate depiction in metaphor of your true Self, of human being, human nature. And in that sense, this was an instruction manual and a true and correct navigator's map for anyone who sought out their Self but not for an individual who might use it for their own egotistical ends.

Back in 1972, when I was just twenty years old, I had penetrated Nietzsche's massive wall. With a vow to spend my entire life learning everything this book could teach me, I set out entirely on my own, undaunted by the prospect of massive and enduring difficulties and with enough love in my heart toward Nietzsche to be sustained by an unwavering faith that everything Nietzsche said was sensible and important and, if he had difficulty expressing it, it was up to me to reiterate it and render the good sense. When I said earlier that my passion for philosophy had turned to love when I discovered Nietzsche's work, the benefit of that love was this faith in sensibility, and it was this faith in sensibility, which others lacked without that love, that enabled me to penetrate his most difficult writing.

Now, in 2020, forty-eight years later, I have learned everything. His ideas of Übermensch, eternal recurrence, and the will-to-power as life have all become a deep and intrinsic part of how I think. I have even learned instinct from him. I now write this book with the hope that I may be able to teach others how to do the same: to learn instinct.

My aim with this book is to teach a philosophically minded college student how to read a dithyramb, how to practice dithyrambic drama, and the value of undertaking this education. By philosophically minded, I do not mean a college student who has discovered dialectic and wishes to engage in it further. Unfortunately, though few ever come to realize it, the enchantment with dialectic is nothing more than precisely the same delight that the poet finds in his rhyming ability. Dialectic, or logic, may be a good study for someone wishing to engage in computer programming, science, or law, but I see little other use for it, and least of all for philosophical inquiry. Instead, here we will engage in intuitive thought and intuitive inquiry. There is no place here for the dialectician.

The other important point I wish to make for the young philosophy student is that philosophy is not merely the sport of genius that really has no practical applications. Sometimes, albeit rarely, philosophers establish new ways of thinking, as Socrates did with science. And sometimes they legislate the most esteemed values, as the Persian prophet Zoroaster did with righteousness, thereby raising moral thought to a level previously unchartered. In the past, the establishment of a new way of thinking and the legislation of high values vastly enhanced the ability of the human species to move forward with life on this Earth. That is the good that philosophy provides.

Part 1: Hermeneutics

Nietzsche Founds a New Culture: Dionysia

The work of a genius can be very difficult to understand. Often, the best place to start is with the vision to which the genius was beholden in the pursuit of his work. In Nietzsche's case, the vision that drove him was that of physician to an ailing culture, as he wrote at the beginning of his writing career in the second preface (1879) to *Philosophy in the Tragic Age of the Greeks*:

> ... where is to be found the instance of a nation becoming diseased whom philosophy had restored to health?[5]

This was Nietzsche's vision, his genius: to restore to health not just a failing German culture but all of Western culture; indeed, one might even say, the species. Toward the end of his writing career, in the second (1886) preface to *The Gay Science*, he again mentioned this vision:

> I still expect that a philosophical *physician*, in the exceptional sense of the word—one who applies himself to the problem of the collective health of peoples, periods, races,

and mankind generally—will some day have the courage to follow out my suspicion to its ultimate conclusions, and to venture on the judgment that in all philosophising it has not hitherto been a question of "truth" at all, but of something else,—namely, of health, futurity, growth, power, life....[6]

And, finally, there is this:

We Aeronauts of the Intellect. — All those daring birds that soar far and ever farther into space, will somewhere or other be certain to find themselves unable to continue their flight, and they will perch on a mast or some narrow ledge—and will be grateful even for this miserable accommodation! But who could conclude from this that there was not an endless free space stretching far in front of them, and that they had flown as far as they possibly could? In the end, however, all our great teachers and predecessors have come to a standstill, and it is by no means in the noblest or most graceful attitude that their weariness has brought them to a pause: the same thing will happen to you and me! but what does this matter to either of us? *Other birds will fly farther!* Our minds and hopes vie with them far out and on high; they rise far above our heads and our failures, and from this height they look far into the distant horizon and see hundreds of birds much more powerful than we are, striving whither we

4

> ourselves have also striven, and where all is sea, sea, and nothing but sea!
>
> And where, then, are we aiming at? Do we wish to cross the sea? whither does this over-powering passion urge us, this passion which we value more highly than any other delight? Why do we fly precisely in this direction, where all the suns of humanity have hitherto set? Is it possible that people may one day say of us that we also steered westward, hoping to reach India—but that it was our fate to be wrecked on the infinite? Or, my brethren? or—?[7]

Frankly, this makes no sense. Indeed, much of what Nietzsche wrote makes no sense — until, that is, you realize that he is speaking in metaphor. One of the most important things to understand about Nietzsche's writing is that, just as the singer breaks out in song, the dancer in dance, and the poet in poesy, Nietzsche the philosopher often breaks out in metaphor. Knowing that, if we reiterate the above quote, then we might see that he is talking about the inevitable death of every culture that has ever existed, that they all have a course to run but that they eventually fade out like a setting sun, such as we see currently with the Christian culture and soon with Socratic culture. But then he makes a prediction and says that this new culture that he has founded, Dionysia, might perhaps see a different fate, that it might just escape the fate of all cultures that eventually die out, and that it might actually persist — *forever*.

For Nietzsche, philosophy was not an intellectual or academic pursuit of truth. For Nietzsche, philosophy was a way to restore an ailing culture to health. Every grand and minute aspect of his work can be understood in this context.

And, as I am about to show you, Nietzsche succeeded in finding a way to restore the health of Western civilization by completely overhauling the two-thousand-year-old culture established by the dominant philosophies of Christianity and Plato and, most importantly, morality. He did this by founding a new culture, which will be called Dionysia.

> … no one before me knew the proper way, the way upwards *[the way to salvation]:* only after my time could men once more find hope, life-tasks, and roads mapped out that lead to culture—*I am the joyful harbinger of this culture.* [Dionysia].[8]

> My philosophy reveals the triumphant [mode of] thought through which all other systems of thought must ultimately perish. It is the great disciplinary thought: those races that cannot bear it are doomed; those which regard it as the greatest blessing are destined to rule. [9]

And finally,

> I wish to teach the thought which gives unto many the right to cancel [or "erase," by Kaufmann/Hollingdale] their existences — the great disciplinary thought.[10]

A Definition of Culture

But what is culture? The simplest explanation I can provide is that it is a way of thinking. And culture as a mode of thought was Nietzsche's understanding as well.

Consider this, from Richard Wagner in Bayreuth:

> Wagner's *poetic* ability is shown by his thinking in visible and actual facts, and not in ideas; that is to say, he thinks mythically, as the people have always done. No particular thought lies at the bottom of a myth, as the children of an artificial culture would have us believe; but it is in itself a [mode of] thought: it conveys an idea of the world, but through the medium of a chain of events, actions, and pains.[11]

The first thing to understand about *Richard Wagner in Bayreuth* is that it is not an essay about Wagner and Wagner's music but rather about Nietzsche and dithyrambic music, of which *Thus Spoke Zarathustra* is the only example. And Nietzsche himself tells us so.

> A psychologist might add that what I heard in Wagnerian music in my youth and early

> manhood had nothing whatsoever to do with
> Wagner; that when I described Dionysian
> music, I described merely what *I* personally
> had heard — that I was compelled
> instinctively to translate and transfigure
> everything into the new spirit which filled
> my breast. A proof of this, and as strong a
> proof as you could have, is my essay,
> *Wagner in Bayreuth*: in all its decisive
> psychological passages I am the only person
> concerned—without any hesitation you may
> read my name or the word "Zarathustra"
> wherever the text contains the name of
> Wagner. The whole panorama of the
> *dithyrambic* artist is the representation of the
> already existing author of *Zarathustra*, and it
> is drawn with an abysmal depth which does
> not even once come into contact with the real
> Wagner.[12]

Reading Nietzsche often requires a labyrinthine odyssey to find a gateway through whose entrance his writing finally makes sense. And the above quote about *Wagner in Bayreuth* is the simplest example of this odyssey and that gateway. But there are many others as well.

In the above quote about myth and thought, Nietzsche elucidates more about myth, which we will cover later and much more extensively. But, for the time being, keep in mind that the word "myth" denotes something that is fundamental and integral to an understanding of the dithyramb and culture, and it denotes something about which, I assure you, you have absolutely no understanding outside of this essay. More accurately, though you have heard and may have used the word "myth," its use has always pertained to a dead myth, which we call a false notion. And it is a living myth that requires a new understanding.

Nietzsche also says that (1) culture is a way of thinking and (2) that the way of thinking is based not on a single idea or a single thought but rather on *an idea of the world*, through which the whole inner world of man becomes interpretable and manageable.

> No particular thought lies at the bottom of a myth, as the children of an artificial culture would have us believe; but **it is in itself a [mode of] thought**: it conveys an idea of the world, but through the medium of a chain of events, actions, and pains.[13] (emphasis added)

Actually, it is the succession of events, actions and sufferings that leads to mythopoeia and brings the myth into existence. And, insofar as those events, actions and sufferings reverberate within the created myth, then, it is true that the myth communicates an idea of the world as a succession of events, but it is important to understand the process of mythopoeia arising out of the succession as well. And we will see this development very clearly when we examine the creation of the myth that Nietzsche called Übermensch.

It is easy enough to understand thought that is founded on a single thought (or a single event), but it is more difficult to understand a way of thinking that is based upon a series of events, and it is the latter we need to understand in order to understand mythical thinking. A man who resolves to become wealthy by adopting the absolute conviction that he must ruthlessly look for and be ready to pounce on any opportunity to make money is an example of a way of thinking that is founded upon a single thought, and it is more a will-power type discipline than a way of thinking. In contrast, we have science as a way of thinking that arises out of a series of events: (1) a belief that the world is categorically knowable; (2) adoption of the passion to obtain knowledge for no other reason than the attainment of knowledge, regardless of its use or benefit, but simply to know something; (3) adoption of the determination to make the world comprehensible; and (4) the discipline of logical thought. These insights and disciplines, upon which the scientific way of thinking arises, develop or unfold within the individual who later becomes a scientist as a series of events within his course of living, over a period of time.

In short, myth is a way of thinking that arises not from a will-power type of psychology but rather from a series of inner events that the mythical thinker has undertaken before arriving at the myth and therewith enabling the mode of thought that ensues. And culture is something that is founded upon myth, by which I mean actually several myths.

But what is the object of culture? What is the object of this mode of thought?

When a human being suffers, they lose their sense of Self and subsequently devolve into a chaotic maelstrom of wayward thought and compulsive emotion. A meaningful and effective culture is one that helps suffering man rise up out of that chaos toward a restoration of Self. That restoration involves a process of growth that defines life itself. We are accustomed to think of "life" as a period of time that we spend here on Earth. But the word also applies to a process of growth that plays out within the human spirit. And philosophers have struggled for thousands of years to understand how that process plays out.

Plato taught that Self is an eternally existent idea of human being that exists high above suffering man, like an ideal. And he taught that the ideal can be attained through a process of thought and contemplation; specifically, rational thought and contemplation of virtue, together which would lead to a presence of Self alongside happiness. All of Western culture is founded upon Platonic philosophy, which means that the highest values that steer Westerners through life derive from it.

Morality and moral thought also weigh heavily on the direction in which individuals are steered by Western values. But no one created moral thought as a new way of thinking. Rather, moral thought and moral values arise naturally from deep within human nature. However, the ancient Persian prophet Zoroaster significantly augmented moral thought with his revelations about the battle between good and evil, and that is an individual creation. According to Zoroaster's teaching, all of human nature can be characterized as either good or evil. And life, as a process of growth, is the pursuit of good over evil. Righteousness, more than anything else, will guide you appropriately through the pursuit, whose aim, as with Platonic philosophy, is happiness. Zarathustra the Persian was the first man to teach the role of righteousness in life, and he elevated it to a high value, which endures today.

And finally, Christianity took Zoroastrianism and developed it even further. Christianity taught that a better life awaits the sufferer in the next life, the afterlife, provided that the battle between good and evil is fought mightily and successfully during this life. If the battle is fought wholeheartedly, meritorious rewards await the sufferer in the next life via resurrection and a subsequent ascension unto heaven.

Nietzsche specifically debunked the philosophies of life put forth by Plato, Christ, and Zoroaster. He taught that Self exists not high above you but rather deep within you and that it awaits discovery not in thought but in emotion. He taught that there is no battle to fight between good and evil but rather between the delineation of Self and the chaotic maelstrom of thought and passion within you. And he taught that while there is such a thing as resurrection and an ascension unto heaven, both phenomena occur only during this life, not in an afterlife.

Plato, Zoroaster, and Christ all founded cultures, which is a way of thinking that aims to heal suffering man. Nietzsche's goal with the founding of a new culture, also, was to establish a new mode of thought that healed suffering man. And it is *Thus Spoke Zarathustra* that teaches his new mode of thought by teaching the myths *and the instincts* out of which the mode of thought arises. Nietzsche's new way of thinking and the culture it founds will be called Dionysia.

The Bad Conscience

The suffering that Nietzsche sought to heal specifically was the bad conscience, which is a phenomenon he delineated and elucidated very well in the *Genealogy of Morals*, the text of which I now quote in its entirety and then, afterwards, I will highlight the significant points and images or ideas.

> At this juncture I cannot avoid trying to give a tentative and provisional expression to my own hypothesis concerning the origin of the bad conscience: it is difficult to make it fully appreciated, and it requires continuous meditation, attention, and digestion. I regard the bad conscience as the serious illness which man was bound to contract under the stress of the most radical change which he has ever experienced—that change, when he found himself finally imprisoned within the pale of society and of peace.
>
> Just like the plight of the water-animals, when they were compelled either to become land-animals or to perish, so was the plight of these half- animals, perfectly adapted as they

were to the savage life of war, prowling, and adventure — suddenly all their instincts were rendered worthless and "switched off." Henceforward they had to walk on their feet—"carry themselves," whereas heretofore they had been carried by the water: a terrible heaviness oppressed them. They found themselves clumsy in obeying the simplest directions, confronted with this new and unknown world they had no longer their old guides—the regulative instincts that had led them unconsciously to safety— they were reduced, were those unhappy creatures, to thinking, inferring, calculating, putting together causes and results, reduced to that poorest and most erratic organ of theirs, their "consciousness." I do not believe there was ever in the world such a feeling of misery, such a leaden discomfort— further, those old instincts had not immediately ceased their demands! Only it was difficult and rarely possible to gratify them: speaking broadly, they were compelled to satisfy themselves by new and, as it were, hole-and-corner methods. All instincts which do not find a vent without, *turn inwards*—this is what I mean by the growing "internalisation" of man: consequently we have the first growth in man, of what subsequently was called his soul.

The whole inner world, originally as thin as if it had been stretched between two layers of skin, burst apart and expanded proportionately, and obtained depth, breadth, and height, when man's external outlet became *obstructed*. These terrible bulwarks, with which the social organisation protected itself against the old instincts of freedom (punishments belong pre-eminently to these bulwarks), brought it about that all those instincts of wild, free, prowling man became turned backwards *against man himself*. Enmity, cruelty, the delight in persecution, in surprises, change, destruction—the turning all these instincts against their own possessors: this is the origin of the "bad conscience." It was man, who, lacking external enemies and obstacles, and imprisoned as he was in the oppressive narrowness and monotony of custom, in his own impatience lacerated, persecuted, gnawed, frightened, and ill-treated himself; it was this animal in the hands of the tamer, which beat itself against the bars of its cage; it was this being who, pining and yearning for that desert home of which it had been deprived, was compelled to create out of its own self, an adventure, a torture- chamber, a hazardous and perilous desert—it was this fool, this homesick and desperate prisoner—who invented the "bad conscience." But thereby he introduced that most grave and sinister illness, from which mankind has not yet recovered, the suffering of man from the disease called man, as the result of a violent breaking from his animal past, the result, as it were, of a spasmodic plunge into a new environment and new conditions of existence, the result of a declaration of war against the old instincts, which up to that time had been the staple of his power, his joy, his formidableness. Let us immediately add that this fact of an animal ego turning against itself, taking part against itself, produced in the world so novel, profound, unheard-of, problematic, inconsistent, and *pregnant* a phenomenon, that the aspect of the world was radically altered thereby. In sooth, only divine spectators could have appreciated the drama that then began, and whose end baffles conjecture as yet—a drama too subtle, too wonderful, too paradoxical to warrant its undergoing a non-sensical and unheeded performance on some random grotesque planet! Henceforth man is to be counted as one of the most unexpected and sensational lucky shots in the game of the "big baby" [great child, per Kaufmann] of Heracleitus, whether he be called Zeus or Chance— he awakens on his behalf the interest, excitement, hope, almost the confidence, of his being the harbinger and forerunner of something, of man being no end, but only a

16

> stage, an interlude, a bridge, a great promise.[14]

Please note that the above elucidation was part of an effort to understand the origin of moral values, which Nietzsche was never able to do. The reason he wanted to understand the origin of moral values is because they pose a huge problem for life, by which I mean a process of growth that is driven by a will to power, as we will see shortly. Nietzsche found the single force of human nature that drives the process of life within the human spirit in a will to power. Later, as we will see, he went on to teach that will to power via dithyrambic drama.

> The question concerning the origin of moral valuations is therefore a matter of the highest importance to me because it determines the future of mankind.[15]

In my early twenties, when I became aware of the need for this understanding and the fact that Nietzsche had missed it, I set out to find it myself, and I found it very quickly. When I tried to reconcile Nietzsche's failure with my quick and easy success, especially given all the extraordinary success he had with numerous other insights, the only explanation I could find is that Nietzsche was not prone to moralizing and therefore could not see the problem out of which moral values arise, but I was prone and I did moralize. I will present my theory on the origin of moral values at a later time in this book. But for the task at hand, which is an understanding of the origin of the bad conscience and its role as something that the new Dionysian culture, the new Dionysian mode of thought, aims to heal, suffice it to say that the bad conscience is a primary, fundamental, and critical malady whose cure would radically transform the species and justify any culture that succeeded in delivering that cure.

To summarize the above quote, Nietzsche theorizes that the bad conscience developed as a consequence of man becoming civilized. Prior to the civilization of man, in the wild, individuals who possessed ferocious and violent tendencies (and, most importantly, a lustful cruelty to inflict pain on others) were a valuable asset that protected members of their tribe from the equally ferocious and violent wilderness around them. But when the tribes erected walls to protect themselves from the wilderness, thereby removing the threats inherent in the wilderness, civilizing forces arose to dictate a new mode of behavior, and violent and ferocious behavior — very suddenly, not gradually — turned from an asset to a threat because cruel and ferocious individuals became a threat to the other individuals living in the same enclosure. As a consequence of civilizing forces, those ferocious individuals could no longer easily discharge their violent urges and instincts. But the urges themselves did not dissipate. Instead, the desire to be cruel turned the ferocity inward upon those individuals themselves who possessed them.

> *[The bad conscience]* … is not, as you may believe, "the voice of God in man"; it is the instinct of cruelty, which turns inwards once it is unable to discharge itself outwardly.[16]

And with that, man became afflicted with a most profound malady, which, to this day, has not been cured: the bad conscience, which constitutes man's suffering of man himself.

Whether or not Nietzsche hit the nail on the head regarding the origin of the bad conscience should not be the focus of our discussion here, though I believe he did. Rather, the focus of our discussion should be the phenomenon of the turning-inward of emotion, the blocking of the discharge of a titanic and destructive emotion. Civilization may have turned ferocious cruelty inward upon man himself, but that turning inward also opened the door for other destructive emotions to turn inward. In fact, the turning inward of destructive emotions leads to deep and endless torment, which is precisely what culture aims to heal. A good example of this blocked discharge phenomenon would be the infliction of pain, humiliation, or fear within an individual. If the fear is not sufficiently discharged with a scream, or the pain with sufficient weeping, or the humiliation with a surge of brave dignity, each titanic emotion instead turns inward onto the conscience of the afflicted individual. And it lingers there forever, deep down inside, beyond the purview of consciousness. And if it is beyond the purview of consciousness, then it is also beyond the purview of action and management. In such a way, the beast in deed becomes a beast in thought. And make no mistake that sublimated thoughts that torment suffering man (or, simply, demons), never die and go away which is something that any suffering individual can confirm. According to Nietzsche himself, "...everything that has been is eternal: the sea will wash it up again."[17] And by "sea," he means sea of unimpeded emotion (i.e., emotion that is not repressed and, therefore, without a limited range of perceptibility).

Going forward with our discussion, when we think of the bad conscience, the image we must envision is that of the individual whose conscience has turned against him and therewith plunged him into abyssal torment. It is not the image of the extroverted and ferocious barbarian who has suddenly grown a conscience and become tamed and introverted that we want to think of, though it was with him that the phenomenon originated.

It is also important to note that the blocking and turning-inward of titanic emotion also gave rise to the soul and to the thoughtful man, as per the above quote. Suffering imparts depth to human being. Indeed, the very depth of a pensive soul, thinking man himself, lies in the development of the bad conscience, the turning inward of ferocious emotion. But it also imparts chaotic thought and passion.

Concurrent with the blocking of a discharge of titanic emotion and its turning inward upon the suffering individual, the bad conscience gives rise to a multitude of other very serious problems.

First, the individual loses his Self, and the loss is cataclysmic because the Self imparts both a sense and an idea of being. Without an idea of being, emotion becomes unanchored, which means wild. In the presence of a ruling Self, emotion becomes attributable to Self as an interpretable and manageable dimension of being and subject to sophrosyne. Without Self, emotion becomes a strange, foreign, and inexplicable phenomenon. (The ancient Greeks had a caricature-symbol for the man in whom emotion had become unanchored and wild, which they called a satyr, a creature that was half man and half animal, and by animal we should understand a creature that is unable to resist or master emotion, stimuli.)

The other problem that arises with the loss of Self is the erection of an immense wall between the individual and his or her emotions that is meant to prevent titanic emotion from entering into his consciousness. The other, imperceptible side of this wall is what we call the subconscious. Emotion whose discharge is blocked and subsequently turns inward upon the individual is too unbearable to bear, which is why the mind erects a wall, a vault.

And lastly, in the wake of the collapse of the Self, the Ego is created. The Ego is a thinking sense of being, while the Self is a feeling sense of being. The difference is striking. Thought can easily go astray and lead the individual into chaos. But emotion is grounded in reality and will easily lead the individual back into a meaningful fray where an equally meaningful resolution is ultimately achievable.

Any attempt to heal suffering man, which is the specific goal of any culture, must include a cure for the malady posed by the bad conscience. Historically, Western culture has offered three ways to cure the bad conscience.

One way is offered by Christianity, which teaches that the bad conscience is caused by sinning. Simply repent, which means turning your back on sin forever and accept Christ into your heart (because Christ died for your sins, so that, if you accept him into your heart, you have no debt for the sins you have committed), and you will be redeemed. I can tell you unequivocally and categorically that repentance and love of Christ will have absolutely no effect on the specific cause of your bad conscience, though it may intoxicate and enchant you sufficiently to assuage or help you forget your bad conscience.

Christianity is steeped in morality, which is a second and older way to clear the bad conscience. Zarathustra, the Persian prophet, was the first man to teach the value of truth and righteousness within the eternal battle of good and evil in life on earth. In short, Zarathustra the Persian taught the individual to follow the straight and narrow path to maintain a good conscience. Tell the truth and always do right, and your conscience will remain clear. Be righteous, and you will be morally upstanding, thus happy.

Both Christianity and Zoroastrianism assuaged and avoided the bad conscience but did nothing to cure it.

The third cure of the bad conscience is provided by science in the form of psychiatry, which teaches the suffering individual to learn to feel again ("to feel is to heal") and, in doing so, eventually reach back in time to the moment and the emotion that turned inward and then properly discharge it, therewith reversing the bad conscience. Eventually, that will work, and it is presently the only valid cure for the bad conscience. But there is a problem with this cure, which we shall see shortly.

The larger problem with both Christianity and Zoroastrianism is that they are each founded on morality. And morality is a huge problem in the quest to undo the blockage caused by the bad conscience. In order to understand the problem and fix it, we need to understand whence arise moral values.

Zoroaster may have taught the value of righteousness and he may have taught value in the pursuit of truth and fairness, thereby augmenting morality, but morality as a way of thinking arises naturally. And Nietzsche was never able to understand how it arises. He wrote an entire book, *The Genealogy of Morals*, in an attempt, and he solved many of life's other, more enduring and deeper mysteries, but he never figured out how moral values arise within man.

Morality arises *only* within the individual who suffers with the bad conscience, by which, I repeat again, I mean the turning inward of a blocked discharge of titanic emotion. If you consider all the problems that arise from the bad conscience — the creation of the subconscious, the loss of Self, the rise of the waywardly thinking Ego, etc. — the most difficult problem is the enfeeblement of the will, the suffering individual's inability to act upon his emotions due to the distance and antipathy between him and his emotions. The need to find a means to act becomes dominantly powerful. And morale fills that need. Morale, better than any other force of human nature, cures the enfeeblement of action. Morale, in and of itself and outside its relevance to the origin of moral values, is a great asset, not a problem. However, it becomes a huge problem *when it is sublimated* and begins to drive and command the spirit via the creation of new values, which is what sublimation leads to. And the highest value it dictates is "Ban all suffering." The reason that sublimated morale legislates "Ban all suffering" as the highest value is because suffering demoralizes, and morale, once it enters the spirit via sublimation, wants itself to become dominant over all the other drives. Indeed, all drives that come into existence each wants to become the dominant drive, as evidenced by the sexual drive or the drive for revenge. Sublimated morale will not allow anything that dampens morale to exist alongside it. Thus, it bans all suffering.

If you ask someone why something is immoral, aside from something being obviously wrong, rarely can they tell you specifically why something is immoral. They just know; it is a gut feeling. And people in one place and time have different morals from other people in other places and times. For instance, Aztec Indians sacrificed human beings in an act of propitiation to the gods. Any attempt to interfere with that holy practice would have been deemed immoral by a moralist living amongst the Aztec Indians. But when Europeans witnessed it firsthand, the moralists among them instead found the practice of sacrificing human beings to the gods itself deeply immoral. The criterion by which something is deemed immoral is inherent in what the beholder values and the resulting demoralization that would be caused by any disparagement of that value. That is what is immoral.

The more curious notion about moral values is that, though they originate in the subindividuated individual, individuated individuals will accept them as high values and adopt them. And why that happens is, to me, a very curious phenomenon that is well worth exploring because it strikes at the heart of the proliferation of morality.

If we accept the working theory that the value of any culture is measurable by its success in healing suffering man of his bad conscience, and we accept the fact that any meaningful and successful manner of healing the bad conscience requires approaching the bad conscience, as evinced by the success that psychiatry has had, then morality is a huge problem because its basic tenet, "Ban all suffering," categorically precludes any such approach.

The problem with the psychiatric approach, though effective, is that it renders the suffering meaningless and worthless. In other words, by achieving a proper discharge, the individual is made whole again, but nothing good comes from all that time spent suffering.

With the birth of Dionysia, a new and fourth cure for the bad conscience is proffered. The approach is very similar to but not a duplication of — the approach put forth by psychiatry: learn to feel again. However, while psychotherapy is nothing more than a talking session, the cure for the bad conscience that Dionysia provides actually requires learning a whole new way to think, which is what makes it a culture. And if you succeed in learning this new way of thinking, the reward is quite extraordinary.

As it turns out, the bad conscience is a gateway into an unchartered and, until now, unheralded realm of the human heart and mind, which we will call the supra-conscience, in contrast to the sub-conscience. Via a willful exertion (and that is the critical factor), the supra-conscience rises directly out of whatever titanic emotion has become blocked and turned inward against the conscience, and it elevates suffering man high above the principium individuationis (or PI), which is another phenomenon that I will explain shortly. The elevation unto the supra-conscience, which exists high above the principium individuationis, is the "over" part in Nietzsche's overman. And he speaks of it prophetically in the above quote about the bad conscience from *The Genealogy of Morals*, at the end:

> Undoubtedly the bad conscience is an illness, but an illness like pregnancy is an illness.[18]

And,

> Henceforth man is to be counted as one of the most unexpected and sensational lucky shots in the game of the "great child" of Heracleitus, whether he be called Zeus or Chance—he awakens on his behalf the interest, excitement, hope, almost the confidence, of his being the harbinger and forerunner of something, of man being no end, but only a stage, an interlude, a bridge, a great promise.[19]

Those last words are straight out of *Thus Spoke Zarathustra*. And when Nietzsche says that "something is announcing itself," he is specifically referring to his Übermensch. Thus, Nietzsche's Übermensch derives from the bad conscience or blocked emotion.

Exactly what constitutes Nietzsche's Übermensch is a matter that requires some lengthy explanation, which I will provide later in this book. But until then, I would ask you to consider again the individual with the bad conscience who has become afflicted with some titanic humiliation, fear, or pain that has turned inward upon him. (And I believe those emotions are generally and most commonly the demons with which most people are afflicted — certainly in a subliminal way.) Simply put, if the emotions are sufficiently intense and haunting, it might be said that individual has gone mad. And it is important to consider that extreme condition because its redemption leads to an equally extreme condition that will soon become the focus of our discussion. The opposite of madness is genius. Genius derives from madness that has been redeemed. And genius is Nietzsche's Übermensch.

But genius is a type of human being, like Mozart and Shakespeare and Napoleon. Yes, but it is also a human condition, a state of being, just as madness is a human condition and a state of being. And *Thus Spoke Zarathustra* teaches its reader how to achieve that enlightened state of being. How that enlightened state of being then becomes incarnate is also something I will elucidate for you later.

When I speak to you about an ascension into the supra-conscious and unto supra-individuation, I understand that you will have no idea what I am talking about. First, you've never even heard of the supra-conscious, and, second, you would have no idea how to ascend into an enlightened state, precisely because you have never fathomed the subconscious where the ascension begins, let alone just simply approached the subconscious. And really, what good would it do you to have a concept of all this? Would a concept help you to attain it? No, it would not. What is really needed is for you to understand supra-individuation as an object of your desire because a desire would definitely help you attain it. But in order to find a desire for the supra-conscious, you must enter into the abyss within the subconscious wherein the bad conscience resides because it is only out of that abyss that the desire for supra-individuation arises. Moreover, the only way to enter into the subconscious is by first finding your Self, which itself first requires a will to Self. And the will to Self is Nietzsche's will to power. The reason he calls it a will to power is because the Self empowers its beholder.

Fundamentally, will is desire. But it differs from simple desire in that it also uses intellect. First, will begins with a decision on what shall be the object of one's desire. What does one wish to obtain or move towards? Using that intellect, then one can harness and use this and that desire to move toward one's goal like a ship being driven by favorable winds. But sometimes it is necessary to move in a direction away from one's goal, perhaps to catch a stronger wind, and that kind of navigation also requires intellect. And sometimes there are forces at work that move to hinder the sailor's journey, and those forces must be extirpated, which, again, requires intellect. Therefore, will is fundamentally desire, but it also requires intellect, and sometimes a labyrinthine navigation.

The effect of finding one's Self is very empowering. Just as the loss of Self leads to a maelstrom of chaotic thought and passion, the reclamation of Self leads to a reordering. It is like inserting a mighty sun into a chaos of wandering planets. Suddenly, they all find their individuals orbits and enter into an orderly system. It is the same with

Self. A new order suddenly arises. Therefore, the reclamation of Self is very empowering. And the will to find one's Self is essentially a will to power. *Thus Spoke Zarathustra* teaches that will to power.

A Journey into the Subconscious

In the dithyrambic drama, Nietzsche takes you by the hand and leads you through the inner world of man to the specific inner conflict or tension out of which a desire for Self arises *and which he wants to show you* so that you may then embody that desire and become motivated or driven by it. If you succeed in reaching that juncture and then embodying that desire for Self and then working for and finding your Self, you will enter into a new place within yourself, where another new and deeper desire for Self awaits and, with it, a deeper sense of Self. This is the art and the practice of dithyrambic drama.

And let there be no doubt *Thus Spoke Zarathustra* is a literary representation of the will to power and that, if the reader achieves an embodiment of that will, first as deconstructed parts and then as an integrated whole, he or she will undertake a journey into the deepest parts of the subconscious, wherein he will encounter his demons, struggle to free himself from their grip, and then ascend into an enlightened state of being in which all his suffering is made worthwhile. Let there be no doubt that is what Nietzsche himself did— because he tells us that is what he did in the preface to *The Dawn*.

> ... I had undertaken something which could not have been done by everybody: I went down into the deepest depths *[of the subconscious]*; I tunneled to the very bottom *[of the subconscious]* ....[20]

However, reconsider the quote without my added clarification:

> ... I had undertaken something which could not have been done by everybody: I went down into the deepest depths; I tunneled to the very bottom ; I started to investigate and unearth an old *faith* which for thousands of years we philosophers used to build on as the safest of all foundations -- which we built on again and again although every previous structure fell in: I began to undermine *our faith in morals*.[21]

Is he saying he dug down beneath our faith in morals? Or is he saying that he dug down deeply into the subconscious and discovered that moral values waylaid him on his journey, which required him to disregard moral values in order to navigate his journey, thereby undermining moral values and their efficacy?

We get a clue from the paragraph that precedes the above quote in the same preface.

> In this book *[The Dawn, or Daybreak]* we find a "subterrestrial" at work.... Does it not seem as if ... he himself desires a long period of darkness, an unintelligible, hidden,

enigmatic something, knowing as he does that he will in time have his own morning, his own redemption, his own rosy dawn? Yea, verily he will return: ask him not what he seeketh in the depths; for he himself will tell you, this apparent Trophonius and subterrestrial, whensoever he once again becomes man. ... Indeed, my indulgent friends, I will tell you — here, in this late preface, which might easily have become an obituary or a funeral oration what I sought in the depths below: for I have come back, and — I have escaped.[22]

Unfortunately, he never does come out and tell us explicitly what he sought in the depths (at least not in this preface), which is typical of Nietzsche. He never says what he means; he only ever alludes to what he means. The fact is that the only way to know exactly what he sought in the depths is to have undertaken and completed *Thus Spoke Zarathustra* oneself, which I have done over the course of nearly fifty years. Then, and only then, do all his very ambiguous allusions become clear.

So, let's read the clues, as disclosed in the above quote:

1. In this book {*The Dawn,* or *Daybreak*};
2. He will in time have his own morning, his own redemption, his own rosy dawn;
3. This apparent Trophonius (Trophonius was a man who was swallowed by the earth and transformed into a demigod; presumably, the transformation was a consequence of his envelopment);
4. Whensoever he once again becomes man;

5. I have escaped.

(RE 4) He discloses what he found in the depths of the subconscious — and along the way — in all of *Thus Spoke Zarathustra*. Read the last sentence of the first dithyramb in Zarathustra's Prologue:

> Take heed! This cup wants to be empty again and Zarathustra wants to become man again.[23]

When Nietzsche says that he will disclose what he found in the depths "whensoever he once again becomes man," he arrives at that moment, "whensoever," with the composition of *Thus Spoke Zarathustra*.

(RE 3) Trophonius is regarded by scholars to have been a demon that resided within a cave of nightmares. Might not the demon-riddled subconscious be regarded as a cave of nightmares?

(RE 2) Subsequent to his descent into the depths, there will come a new morning, a rosy dawn, and, with it, redemption. Read the second sentence of *Thus Spoke Zarathustra*: "one morning he rose with the dawn, stepped before the sun, and spoke to it thus…."

(RE 1) The reason he named the book from which I am quoting here, *Dawn* or *Daybreak*, is because this was the period in his life after he emerged from the depths of the subconscious in which he had fought with his inner demons.

(RE 5) After fighting with his demons and struggling to free himself from their grip, he succeeded. He escaped from their grip.

Therefore, I repeat that the following quote sums up the entire experience that Nietzsche offers in *Thus Spoke Zarathustra*.

> ... I had undertaken something which could not have been done by everybody: I went down into the deepest depths *[of the subconscious]*; I tunneled to the very bottom *[of the subconscious]* ... And I have escaped.[24]

You need to think a long time about that declaration if you want to understand *Thus Spoke Zarathustra* because the book provides a map for anyone so inclined and brave enough to take the journey themselves. I cannot put it more simply for you. But more importantly, who themselves would have been inclined to brave the subconscious? Who would have known where to begin such a journey? Who would have been inclined to deem such a journey the most meaningful, most rewarding, and most fundamental effort that might ever be taken in the course of their life? Who would have been able to stick to it and see it through to the end? Apparently, only Nietzsche himself, or so history shows. Here is a journey which has never before been undertaken, except once (by Nietzsche).

And everything that Nietzsche discovered about life, particularly its process and its meaning, was discovered on this journey, and only on this journey, specifically:

- How life manifests itself within the soul;
- What one becomes through that process of growth (i.e., the meaning of life);
- The critical and integral role that tragedy plays in life;
- And the meaning and value of suffering in life.

But, without a doubt, the most important discovery Nietzsche made happened when he uncovered the profound illness from which humankind has suffered since the dawn of civilization and entirely without hope. And if only you will take the same journey, then you will discover the same things. And outside of that journey, you will never understand these things.

Nietzsche's discoveries, as I specified above, constitute a new way of thinking, which is much more than a simple set of beliefs. Rather, this new way of thinking is founded upon a will to power, which is not will power, and that way of thinking constitutes a new culture, which has been named Dionysia. Under this new culture, some of life's most meaningful phenomena have been re-evaluated and now assume new meaning.

For instance, like Christianity, Dionysia also teaches resurrection, but it teaches resurrection here on Earth, in this life, not in an afterlife. And it teaches an ascension unto heaven, but again, in this lifetime. It teaches eternal life, blissful salvation, and redemption of suffering — all in this lifetime. Now, I ask you, which possibility would you prefer to pursue: heaven on earth or heaven in an afterlife, which may or may not even exist?

The first step in founding a new culture is a crucial step forward. To whom do you speak? Christ spoke to the masses. And Nietzsche viewed that is a huge mistake, which he stated explicitly.

> The Founder of Christianity had to pay dearly
> for having directed His teaching at the lowest
> classes of Jewish society and intelligence.
> They understood Him only according to the
> limitations of their own spirit.[25]

Nietzsche's first crucial step was to speak to individuals and only individuals. Therefore, his masterpiece, *Thus Spoke Zarathustra*, is written for individuals, not the masses. The next question to ask is what kind of individual is *Thus Spoke Zarathustra* written for. About this, I have discerned the following:

- The person must possess a deep and lasting desire to find his or her Self, which presupposes that he also possesses (or will come to possess) the highest integrity with regard to his or her Self;
- The person must be capable of highly abstract and symbolic thought and able to think in leaps and bounds;
- The person must be keenly perceptive and capable of holding on to truth that may be transient, shallow, or illogical;
- And lastly, though not required, it would be to his or her advantage if the person was the victim of a crime and possessed a sense of horror; the greater, the better.

Finally, if there is any doubt in the reader's mind that *Thus Spoke Zarathustra* is indeed written for individuals, I would ask you to consider the following, which Nietzsche himself wrote:

> I teach that there are higher and lower men, and that a single individual may under certain circumstances justify whole millenniums of existence —that is to say, a wealthier, more gifted, greater, and more complete man, as compared with innumerable imperfect and fragmentary men.[26]

Genius as the Aim of Culture

Eventually, he will move to the point (although he never does it explicitly, so I will have to do it instead), that genius is what humanity produces as a justification for its existence, as the reason it suffers, as the meaning of life. In fact, genius is the incarnation of his Übermensch.

> The problem that I set here is … … what type of man must be *bred*, must be *willed*, as being the most valuable, the most worthy of life, the most secure guarantee of the future. This more valuable type [the genius, e.g., Beethoven, Mozart, Shakespeare] has appeared often enough in the past: but always as a happy accident, as an exception, never as deliberately *willed*. Very often it has been precisely the most feared [e.g., Napoleon, Caesar]; hitherto it has been almost *the* terror of terrors….[27]

And,

Mankind surely does not represent an evolution toward a better or stronger or higher level, as progress is now understood. This "progress" is merely a modern idea, which is to say, a false idea. The European of today, in his essential worth, falls far below the European of the Renaissance; the process of evolution does not necessarily mean elevation, enhancement, strengthening.

True enough, it *[mankind]* succeeds in isolated and individual cases in various parts of the earth and under the most widely different cultures, and in these cases a *higher* type certainly manifests itself; something which, compared to mankind in the mass, appears as a sort of superman. Such happy strokes of high success have always been possible, and will remain possible, perhaps, for all time to come. Even whole races, tribes and nations may occasionally represent such lucky accidents.[28]

In any case, the point to be taken here is that the creation of great individuals is the goal, not the elevation of the masses.

The *fundamental errors* of the biologists who have lived hitherto: it is not a matter of the species, but of rearing stronger individuals (the many are only a means).[29]

> *Fundamental errors*: to regard the *herd* as an
> aim instead of the individual! The herd is
> only a means and nothing *more*! But
> nowadays people are trying to understand *the
> herd* as they would an individual, and to
> confer higher rights upon it than upon
> isolated personalities. Terrible mistake!![30]

And, therefore, if his first step in founding a new culture is
to speak to individuals, and if great individuals is what he aims
for, it makes sense that he would address himself only to great
individuals to begin with, which I believe is precisely what he
says in the next statements.

> *The order of rank*: he who *determines* values
> and leads the will of millenniums, **and does
> this by leading the highest natures**—he *is
> the highest man.*[31] (emphasis added)

> Here it is not a "prophet" who speaks, one of
> those gruesome hybrids of sickness and will
> to power, whom men call founders of
> religions. [32]

And to those who would say that Nietzsche wanted no
followers, clearly, he wanted followers; he just did not want a
cult following.

I define culture as the convergence of philosophy,
religion, and art into a mode of thought that successfully
heals suffering man in such a way as to render his suffering
meaningful and worthwhile. In *Philosophy in the Tragic Age of
the Greeks*, Nietzsche states clearly and simply that the focus

of his lifelong work will be to restore the failing health of Western culture. And he succeeded. With his philosophic work, he delved into the foundations of our modern way of thinking, found the errors, and corrected it. And the corrections he made went very, very deep.

Previously, Western civilization's most fundamental premise for a philosophy of life was founded on the belief that life manifests itself with human being as a state of being (e.g., Plato's ideal of the higher and already existing Self). Nietzsche replaced that single and most fundamental premise with a belief that life manifests itself as a process of becoming. And every idea that Nietzsche put forth as a prerequisite of life (the will to power, the Übermensch, and the eternal recurrence) all facilitate life as a process of becoming. This facility is the common characteristic in all of Nietzsche's philosophical ideas, and I will show you that fact in detail.

The introduction of a new way of thinking is not itself something new. Socrates did it with science. But the mode of thought that Nietzsche developed and introduced is very new, and therefore it is also very unfamiliar; it requires learning. And whereas Socrates' new mode of scientific thought provided a way of thinking about the world, Nietzsche's new mode of thought provides a way of thinking about the inner world, by which I mean our feelings, our thoughts, our ideas, and our beliefs. And in the same way that Socrates' new mode of scientific thought enabled man to better manage the world around him, Nietzsche's new mode of thought enables man to manage the world *within* him.

Nietzsche's new mode of thought replaces a mode of thought that has existed, in some respects, since Socrates' time, and in other respects, going back even further to the time of the Persian prophet Zoroaster, who taught the value of righteousness as the vanguard of moral thought. Additionally, with respect to morality in general, which Nietzsche's new mode of thought completely devalues, it goes back to the beginning of time, or at least to that time in history when the bad conscience developed. In other words, this overhaul, which is intended to restore Western culture to a robust and healthy state, is extensive and very, very fundamental.

The development of a new mode of thought is — in itself — a remarkable achievement. And the development of a new mode of thought that applies to the management of the inner world, as opposed to the outer world, by which I mean Earth but not the soul, is one that merits special attention. But, insofar as Nietzsche "hit the nail on the head" with his two most fundamental premises, that life is a process of becoming and not a state of being *and* that the process is driven by a will to power, Nietzsche's new mode of thought is a spectacular achievement. I can tell you most assuredly, as one who has learned his new way of thinking *and spent nearly five decades living it,* that it renders life meaningful. But for me to speak of life that is meaningful to a seed that has forgotten how to grow *is a far stretch.* In fact, it is not possible to explain life to something that has lost its way and forgotten how to grow. Rather, life must be shown. Life must be attempted. The pupil must be taken to each and every gateway and shown how to walk through that gateway. No manner of explanation will compel a pupil to take the first steps of life. But a good explanation might encourage him to try to do so himself. And that is all I can hope to do for you in this book.

After having learned life's most precious secrets, specifically its process and its meaning, the next major task for Nietzsche was to find a way to teach all that he had learned and to do it in such a way as to preserve and protect the lessons from one generation to the next against the onslaught of egotistical distortions that would surely ensue. And for that he invented dithyrambic drama and the New Dithyramb.

In order to begin to understand dithyrambic drama, you must first understand that Nietzsche makes a very definitive distinction between the outer world of the cosmos, which is perceptible to the body's five senses, and the inner world of man, which is perceptible only to the sixth sense of intuition. And as much as the outer, physical world is a wondrous, animated, and dynamic interaction of natural forces, so too is the spiritual inner world a wonderous interaction of human forces. For Nietzsche, the inner world of man was a complete world unto itself, and he devoted his entire life and all his labor to an understanding of that world. Thus, to study Nietzsche is to study the inner world of man. And it is important to understand that whenever Nietzsche speaks of the "world," he is always speaking about the inner world. To show the importance of keeping this distinction in mind, I have seen it argued that when Nietzsche speaks of a categorical affirmation of everything in the world, scholars stumble on this point because it is simply inconceivable to them that Nietzsche would argue for an affirmation of some of the horrible things that exist in this world in which we live. In fact, Nietzsche does not argue for a categorical affirmation of everything that exists in this world in which we live. But he does argue for a categorical affirmation of everything that exists within the inner world and specifically everything that exists within the subconscious. Remember that he is always talking about the inner world when he speaks of the "world," always. As you yourself will hopefully discover, *Thus Spoke Zarathustra* is a journey into the subconscious for the purpose of redeeming the horror that exists within it. And a categorical affirmation of the subconscious is a prerequisite of completing that journey. Everything that exists within the subconscious, regardless of the terror associated with it, must be affirmed. Otherwise, without affirmation, it remains a part of the subconscious and completely out of reach. Once you know how to redeem suffering, which is what *Thus Spoke Zarathustra* will teach you, in order to proceed with that redemption, you must be able to access your suffering, especially the suffering within the subconscious. It is in this sense that he argues for a categorical affirmation of everything that exists within the "world."

But the most supreme entity within the inner world of man is the Self, an idea and a sense of being, which exists amidst a world of chaotic forces acting upon it. The Self is the being in human being. And the insertion of Self into a chaotic maelstrom of emotions, which is a world of sometimes titanic and always contradictory forces, is like the insertion of a sun into a planetary system: it creates order. In fact, I will show you that the existence of Self gives rise to the will to power. In its absence, there is no will to power.

The New Dithyramb

Thus Spoke Zarathustra is Nietzsche's new dithyrambic drama, and it is a new art form with which the world is completely unfamiliar. Keep in mind that Nietzsche wrote it toward the end of his life. Though he knew he needed to leave some instruction in the manner of its interpretation and practice, he simply ran out of time and did not do so.

> [My] work would not have been complete had [I] handed it to the world only in the form of silent manuscript. [I] must make known to the world what it could not guess in regard to [my] productions, what was [mine] alone to reveal—the new style for the execution and presentation of [my] works, so that [I] might set that example which nobody else could set, and thus establish a *tradition of style*, not on paper, not by means of signs, but through impressions made upon the very souls of men.[33]

A new dithyramb is comprised of a multitude of idioms. For instance, consider the following idiom, which can be found in the dithyramb entitled Of the Tree on the Mountainside:

Zarathustra came to understand that a youth was avoiding him. And as he was walking alone one evening upon the mountains surrounding the town called "the Cow of Many Conflicting Appearances," lo and behold, he found the youth sitting and leaning against a tree and gazing with a wearied look into the valley. Zarathustra took hold of the tree beside which the youth was sitting and spoke thus:

"If I wanted to shake this tree with my hands, I would not be able to do it.

"But the wind that we do not see troubles and bends it wherever it blows. We are swayed and troubled the worst by invisible hands."

Then the young man stood up in dismay and said: "I hear Zarathustra and I was just thinking about him."

Zarathustra replied: "Why are you startled? – But it is with men as with this tree.

The more it wants to go up and up, the more his roots strive downwards, downwards, into darkness, deepness, into evil."[34]

Clearly, this passage appears to be telling a story. And there appear to be two characters in this part of the story: the main character named Zarathustra and a young man. But there is no story in *Thus Spoke Zarathustra* and there are no characters, not one.

Each of the above statements is an idiom. Some people call them aphorisms, but "idiom" is a more accurate description because an idiom is not meant to convey a literal meaning. And none of Nietzsche's dithyrambs contain anything that is meant to be taken literally

If I wrote a simple sentence, like "the dog ran up the stairs," you would read the sentence and reference in your thoughts the concepts "dog" and "running" and "up the stairs." That is how you read. And it's as simple as that.

But in a dithyramb, an idiom is written entirely in metaphor. So, what is being referenced is not something literal but rather something symbolic.

But, if the dithyrambic idiom is merely a clue that points to something which has to be figured out, where does one begin to look?

Within yourself! Within the inner world. Always within the inner world. And you must use your intuition to find what is being referenced in metaphor.

The metaphors are merely like *facial gestures* with which to figure out what *feeling* or inner circumstance (tension) is being referenced. The actor must learn to read a dithyramb in the same way one reads a face, using the metaphors as gestures that point to how the person behind the face is *feeling*. And then you must find that feeling within yourself and do with it as the dithyramb instructs.

Nietzsche's dithyrambic idioms reflect your manner of thinking toward your Self, your feelings, and the various conflicts between your will and your conscience. The idioms are metaphors of how you think and feel. And every idiom offers a different way to think about the inner circumstance of will and conscience that is being highlighted in any particular dithyramb, so that, if you miss one, there are numerous others that might hit the mark for you.

But how does Nietzsche know how you think?

There are some thought processes that are basic and fundamental and can be found in every human being who is part of the culture in which the thought processes have become inbred. And there are some thought processes that are unique to each individual, due to their unique history, their Ego. The cultural, universal thought processes are what Nietzsche addresses in his dithyrambs, not the egotistical, idiopathic thought processes. Therefore, the idiomatic representations that comprise Nietzsche's dithyrambs are *universally* applicable, and it is for that reason that the book is dedicated "For All." But there is not one idiomatic representation that is idiopathic and representative of any one particular Ego, and certainly not Nietzsche's, and it is for that reason that the book is dedicated "For None."

Theory of the Will to Power

Having spent my entire life studying Nietzsche, now I must explain him, and that is certainly no easy task. I could make the task a little easier if I found a Heraclitean logos within the development of his discoveries and then simply articulated that logos for you. But there is no logos, unless we are talking about the will to power, which most definitely follows a pattern, though it be musical and not logical. But I am talking about something grander. I am talking about what Nietzsche was driven to do and eventually succeeded in doing. And for that, there are only his visions, which he then went on to develop in much the same way that Einstein had a vision about relativity in his youth and then went on to prove it. Fortunately, I know Nietzsche's work well enough to glean those visions from within his early writing so that I am able to articulate those visions, which I will now do.

The most comprehensive vision that Nietzsche pursued very early on was a goal to restore a failing culture to a robust health, specifically Western culture. The second most important vision he had was to achieve this goal within an individual, not a mass of people. The third most important vision he had was to find a paradigm for a life as it plays out within human being in the same plain and obvious way that it plays out within the plant. He found that paradigm in the extension of the limits of individuation, the limits of Self, and specifically the limits of Self to incorporate the subconscious into the conscious, just as the seed endeavors to extend its limits into the seedling, then the plant, then the tree. The fourth most important vision that Nietzsche pursued was to find a *single* force of human nature through which that process of growth was enabled. And lastly, near the end of his life, he had a vision to find a way to teach the process of life that he uncovered *to an individual* in such a way as to prevent those others who might not understand him and might, *therefore*, distort and endanger what he was teaching. These five visions represent the sum of Nietzsche's work.

Nietzsche found the single force of human nature that drives the process of life within human being in the will to power. Therefore, we need to begin with an understanding of the will to power.

The will to power derives from the need for Self. And Self arises from the mythopoeic instinct. Therefore, in order to understand the mechanism of Self and the will to power that derives from Self, we need to understand the mythopoeic instinct. I emphasize that it is crucial to both your understanding of the will to power and the hermeneutics of the New Dithyramb that you first understand the mythopoeic instinct.

Myth is something that Nietzsche embraced as the object of his new art form. It was his view that, during ancient times, the production of myth as an art form had flourished but that it had perished shortly afterward. And it was his goal to restore it as an art form.

> What part did myth and music play in modern society, wherever they had not been

> actually sacrificed to it? They shared very much the same fate, a fact which only tends to prove their close relationship: myth had been sadly debased and usurped by idle tales and stories; completely divested of its earnest and sacred virility .... Here the artist distinctly heard the command that concerned him alone—to recast myth and make it virile, to break the spell lying over music and to make music speak....[35]

In other words, the student who learns how to read a dithyramb and how to practice dithyrambic drama will experience the creation of myth, or mythopoeia, as a direct result of that practice. More specifically, dithyrambic drama creates myth within the heart and mind of its actor. And it is in this sense that Nietzsche "establish[ed] a *tradition of style*, not on paper, not by means of signs, but through impressions made upon the very souls of men."[36] Therefore, for the purpose of understanding the hermeneutics of the dithyramb, it is necessary to formulate a concept of myth, although myth itself is something much grander than a mere concept.

Toward an understanding of myth, it is important to distinguish between living myth and dead myth. And we already have an understanding of what is meant by dead myth. Dead myth refers to a notion of cause that is no longer believed to be true. In such a way, when we refer to something as a myth, we mean something that has been proven false. But our use of the word "myth" makes no distinction between what has become a dead myth and what is still a living myth. And it is living myth that is important to understand.

Consider the plight of the fisherman making his way up the coast toward home port when he encounters a terrific storm and is forced to find shelter on an island. He finds an unoccupied summer home and stays for the night. The next morning, he awakes to find evidence that someone is occupying the house alongside him. And though he looks and finds no one, the evidence is irrefutable that someone else is in the house. Unable to find any "earthly" explanation, he makes a tremendous leap of faith and posits the existence of a ghost in the house. But why does he make this tremendous leap of faith? There are two reasons. First, he asks "why." And he cannot help but ask why the phenomena he observes happen in the first place because his instincts compel him to ask. And secondly, the only answer to the question "why" is something he identifies as a cause, as in cause and effect, and, if he cannot find a cause, he creates one. Myth is a fictive being that is postulated as a cause of observed phenomena. And the creation of myth, which is called mythopoeia, also arises from an instinct, which is itself preceded by the instinctual posing of the question "why." Thus, we have the occurrence of certain phenomena, the asking of "why," immediately preceding the creation of the myth. And it is important to understand that myth is founded upon and arises from instinctual phenomena that precede it because, if you can recreate those instinctual phenomena within someone, then you can create the myth that arises out of them.

Mythopoeia empowers its beholder by enabling his will. With the postulation of a ghost as the cause of the phenomena he is observing, the fisherman is no longer "in the dark." Moreover, he can now endeavor to manage the phenomena, in addition to understanding it, by pleadings with the ghost for this or that. And, most likely, he will endeavor to divine the intent of the ghost, be it good or evil, so as to *predict* its actions. This is precisely what ancient man did with his gods as much as it is what modern man does with his God. Myth empowers man. It imparts knowledge of phenomena, and it imparts management of phenomena.

The ancients were compelled by the same instinct. When a huntsman looked out upon a vast plain and witnessed a stroke of lightening appear literally out of nowhere and in the middle of nowhere, he asked why. And when he could find no "cause," he instinctively created one: a god. And when he asked why the god struck down one particular tree as opposed to another, then, too, he endeavored to divine the intent of the god, be it good or evil. And the ancients invested substantial time and effort to their pleadings with the gods in order to influence their gods' intentions. All of this constituted enablement of the will, which rendered the world interpretable, intelligible, and manageable.

Myth is an idea, but it is a grand idea, and that is what distinguishes it from mere idea. For instance, a man goes on a journey and finds his way impeded by this or that obstacle. Then he gets an idea that assists him in such a way that he overcomes the obstacle and proceeds with his journey. Idea always enables the will in such a way as to allow the will to move forward. That is the purpose it serves in life. But myth is a much grander idea. For instance, if you knew the meaning of life, provided life has meaning and provided the meaning can be discovered, that would be a very grand idea. And it would be a very grand idea that would enable the will in *many different* instances, which is what makes it grand. That is myth. In some instances, myth is the postulation of a fictive being as cause that enables the will by empowering man to make an entire realm of phenomena interpretable and therewith manageable. In other instances, it is a supposition or presumption, such as in the case of the meaning of life, that frees the will as if through a gateway, therewith enabling the will to move forward in *many different* circumstances. Idea enables the will in a particular instance, but myth enables the will universally. Myth founds a mode of thought out of which many ideas arise. In some instances, myth is a fictive being, which we will designate as mythical being, and, in other instances, it is a gateway, which we will designate as a mythical gateway. And, in both instances, myth enables thought, knowledge, and manageability but, most importantly, myth enables forward movement toward a goal.

Science, for instance, is a gateway myth that presupposes that the world is knowable. In fact, the world is not knowable. There are some phenomena for which we have no sense, But the presumption that it is knowable makes the process of *making* it knowable — possible.

The significance of myth lies in its effect upon the will. Idea enables the will, but myth extends the purview of the will. And myth that has not been disproven and is held as truth — is a living myth, which we call "reality."

Unfortunately, in the examples of myth that I gave you above — those of ancient Greek gods and the fisherman's ghost — you know to be false notions of cause, which are dead myths. The new idea I need to bring to you is that of a living myth. Gravity is an example of a living myth. Most people take the example of gravity as proven science, which makes it reality. But actually, gravity is only a theory, which, as I understand it, is still being developed. Gravity is ultimately an unprovable notion of cause that renders an entire world of phenomena explicable, interpretable, and manageable. That is what myth does: it makes the world interpretable and manageable. No myth is provable because it exists only in the human mind, but it can be contradicted by phenomena it purports to explain and account for. And when a myth is contradicted, it quickly dies and becomes a false notion of cause. But until that happens, myth constitutes reality.

If I told you that gravity does not exist, unless you were a scientist trying to develop the theory of gravity, you would think I was crazy. And if I had been living in ancient times and told someone that the gods do not exist, he, too, would have thought I was crazy. That is the difference between dead myth and living myth: a myth that has died becomes a false notion of cause, but a living myth is truth and reality.

The reason that an understanding of living myth is so important to our discussion is because dithyrambic drama teaches many, many *living* myths. And how it does that is something we will soon discover.

All of these insights about the instinctual questioning of "why" and the subsequent mythopoeia of a fictive being as cause become highly illuminative when they are applied to the inner world.

Human Being and Sub-Individuation

When man feels sensation emerging from within himself, he instinctively postulates the existence of a fictive being as the cause of that emotion. Descartes celebrated this instinct with his famous dictum "I think; therefore, I am," although he was referencing the postulation of the Ego upon the perception of thought. Nietzsche countered Descartes with "I feel; therefore, I live," taking the postulation of myth much deeper.

The myth that man creates as the originator of emotion is called Self. And make no mistake that this creation, which is made entirely out of nothing with the aid of the mythopoeic instinct, is a work of art, an artistic creation of something *that does not exist*. In the fundamental act of mythopoeia, we witness man as artist within the inner world of man. Later, when we discuss Nietzsche's essay entitled *The Birth of Tragedy*, we will render the essay sensible by understanding that his major Thalesian insight stated in the very first sentence of the book, that art owes its evolution to the Dionysian-Apollonian duality, is precisely this art: the creation of myth.

And the mythopoeia of Self does more than just found a mode of thought within man; it establishes an idea and a sense of being within the inner world that man himself becomes, which takes our discussion of myth (or living myth) to a whole new level.

When we perceive sensation within ourselves, like the fisherman postulating the existence of a ghost, we instinctively postulate the existence of a being as the *cause* or the origin of that sensation. The other point to consider is the human need for illusion.

If I asked you to find just one example of being in the universe, by which I mean something that has always existed and will never go away, you could spend the rest of your life searching and you would never find it, with one exception. Some people might say that God is the one true being. That would be the one exception. But God, like all the gods that preceded him in history, is a myth, specifically a mythical being. In fact, there is nothing in this universe that exists unendingly. Even the stars that have existed for billions of years eventually die. There is not one thing in this world that has always existed. Everything that comes into existence, eventually passes out of it. In short, there is no being in this world.

But if there is no being in this world, how, then, do we find it? The answer is that we create it, like artists.

> To *stamp* [re-characterize or re-image]
> Becoming with the character of Being—this
> is the highest will to power.[37]

Thus, when man perceives sensation within himself, he postulates the existence of a being, his Self, as the origin and cause of that sensation. In this postulation, man is acting as an artist in the creation of illusory being. And the reason we create being is because life, as it plays out within us as a process of growth, requires the illusion of being. It is also important to point out that illusion satisfies a very deep delight, which, quite simply, is evidenced by our delight in dreams, as when we awake from a pleasant dream wishing to return to sleep so that the dream might resume. In fact, as we will see later in this essay, the illusion of Self is profoundly transformative — and redemptive. In order to understand how it is redemptive, first we must understand how it is profoundly transformative.

Self is the being in "human being." The mythopoeia of Self creates an edification atop the swirling sea of emotion, whose best analogy Nietzsche's teacher, Schopenhauer, provided, as quoted in *The Birth of Tragedy*:

> *Welt als Wille und Vorstellung,* I. p. 416: "Just as in a stormy sea, unbounded in every direction, rising and falling with howling mountainous waves, a sailor sits in a boat and trusts in his frail barque: so in the midst of a world of sorrows the individual sits quietly supported by and trusting in his *principium individuationis* [principium individuationis; hereafter, sometimes 'PI']."[38]

The mythopoeia of Self individuates man, making him an entity unto itself within the inner world of man, separate from the realm of sensations, which, outside the domain of Self, is the only other thing that exists within the inner world of man, until, that is, the realm of ideation develops. Before we begin elucidating how the principium individuationis (PI) interacts with the realm of sensation, it is necessary first to understand more about the nature of the PI itself as an edification, a sense of being, and the protection and perspective that it provides. And it would be better to apprehend it rather than merely conceive it. At the same time, this exercise in thought that is designed to achieve that apprehension will give you your first experience with dithyrambic drama.

Focus on some fear that you have deep down inside but always avoid. Then allow that fear to well up unbridled. At some point, you will stop it, but, before you do, you will experience in a controlled manner the shattering of the principium individuationis (PI), as if falling out of Schopenhauer's "rowboat" that sits atop the sea of emotion. The PI protects you from being overwhelmed by titanic emotion, and, when a man is overwhelmed by emotion and falls out of the boat, we say he is insecure, in mild cases, or that he lost his mind, in severe cases, be it either from fear or humiliation or pain *or any titanic emotion*. And the transformation is nothing less than a profound and utter transformation of the individual. Let us designate this state of being that follows from the shattering of the PI as sub- individuated being.

It is also important to understand that the mythopoeia of Self introduces into the inner world of man, in addition to an idea and a sense of being, the quality of constant, unwavering permanence in stark contrast to the quality of unending transition that is imparted by the sensations, which come and go and in varying intensities. And, unlike sensation that commands feeling, Self as being commands contemplation and visionariness. But perhaps the most important attribute attributed to the inner world by mythical Self is the ability to heal. It is one thing to be driven into maddening compulsion by the unspeakable rumblings of repressed pain and suffering, but, then, to raise the repressed emotions into the light and to see one's Self in that pain and suffering — is to be healed. The illusory image of being heals!

On the one hand, a man experiencing horrendous emotional pain is rocked to and fro by the tumult, and then, seeing his Self in the pain, he is comforted by the restrained and tranquil contemplation that is imparted by the image of his Self into emotion. To put it another way, in the words of Nietzsche himself,

> When, after a vigorous effort to gaze into the sun, we turn away blinded, we have dark-coloured spots before our eyes as restoratives, so to speak; while, on the contrary, those light-picture phenomena of the Sophoclean hero,— in short, the Apollonian of the mask, [or mythical Self]—are the necessary productions of a glance into the secret and terrible things of nature, as it were shining spots to heal the eye which dire night has seared.[39]

Lastly, note also that the introduction of mythical being into the inner world of man juxtaposes three very contrary realms: one, the totally physical realm of exigent sensation, two, the illusory domain of the contemplative image of being, and, three, the ideational realm that rises out of mythical Self as an interaction with sensation. In his essay, *The Birth of Tragedy*, Nietzsche denoted the realm of sensation as "Dionysian" and the realm of ideation as "Apollonian." And he denoted the domain of Self as simply "myth." In short, everything about mood that can be detected in tone of voice or facial gesture is Dionysian, while everything about ideation and myth is totally invisible. Since the dithyramb is composed entirely in gesticulative metaphor, everything that is referenced is sensational in nature. In other words, in the course of reading a dithyramb and rendering its metaphors, in every instance, what you should be looking for in the metaphors are your feelings. And it is out of those feelings — and your struggle with their contradictions — that everything which is Apollonian arises. Otherwise, everything that is Apollonian is totally invisible in the drama. Ideas and myth, both of which are entirely contemplative in nature, are nowhere to be found in the dithyrambic drama. They arise only out of that which is Dionysian, one's feelings. This is the essence of Nietzsche's fundamental Thalesian insight, presented in the first sentence of *The Birth of Tragedy*, that "art," or mythopoeia, the creation of Self, "owes its continuous evolution to the Apollonian-Dionysian duality."

The fall from Schopenhauer's "rowboat" into the sea of emotion is a fall from wholesome reasonableness into emotional instability, insecurity, and even madness. The fall is a cataclysmic event, but it is not a rare event. Quite the contrary, due to the nature of individuated being, which provides strictly defined limits and boundaries to the individual, and the nature of life, which can be reckless, haphazard, and overwhelming, everyone is sub-individuated to some extent, some more than others, and some less than others. But everyone has experienced a violation of their limits, their boundaries, their capacity to bear titanic emotion, inasmuch as they are individuated individuals.

The fall from individuation into sub-individuation profoundly transforms suffering man in three ways. It dismembers him from his emotions so that he no longer has any affinity with them and feels, instead, an antipathy towards them. It creates the subconscious, wherein the unmanageable emotions that caused his fall remain largely imperceptible and, to that extent, unmanageable. And it gives rise to the Ego, whose primary instinct is to keep the subconscious vaulted in order to maintain the Ego in place of the Self. And the confluence of these three conditions severely disenfranchises suffering man and nullifies the empowerment imparted by the mythopoeia of Self.

If you are going to find your Self, these conditions must be overcome. And that overcoming is the most difficult task you will ever undertake in the course of your life, bar none. It is important to note that all these conditions are present in someone with a past, be it a mildly tumultuous past or a severely tumultuous past. Thus, Nietzsche's dithyrambic drama is written for someone with such a past. And it is especially intended for someone with a severely tumultuous past.

> May I commend them particularly to the ears and hearts of those who are afflicted with some sort of a "past," and have enough intellect left to suffer even intellectually from their past? But above all would I commend them to you whose burden is heaviest, you choice spirits, most encompassed with perils, most intellectual, most courageous, who must be the *conscience* of the modern soul and as such be versed in its *science*: in whom is concentrated all of disease, poison or danger that can exist to-day: whose lot decrees that you must be more sick than any individual because you are not "mere individuals"....[40]

First, you must want to find your Self. That is the prerequisite for undertaking a study of *Thus Spoke Zarathustra*. The book is written for someone who wants to find their Self.

Second, you must learn to recognize your Self amidst a chaotic maelstrom of thought and passion. Third, you must learn to feel again, and, in doing so, incorporate the entire subconscious realm into your consciousness, which is a gradual and incremental process and by no means a sudden or quick achievement. And lastly, you must allow your Ego to give way to your waking Self. In other words, your Ego must crumble, collapse, die. So long as the Ego remains alive and functioning, the subconscious will remain vaulted. The two absolutely go hand in hand: the death of the Ego and the resurrection of the Self.

In order to achieve all this difficult work, a whole new way of thinking must be learned. And that is what *Thus Spoke Zarathustra* teaches. It teaches a new way of thinking, whose rethinking, itself, requires that huge obstacles be overcome.

It is very important to understand that the resurrection of Self from deep within the subconscious necessarily requires the collapse of the Ego. And it is important as well to understand how very difficult it is to achieve that collapse, which is entirely a wilful development. Although there is something of the musical nature that inheres in life to be found in this phenomenon as well, thereby assisting it, by and large, it does not happen naturally; it is something that you must want to happen, and it is something you must assist as well. It is probably the most fundamental and integral rite of passage in the long process of re-integrating the subconscious into consciousness, which is the very definition of how life manifests itself within human being, insofar as life is a process of growth whereby boundaries are continually extended. Let us call this rite of passage proto-tragedy to distinguish it from the modern and *false* understanding of tragedy that has endured for thousands of years.

The revelation of the role that proto-tragedy plays in the life process is a milestone in the history of Occidental philosophy. Philosophers struggled for centuries to understand why the ancients celebrated the destruction of magnificent individuality as evidenced in their tragedies, which is a form of drama that they themselves invented. Aristotle, who was one of the first philosophers to try and understand the value that the ancients found in tragedy, incorrectly surmised that it provided pleasure in a catharsis of pity and terror. I would ask you to compare Aristotle's negligible cathartic pleasure with the more obvious and much deeper pleasure that derives from a resurrection of a long-lost Self from the collapse of an inflated and stalwart Ego.

Having lost knowledge of life's most precious secret, then, too, the whole rite of passage devolved into the purely theatrical art form we know today, instead of the fundamental inner phenomenon of the soul that it had once been.

Under the prejudice of the moralist, who believes in the absolute dominion of morale and is driven by its dictate to ban all suffering, thereby protecting morale, proto-tragedy became an impossibility, whose value was lost forever, and its meaning was reduced to the catastrophic and utter destruction of morale, an entirely worldly event that bore no significance whatsoever on the inner world.

The Dithyramb and Dithyrambic Drama

The dithyramb is a representation of will, specifically will to power. But will itself is a representation of something else. It is a representation of something deeper, more intrinsic, and more fundamental than will, which Nietzsche calls music. And by music, he means mood. Thus, a true representation of will is a true representation of mood.

Nietzsche actually wrote a very short essay on his view and understanding of moods, which he entitled *On Moods*. He would have more aptly entitled it *On Music and Moods*, in the same spirit that he entitled the next essay we shall discuss, *The Birth of Tragedy Out of the Spirit of Music*, but he did not do that. He was only nineteen years old when he wrote *On Moods*. And it precedes his first major publication, *The Birth of Tragedy* by eight years. Therefore, I regard this essay as very fundamental to his whole way of thinking.

I will now cite the essay in its entirety. (Please note that this article is used by permission of The Pennsylvania State University Press.) It is very short. Keep in mind as you read it that what we are trying to collect from it is an understanding of how Nietzsche equates moods with music.

On Moods[41]
Part One

Let the reader imagine me sitting at home, wrapped in a dressing gown, on the evening of the first day of Easter. A fine rain is falling outside, and I am alone in the room. I stare for a long time at the blank sheet of paper lying in front of me, pen in hand, vexed by the confused crowd of things, events, and thoughts all demanding to be written down. Some of them are tempestuous in their demands, being young still and effervescent like new wine; but in opposition to these many an old, ripened, clarified thought arises, like an old master who surveys the strivings of the youthful world with an equivocal eye. Let us say it openly: our temperament is conditioned by the conflict between these old and new worlds, and the current situation of the conflict is what we call 'mood' or also, with some disdain, 'temper'.

Like a good diplomat I rise above the quarreling parties and describe the state of the commonwealth with the impartiality of a man who every day attends inadvertently the sessions of all the parties, applying in practice the very principle that he mocks and scorns from the rostrum.

Let us admit it: I am writing about moods, insofar as I am right now in a certain mood;

and it is fortunate that I am just in the mood for describing moods.

Today I played Liszt's Consolations many times over, and now I feel how its tones have penetrated my being and continue, spiritualized, to resonate within me. I recently underwent a painful experience that had to do with a parting or a not-parting, and now I notice how this feeling and those tones have fused together, and I see that the music would not have appealed to me had I not just had this experience. So the soul strives to attract what is like it, and the current mass of feelings squeezes like a lemon the new events that impinge upon the heart, but always in such a way that only a part of what is new fuses with what is old, and a residue is left over which is not yet able to find anything related to it in the household of the soul, and thus lodges here alone, quite often to the displeasure of the older residents with whom it often comes into conflict. But look! Here comes a friend, there a book is opening, a girl passes by. Listen! Music! Already new guests are streaming in from all sides into the house that stands open to all, and the one who was just now standing alone finds many noble relatives.

It is quite marvellous: it is not that the guests come because they want to, nor that the guests come as they are; but rather those guests come who must, and indeed only those who must come. Anything the soul cannot reflect simply does not touch it; but since it does not lie within the power of the will to make the soul reflect or not, the soul is touched only by what it wants. And that seems absurd to many people: for they recall how there are many sensations that they resist. But what is it that ultimately determines the will? Or how often the will sleeps and only the drives and desires are awake! But one of the strongest desires of the soul is a certain curiosity, a taste for the unusual, which explains why we often allow ourselves moods that are unpleasant.

But it is not only through the will that the soul assimilates things: the soul is composed of the same or similar stuff as experiences, and thus it is that an event which finds no sympathetic resonance can lie so heavily on the soul as a burdensome mood, and can eventually assume such a preponderance that it compresses and constricts the other contents of the soul.

Moods thus arise either from inner conflicts or else from external pressure on the inner world. Here there is a civil war between two enemy camps, there an oppression of the populace by a particular class, a small minority.

Often, when I eavesdrop on my own thoughts and feelings and silently attend to myself, it is as if I heard the hum and buzzing of those wild factions, as if there were a rushing through the air as when a thought or an eagle flies to the sun.

Conflict is the constant nourishment of the soul, and the soul knows how to extract from it much that is sweet and fine. The soul destroys and thereby gives birth to new things, it fights energetically and yet gently draws the opponent over to its own side for an intimate union. And the most marvellous thing is that it never pays attention to the exterior – names, persons, places, fine words, handwriting are all relatively unimportant – but it treasures what lies within the covering.

That which is perhaps now your whole happiness or your entire sorrow may soon turn out to be only the garment of a yet deeper feeling, and will thus disappear when the greater thing comes. And thus our moods deepen themselves continually: no one of them is quite the same as the next, but each is unfathomably young and the birth of the moment.

I think of many a thing that I used to love; names and persons changed, and I don't want to claim that in actuality their natures would have become ever more beautiful and profound. What is true, though, is that each one of these similar moods signifies a step forward for me, and that for the spirit it is intolerable to go through the same stages again that it has already gone through: it wants to keep on extending itself into the depths and heights.

Part Two

Dear moods, I salute you, marvellous variations of a tempestuous soul, as manifold as nature itself, but more magnificent than nature, since you eternally transcend yourselves and strive eternally upwards, whereas the plant still exhales the same fragrance it did on the day of creation. I no longer love as I loved some weeks ago; I am no longer this moment in the mood I was in as I began to write.

First I tried it in music, but it didn't work: the heart stormed on, and the music remained dead. Then I tried in verse: no, rhyme failed to capture it, at least not calm and measured rhythms. Away with the paper: take a new sheet, and now pen quickly scribble, ink – quick – here!

Mild summer evening, twilight streaked with pallor. Children's voices in the lanes, in the distance noise and music. A fair: people are dancing, colourful lanterns blaze, wild animals growl; here a shot rings out, there a rattle of drums, steady and insistent.

Inside the room it is darker. I light a lamp, but the eye of the day looks inquisitively through the half-drawn curtains. It would like to see farther, right into the middle of this heart which – hotter than the light, duskier than the evening, more animated than the voices in the distance – reverberates deep within, like a huge bell sounded in a storm.

And I implore a thunderstorm; does the tolling of the bell not attract the lightning? Now, you approaching thunderstorm, clarify, purify, blow fragrances of rain into my dull nature; welcome, at last, welcome!

There! You first bolt of lightning, there you flash, right into my heart; and from it arises something like a long, pale column of mist. Do you know it, the dark, treacherous one? My eye is already brighter, and I stretch my hand out after it, as if to curse. The thunder growls, and a voice rang out: 'Be cleansed!'

Heavy sultriness; my heart swells. Nothing moves. There – a light breath, on the ground the grass trembles – welcome, rain, soother, my saviour! Here it is desert, empty, dead: plant anew!

> There! A second bolt! Dazzling and two-edged, right into my heart! And a voice rang out: 'Hope!'
>
> A gentle fragrance rises from the ground, a wind comes up, and the storm follows, howling in pursuit of its prey. It drives broken-off blossoms before it, as the rain swims joyfully after.
>
> Right through the middle of my heart. Storm and rain! Thunder and lightning!
>
> Right through the middle! And a voice rang out: 'Become new!'

The divisions, Part One and Two, are not part of the original text and were inserted by me to assist with our clarification of this brief essay.

In the first part, Nietzsche talks about mood per se. And what does he say or observe about mood? One, that it arises from inner conflicts, say, perhaps, a conflict between passion and conscience. He also says that mood has the quality of tone, much like voice has the quality of tone, in that some moods can be harsh and some can be soothing. In other words, moods have their ups and downs; they can also be intense and mild. And he says that mood can become spiritualized and endure within the spirit long after the mood has subsided. He also says that music (music proper; i.e., audible music) mimics mood insofar as the pleasure that music might make him feel is conditional upon the mood during which he listened to it. More specifically, he says that the tones of the audible music *fused* with the feeling he had when he began listening to the music. From this observation, he draws a mystical and intuitive insight: the soul strives to attract what is like it. This is an extremely abstract insight. In fact, it is so abstract that some people might find it utterly incomprehensible. But think of it another way. In the course of trying to incorporate your subconscious into your consciousness, you may succeed in bringing up a deep feeling that you previously suppressed. And that deep feeling will trigger your mythopoeic instinct, which will prompt you to sense your deeper Self in that deeper feeling. In such a way, the soul attracts what is like it. And then, even more to the point, that deeper feeling that you succeeded in bringing into consciousness (along with the deeper Self) will begin to bring other deeper feelings into your consciousness. And it may happen with little or no willful exertion by you. We will call on this insight about the soul attracting that which is like it later, when we discuss the origin of tragedy from out of the spirit of music, specifically the origin of proto-tragedy out of dissonance.

Continuing with this phenomenon of the soul striving to attract what is like it, he says that when the soul attracts things that are like it into itself, that which is new is always assimilated only in part according to whether or not it finds something old that is similar. If it does not find something old and similar, it remains but always as a loner, by itself. And then, he observes, something unusual happens when the loner itself begins to bring into the soul things that are like itself. In such a way does the soul undergo a process of growth.

All of this will make much more sense to you if you consider the process of growth via the assimilation of unknown parts as it applies to finding your Self. As you scan the subconscious looking for remnants of your old shattered Self, you will find parts that you recognize and parts that you do not recognize, which does not mean that the unrecognizable parts are, in fact, not a true and original remnant of your old Self, only that you do not recognize or remember it (mostly due to a lack of courage). But the unrecognizable part will remain somewhere within your soul and, later, may draw more old, similar, and unrecognizable parts of your Self into itself, as the soul does, so Nietzsche says. Then one day, and perhaps quite suddenly, you will find a much deeper and more vivid apprehension of Self that was gathering all along, quite outside the scope of your consciousness, entirely of its own doing, simply because "the soul attracts what is like it." Insofar as the process of growth by which the Self extends its limits into the subconscious defines how life manifests itself within human being, and insofar as that same process employs the rule by which the soul attracts to itself things that are similar to itself — and does so outside the scope of consciousness, then life requires mysticism, which contradicts some of what Socrates the logician and scientist taught. And that is a very important point to remember because mysticism and dithyrambic drama go hand in hand.

Continuing with his essay, in the next paragraph, which begins with the words "It is quite marvelous," Nietzsche goes on to discuss other attracting properties of the soul, but now he seems to begin writing in metaphor: "it is not that the guests come because they want to, nor that the guests come as they are; but rather those guests come who must, and indeed only those who must come."

Then he introduces the interplay of will within the soul and upon the moods, and he says that, though the will assimilates things into the soul, it is not the only via the will that things get assimilated into the soul because the soul itself has an innate curiosity by which things are drawn into it. And he notes that the will cannot move the soul to reflect, by which I presume he means reflect upon and not deflect away. And he asks the question, what determines the will, by which I presume both its makeup and its direction. And lastly, he asks what determines when the will becomes dormant, even while the drives and desires comprising the will remain active.

Lastly, he concludes that, due to the soul's innate curiosity, things come into it that may be incongruent with an existing will and existing drives and desires, so that there is war amongst the parts of the soul, but that this warring is good for the soul.

And then resorting to metaphor again, he says something that will prove very telling in our disquisition:

> Often, when I eavesdrop on my own thoughts and feelings and silently attend to myself, it is as if I heard the hum and buzzing of those wild factions, *as if there were a rushing through the air as when a thought or an eagle flies to the sun*. (emphasis added)

And finally, he reveals two things about the soul that are also very telling:

> That which is perhaps now your whole happiness or your entire sorrow may soon turn out to be only the garment of a yet deeper feeling.... And thus our moods deepen themselves continually....

And

> ... [the soul] wants to keep on extending
> itself into the depths and heights.

Before continuing on to the next point, which is most important, I need to take the reader aside to point out what is probably the most telling insight I have ever discovered into the one thing that singularly enabled Nietzsche to achieve all that he achieved. And that one thing is revealed in the above two citations. Keep in mind that Nietzsche was only nineteen or twenty years old when he wrote them. In the above, he says that he discovers "yet deeper feeling[s]" underlying his moods and he observes that the soul "wants to keep on extending itself into the depths and heights."

I have always found it curious to understand how Nietzsche was driven to the extraordinary achievements that he succeeded in making. He was the first philosopher to elucidate the process of life, the first to figure out the meaning of life, and the first to unravel the mystery of how pleasure derives from tragedy. And I have concluded that all those achievements derived from his penchant to plumb the depth of his feelings, which, I contend, is far from common. Generally speaking, people do not plumb their feelings. On the contrary, the common tendency is to avoid the depth of one's feelings. Yet Nietzsche had a strong proclivity to do just the opposite. It is as simple as that; that is the key ingredient in Nietzsche's success. And that key ingredient is also what illuminates the journey that Nietzsche's dithyrambic drama provides.

Returning to our disquisition at hand, I divided Nietzsche's essay about moods into two parts because something very significant becomes apparent in the second part: he bursts into metaphor — in the same way that a songwriter would burst into song or a poet would burst into rhyme. And in the second paragraph of Part Two, he says "First I tried it in music." Tried what? He does not say explicitly. But I believe he is looking for a way to represent mood in words on paper. He tried also but could not find a way to represent mood in audible music. In the next sentence, he says he tried to find a way to do it in poetry, but that did not work either. But in the paragraphs that follow in Part Two, where he bursts out in metaphor, there he found a way.

If you compare those latter paragraphs in Part Two with the dithyramb in *Thus Spoke Zarathustra* entitled Of the Tree on the Mountainside, the similarity of images should be apparent, specifically the image of lightening striking and thereby renewing life. And in another dithyramb, entitled Of Great Events, there is a similarity of the metaphor of a voice calling out in that dithyramb.

Writing in metaphor was the way Nietzsche found to represent mood in words. And insofar as "our moods deepen themselves continually" and, through our moods, the spirit "wants to keep extending itself into the depths and heights" of the soul, the representation of mood in words (with its highs and lows), constitutes music, specifically dithyrambic music. Shortly, when I explain the process by which Nietzsche's metaphor of moods is rendered and embodied, then you will see how dithyrambic music is dramatic music. And by dramatic music, I mean a natural continuity of moods whose confluence comprises will.

What is important to take away from Nietzsche's essay on mood is evidence of an extremely focused and deeply penetrating eye on the workings of our inner world, and not only with regard to mood, but including also the drives and desires, will, consonance and conflict of the drives and desires, even thought. And, most importantly, he sees the quality of music in this interplay. And all of *Thus Spoke Zarathustra* is a representation in metaphor of the inner world. Everything that is referenced in his dithyrambs is a reference to something within the inner world. That is the only world with which Nietzsche has any concern whatsoever. And the moment you lose sight of that fact and begin reading the dithyrambs as if they were not written in metaphor and instead look for something in reference to the physical world, you stop hearing the music. And when you stop hearing the music, all is lost. Make no mistake that *Thus Spoke Zarathustra* is written *entirely* in metaphor and all of the metaphors point to something within the inner world, specifically mood.

The other important point to take away is that mood does not equate to will; the two are separate phenomena. And mood by itself does not create will. Rather, will is an intellectual decision, a choice. Mood is to will like the wind is to the sails of a ship. Mood carries the will, but will makes its own choice as to where it wants to go, in the best circumstances. And just as a sailing ship sometimes must temporarily sail away from its destination in order to capture a wind in the general direction it wants to go, so too must the will sometimes temporarily move in a direction away from its ultimate goal in order to eventually reach it, which may seem illogical. In fact, as you will learn, sometimes the will must go in the exact opposite direction in order to reach its goal. And it is due to this particular quality that will is much more sophisticated than mere will power, which is basically just rude and ruthless willing toward a single goal, in that will must go in different directions and requires the intellect needed to make a choice in direction as well as to discern which desires will assist that movement and which obstacles will hinder it.

Before we leave the teenage Nietzsche's essay on mood, I would like to provide a very brief demonstration of the process by which his dithyrambic music is rendered. At the end of the first part of the essay, he writes:

> Often, when I eavesdrop on my own thoughts and feelings and silently attend to myself, it is as if I heard the hum and buzzing of those wild factions, as if there were a rushing through the air as when a thought or an eagle flies to the sun.

The first thing to note is that he is referencing his thoughts and feelings.

In the first part of this sentence, he writes literally. And in the second part, he writes metaphorically. But both references, the literal and the metaphorical, refer to the same thing: an epiphanic thought. The "rushing through the air" metaphor is what suggests an epiphany. But what is the thought about? We do not know because he writes it only in metaphor: "the sun." However, now that we know that Nietzsche's metaphors constitute dithyrambic music and that dithyrambic music is a representation of mood, or the drives and desires, their conflicts and resolutions, also the will and even thought itself, then we know where to begin looking for what the metaphor points to: always, we look within the inner world.

After having spent decades practicing dithyrambic drama, I can tell you very confidently that the "sun" is a metaphor for Self. Thus, the eagle, which is a common metaphor in *Thus Spoke Zarathustra*, is any sudden desire to go out into the wild (the passions) and find one's Self, and the snake wrapped around the eagle's neck, which is another common metaphor, is knowledge of the newfound Self that is gained via that desire (eagle). And the reason he chose a bird for his metaphor is because finding one's Self is often exhilarating and the discovery makes the discoverer feel as if he is rising above himself, out of chaos, after which his "eagle" continues in time to rise even higher still. And the reason that the "eagle" and the "snake" are called "Zarathustra's animals" is because they come and go without any rhyme or reason; they come and go like animalistic urges.

In his essay, *On Music and Words*, Nietzsche continues to explore the possibility of representing the entire inner world of man in words, specifically metaphor, and he enunciates the use of metaphor *as gesture* to indicate which elements of the inner world are being referenced in dithyrambic music. The sum of the essay is the goal of understanding language as a means of communicating dithyrambic music via metaphor. And by "dithyrambic music," he does not mean audible music but rather the entire spectrum of human emotion, volition, mood, and sensation, which is an entirely new use of the word "music."

In the first paragraph, he elucidates the fact that mime is intensified symbolism of a person's gestures and is, in fact, a simile or a metaphor that can be used to express music (mood). Then he goes on to cite Schopenhauer's insight into the expression of music or mood through language.

> "It might be admissible, although a purely musical mind does not demand it, to join and adapt words or even a clearly represented action to the pure language of tones, although the latter, being self-sufficient, needs no help; so that our perceiving and reflecting intellect, which does not like to be quite idle, may

meanwhile have light and analogous occupation also. By this concession to the intellect man's attention adheres even more closely to music, by this at the same time, too, is placed underneath that which the tones indicate in their general metaphorless language of the heart, a visible picture, as it were a schema, as an example illustrating a general idea . . . indeed such things will even heighten the effect of music." (Schopenhauer, Parerga, II., "On the Metaphysics of the Beautiful and Æsthetics," § 224.)[42]

In order to understand the above statement, it must be deconstructed. Simply put, Schopenhauer seems to be saying that words and action can be made to synchronize, as it were, with the tone of an actor's voice or the tone of music. And, most importantly, the synchronized words and action will heighten the effect of the actor's tone of voice or the tone of the music. By a grand leap of thought and insight, Nietzsche will take Schopenhauer's insight to a new insight, which lies at the heart of the New Dithyramb.

Somehow, and I have yet to find the exact moment when he did it, Nietzsche came to the conclusion that when sensation, emotion, volition, impulse, and instinct (in short, everything that is Dionysian) come together to form an idea and, more importantly, a myth, the confluence they form immediately preceding the production of the idea or myth constitutes a phenomenon he calls "music," by which he means dramatic music.

Thus, taking Schopenhauer's insight as stated above, Nietzsche would go on to conclude that metaphor can be made to "synchronize" *or reflect* sensation, emotion, volition, impulse, and instinct, in short, "music." And most importantly, using those metaphors and relying on the listener's ability to render the metaphors and "hear" the "music," the actor can be brought into the musical confluence and will necessarily be led to the idea or the myth arising out of that music. Bring the actor into the moods, the states of mind, *and he will see the idea or the myth*. That is one of the most fundamental rules of dithyrambic drama: dithyrambic drama teaches ideas and myth by representing the moods or the states of mind out of which the idea or myth arises naturally.

With all of this said, then we can make sense of the following statement that Nietzsche made regarding his *Thus Spoke Zarathustra*.

> The whole of *Zarathustra* might perhaps be classified under the rubric music. At all events, the essential condition of its production was a second birth within me of the art of hearing.[43]

Lastly, the above citation of Schopenhauer's writing states that the idea or myth arising out of that musical confluence will be heightened (or enlivened) by that "music," by the emotions out of which the idea or myth was created. And that insight goes directly to the creation of the mythical Übermensch. As the actor embodies the "music," the inner conflict, that is found in each dithyramb, he takes a step closer to his Self in direct proportion to his ability to uncover and "hear" the deeper mood and "see" his deeper Self in that mood. The apprehension of that deeper Self, which lies beyond the existing Self, is the myth that Nietzsche calls

Übermensch and which I call the supra-Self. And insofar as the deeper mood enlivens or animates the deeper Self that the actor finds in it, that deeper sense of Self then becomes reality, which prompts the proto-tragic phenomenon by which the former Self collapses in the wake of the emerging deeper reality. This whole process of listening for the deeper mood, creating the deeper mythical Self, and letting the old Self die away is the very process by which life constitutes itself within the human spirit. Clearly, this is a process of becoming, and it is a process of becoming in which being plays only a proto-tragic role. Moreover, it is a process that unfolds continually, until the very deepest supra-Self is reached. As we shall see, however, the meaning or ultimate aim of the whole process *is not* the visualization or apprehension of the deepest Self but rather the *transcendence* of the deepest Self, a passage beyond the limits of all individuation into supra-individuation, which I will explain further a little later.

Returning to our discussion of the structure of the new dithyramb, *Nietzsche's metaphors are gesticulative metaphors that reflect an inner state of mind.* And that is a huge advance in the history of writing. In the beginning of the history of writing, written symbols reflected numbers, quantity. Then, other symbols reflected the objects, like grain or animals, that were being counted. Eventually, writing went on to reflect numerous things, all nouns, in the world. Then written symbols went on to reflect the sounds that people spoke, so that more than mere nouns could be reflected in written symbols, like movement, which made the composition of whole sentences possible. Eventually, writing developed into the reflection of ideas and concepts. With Nietzsche, writing has now developed further into the reflection of inner states of mind. And that is an extraordinary achievement. *That is Nietzsche's achievement in the new dithyramb.*

But for what purpose would a writer want to represent a state of mind? For the purpose of creating living myth within its readers. Except that reading literature that reflects an inner state of mind requires more than a mere reading. What is really intended in the representation is that the reader *embody* the represented state of mind, that he enters into it himself. Because it is only via that embodiment that the reader, who has now become an actor via that embodiment, will "see" the myth, provided the representation is properly mythopoeic, provided the writer has chosen a state of mind that leads to mythopoeia. In other words, if I can transport you into a state of mind in which you would discover a deeper sense of Self, that would be a mythopoeic moment. And that is what the dithyramb and dithyrambic music does. And it is only if the represented state of mind *truly* prompts mythopoeia that the representation may then rightly qualify as "music." When Nietzsche speaks of dithyrambic music, that is precisely the qualification he is referencing: the ability to prompt mythopoeia.

The other point to consider is whether it is possible to simply compose a single dithyramb that, through embodiment, would lead the actor directly into a state of mind in which his deeper Self would be revealed to him. The answer is no. There is an entire series of dithyrambs that must be undertaken in order to lead up to the mythopoeic moment. For instance, insofar as a deeper Self is only revealed by plumbing the subconscious, and insofar as the subconscious is a place where deeply intractable and deeply disturbing emotions reside, it is first necessary to learn that process of plumbing. And there are dithyrambs that teach the actor to do that, but only by entering into the various states of mind in which resistance to the subconscious is made manifest, so that the actor may then learn the "fix" to overcome them and that resistance. Thus, there is a continuum of inner states of mind (or melodies) through which the actor must pass along the way to the moment of mythopoeia.

> ... he really did succeed in discovering a novel method of expressing the grand and vaulting arch of passion. He merely selected certain portions of its curve; imparted these with the utmost clearness to his listeners, and then left it to them to *divine* its whole span.[44]

That continuum renders those various states very meaningful to each other. And that meaningful continuum, as a whole and as represented in the whole dithyrambic drama, is something Nietzsche calls "dramatic music." It is musical in the sense that one state of mind that precedes another — necessarily precedes, and another that follows — necessarily follows, just as notes in a melody necessarily precede and follow one another.

It is especially important to understand that the various states of mind leading to mythopoeia are not contrived; there are relationships among them that are real and entirely natural.

> Not that [Nietzsche] invented or was the first to create this relationship, for they must always have existed and have been noticeable to all; but, as is usually the case with a great problem, it is like a precious stone which thousands stumble over before one finally picks it up.[45]

Continuing with our discussion of the essay *On Moods*, in the next paragraph, he says that words are symbols of concepts and that tone is a gesture of pain and pleasure. He also says that tone can be represented by the vowels and consonants that comprise a word or sentence. (However, the only way I found that Nietzsche was ever able to indicate tone in words was with italics). And he also says something that is very telling: "The whole life of impulses, too, the play of feelings, sensations, emotions, volitions, is known to us ... after a most rigid self-examination."[46] This statement is telling because it means any representation of the elements of the inner world is meaningless to someone who has not already undertaken a rigid self-examination. And the reason this insight is so important to consider in our quest to understand the hermeneutics of the new dithyramb is because, as we will see, rendition of the metaphors in which dithyrambic music is composed *leads* the reader/actor to undertake that rigid self-examination simultaneously with his effort to decipher the symbolic metaphors, the gestures. In other words, it is not possible to see the gestures in written metaphors without also feeling or intuiting that which is being represented in metaphor. The metaphors provide clues to the inner pathos that is being represented, and, until the actor reckons what those clues point to *and then embodies that pathos*, only then, can the reader/actor proclaim, "Oh, yes, I see the similarity (between mood and metaphor)."

In the third paragraph, he states his goal: to transcribe music, by which he states that he means will (or, more specifically, a cadent chain of moods, a melody of moods), into metaphors. Keep in mind that, in the essay *On Moods*, he was looking for a way to communicate mood in words. And by mood, we now know that he meant all the inner world, except ideation: just moods, drives and desires, their conflicts and their resolutions — in short, will, or, as we shall see shortly, everything within the inner world that he would come to label as Dionysian.

> This original phenomenon, the "Will," with its scale of pleasure-and-displeasure-sensations attains in the development of music an ever more adequate symbolic expression: and to this historical process the continuous effort of lyric poetry runs parallel, the effort to transcribe music into metaphors: exactly as this double-phenomenon, according to the just completed disquisition, lies typified in language.[47]

In the next paragraph, he states another goal: after finding a way to transcribe mood into metaphor, then to find a way to enable mood to produce idea. If he found a way to produce idea via the representation of dithyrambic music in metaphor, it is very important for us to understand that process of production because that would be a fundamental rule in the entire hermeneutics of the new dithyramb. In fact, he did find a way, and that is how he communicates his ideas of the Übermensch and the idea that all things within the inner world of man recur unendingly.

Words are symbols of concepts, except in dithyrambic music where they are symbols of moods from within the inner world and gestures pointing to those moods: drives, passions, and volitions. We are accustomed to read words while simultaneously interpreting them as symbols of things that exist within the *outer* physical world. In dithyrambic music, what is needed instead is to read words and, rather than interpreting them as symbols of things that exist within the outer world, interpreting them as *gestures* that point to feelings and moods within the inner world. I repeat, the metaphors in which dithyrambic music is composed are gestures, like facial gestures. And to read the gestures is exactly like reading the gestures a speaker makes when he is speaking *in order to* better understand his state of mind, his mood, as bespoken by his tone of voice and facial gestures.

> The sentence quivers with passion. Eloquence has become music. Forks of lightning are hurled towards futures of which no one has ever dreamed before. The most powerful use of [metaphor] that has yet existed is poor beside it, and mere child's-play compared with this return of language to the nature of imagery. [48]

The process of reading gestures is not a complicated or difficult process. Children do it regularly. And children do it much more adeptly and naturally than adults. A child can watch his mother speak and very quickly ascertain those elements of his mother's inner world that are revealed in his mother's tone of voice and the gestures she makes with her face and her limbs, be it anger, love, pain, frustration — anything that is bespoken in those tones and gestures. It is the same with dithyrambic music; you simply read the metaphors as you would read facial gestures. But you certainly do not read them as literal text. Or, to put it another way, the moment you catch yourself thinking conceptually rather than intuitively while reading the dithyrambs, that is when you must refocus your thinking on metaphors of your feelings. And in the beginning, after learning to read it intuitively, as music, you will occasionally revert to reading it conceptually, purely out of habit.

> Now, it is true that language also has this task *[of intensifying the expression of feeling]*, but it is much more difficult for it to achieve it, and it can only do so by indirect means. Language has an impact primarily on the conceptual world, and only secondarily on the emotions, and frequently it does not, because of the length of the path, reach its goal at all. Music, however, immediately strikes the heart *[intuitively]*, as the true universal language that is understood everywhere.[49]

And in case there is any doubt that the dithyramb is a depiction of an inner state of mind and that the "listener" must be capable of that inner state of mind, I would direct the reader to Nietzsche's own statement on the matter.

> I will now pass just one or two general remarks about my *art of style*. To communicate a state an inner tension of pathos by means of signs, including the tempo of these signs,—that is the meaning of every style; and in view of the fact that the multiplicity of inner states in me is enormous, I am capable of many kinds of style—in short, the most multifarious art of style that any man has ever had at his disposal. Any style is *good* which genuinely communicates an inner condition, which does not blunder

over the signs, over the tempo of the signs, or over *moods*—all the laws of phrasing are the outcome of representing moods artistically. Good style, in itself, is a piece of sheer foolery, mere idealism, like "beauty in itself," for instance, or "goodness in itself," or "the thing-in- itself." All this takes for granted, of course, that there exist ears that can hear, and such men as are capable and worthy of a like pathos, that those are not wanting unto whom one may communicate one's self. Meanwhile my Zarathustra, for instance, is still in quest of such people—alas! he will have to seek a long while yet! A man must be worthy of listening to him.... And, until that time, there will be no one who will understand the art that has been squandered in this book. No one has ever existed who has had more novel, more strange, and purposely created art forms to fling to the winds. The fact that such things were possible in the German language still awaited proof; formerly, I myself would have denied most emphatically that it was possible. Before my time people did not know what could be done with the German language—what could be done with language in general. The art of grand rhythm, of grand style in periods, for expressing the tremendous fluctuations of sublime and superhuman passion, was first discovered by me: with the dithyramb entitled "The Seven Seals," which constitutes the last discourse of

> the third part of *Zarathustra*, I soared miles above all that which heretofore has been called poetry.[50]

However, in order for this gesture-reading process to work, two conditions must exist. The dithyrambic music must be an accurate depiction of the inner human reality being referenced in the metaphors, and the actor must be capable of the same passion that is being depicted. In fact, it is the accuracy of the reality of that depiction, down to the smallest detail, that prompts Nietzsche to call his dithyrambic compositions "music," by which he means dramatic music. All that he means when he speaks of dramatic or dithyrambic music is the quality of detailed reality, and that reality includes *melos*, by which I mean the specific and naturally occurring order of the states of mind that precede the idea or myth arising out of that chain of states. For instance, the accumulation of empowerment arising from an increasingly brilliant vision of Self necessarily leads to a moment of dissonance that necessarily leads to proto-tragedy. That is a good example of dithyrambic melos. Melos is reality in the sense that it is not something that can be concocted; it exists only in nature (in this case, human nature) and must be perceived and then accurately depicted, and that is what the dithyramb depicts.

As for the accuracy of Nietzsche's depictions of reality in his dithyrambs, this is a point that requires extensive and persuasive documentation, which I will provide later in a reiteration of *The Birth of Tragedy* and in a reiteration of his essay called *Richard Wagner in Bayreuth*. But for the time being, consider what Nietzsche wrote in *Wagner in Bayreuth*, which, I would remind the reader is not a disquisition on Richard Wagner and his music but rather on Friedrich Nietzsche and his dithyrambic music, according to Nietzsche himself, as noted above.

> ... he really did succeed in discovering a novel method of expressing the grand and vaulting arch of passion. He merely selected certain portions of its curve; imparted these with the utmost clearness to his listeners, and then left it to them to *divine* its whole span. Viewed superficially, the new form seemed rather like an aggregation of several musical compositions, of which every one appeared to represent a sustained situation, but was in reality but a momentary stage in the dramatic course of a passion. The listener might think that he was hearing the old "mood" music over again, except that he failed to grasp the relation of the various parts to one another.[51]

And,

> Taken as a whole, [Dithyrambic] music is a reflex of the world as it was understood by the great Ephesian poet—that is to say, a harmony resulting from strife, as the union of justice and enmity. I admire the ability which could describe the grand line of universal passion out of a confusion of passions which all seem to be striking out in different directions.... [52]

In those essays, as we will see, Nietzsche argues that it was a disregard of "music," a disregard of reality, that the later writers of tragedy perpetrated, which, in turn, led to the disintegration of myth as an art form and, with it, proto-tragedy.

And, as for the actor being capable of the passion being depicted in any particular dithyramb, this is a central point out of which many points regarding hermeneutics arise.

There are people, for instance, who know nothing of jealousy. When they were young and just learning about life, if they had not yet learned about jealousy, seeing it in other people would have gone entirely unnoticed. The same can be said for vengefulness. There are people who are not prone to vindictiveness. Eventually, as they grow older, they learn about revenge, and they learn about the satisfaction that derives from "an eye for any eye." But as souls not inclined to revenge, and as children who have not yet learned of life, seeing a gesture of revenge in the soul of another human being will go completely unnoticed, so that the meaning of someone saying to them "I did not want to give him the satisfaction" will seem meaningless to them.

Therefore, with regard to the dithyramb, which depicts passions via metaphorical gestures, the actor wishing to render the dithyramb and embody the passion it depicts must be capable of that passion to begin with. Otherwise, a metaphorical depiction will go totally unnoticed. In the instances presented by Nietzsche in his dithyrambs, however, the passions depicted do not rise from a petty soul but rather from a lofty soul, and those lofty passions may arise only from a height that not all readers are capable of reaching, but that remains to be seen, and I certainly do not wish to exclude anyone from Nietzsche's dithyrambic drama.

Keeping in mind that Nietzsche's dithyrambic drama is a journey into the subconscious for the purpose of freeing oneself from the grip of one's own demons, when the moment of confrontation finally occurs, it will require an uncommon effort to break that grip and attain freedom. And some people may not be equal to that effort, which means that a metaphorical depiction of the passion and inner circumstances comprising that effort will go totally unnoticed by those people.

> After all, no one can draw more out of things, books included, than he already knows. A man has no ears for that to which experience has given him no access. To take an extreme case, suppose a book contains simply incidents which lie quite outside the range of general or even rare experience—suppose it to be the *first* language to express a whole series of experiences. In this case nothing it contains will really be heard at all, and, thanks to an acoustic delusion, people will believe that where nothing is heard there is nothing to hear.[53]

The actor must also be able to think in leaps and bounds in order to complete the journey. And what does it mean to think in leaps and bounds? Nietzsche himself provides a good analogy in the following quote from *Philosophy in the Tragic Age of the Greeks*.

> How despotically such a faith deals with all empiricism is worthy of note; with Thales especially one can learn how Philosophy has behaved at all times, when she wanted to get

beyond the hedges of experience to her magically attracting goal. On light supports she leaps in advance; hope and divination wing her feet. Calculating reason too, clumsily pants after her and seeks better supports in its attempt to reach that alluring goal, at which its divine companion has already arrived. One sees in imagination two wanderers by a wild forest-stream which carries with it rolling stones; the one, light-footed, leaps over it using the stones and swinging himself upon them ever further and further, though they precipitously sink into the depths behind him. The other stands helpless there most of the time; he has first to build a pathway which will bear his heavy, weary step; sometimes that cannot be done and then no god will help him across the stream. What therefore carries philosophical thinking so quickly to its goal? Does it distinguish itself from calculating and measuring thought only by its more rapid flight through large spaces? No, for a strange illogical power wings the foot of philosophical thinking; and this power is Fancy. Lifted by the latter, philosophical thinking leaps from possibility to possibility, and these for the time being are taken as certainties; and now and then even whilst on the wing it gets hold of certainties. An ingenious presentiment shows them to the flier; demonstrable certainties are divined at a

> distance to be at this point. Especially
> powerful is the strength of Fancy in the
> lightning-like seizing and illuminating of
> similarities; afterwards reflection applies its
> standards and models and seeks to substitute
> the similarities by equalities, that which was
> seen side by side by causalities. But though
> this should never be possible, even in the
> case of Thales the indemonstrable
> philosophising has yet its value; although all
> supports are broken when Logic and the
> rigidity of Empiricism want to get across to
> the proposition: Everything is water; yet still
> there is always, after the demolition of the
> scientific edifice, a remainder, and in this
> very remainder lies a moving force and as it
> were the hope of future fertility.[54]

In short, there will come a time in the course of your journey through this drama when you cannot go forward. When that happens, reason and logic will not help you. Instead, you must be inclined to leap forward upon plausible possibilities that will avail themselves only to your intuition. In such a way, you must be able to think in leaps and bounds. And being able to think in leaps and bounds is an uncommon trait.

The other most obvious prerequisite for an undertaking of Nietzsche's dithyrambic drama is a desire for Self, a desire to find your Self, since the entire drama is about finding your Self for the purpose of freeing yourself from the grip of your demons.

Given these prerequisites, it should not surprise anyone that Nietzsche was very concerned that his drama would not be understood. In fact, he was much more concerned that his drama would be misconstrued. And there are numerous instances throughout his writing when he expresses this concern, which I now cite to persuade you that this concern was quite prevalent in Nietzsche's thinking.

With [critics of Heraclitus] also originate the numerous complaints as to the obscurity of the Heraclitean style; probably no man has ever written clearer and more illuminatingly; of course, very abruptly, and therefore naturally obscure to the racing readers. But why a philosopher should intentionally write obscurely—a thing habitually said about Heraclitus—is absolutely inexplicable; unless he has some cause to hide his thoughts or is sufficiently a rogue to conceal his thoughtlessness underneath words. One is, as Schopenhauer says, indeed compelled by lucid expression to prevent misunderstandings even in affairs of practical every-day life, how then should one be allowed to express oneself indistinctly, indeed puzzlingly in the most difficult, most abstruse, scarcely attainable object of thinking, the tasks of philosophy? With respect to brevity however Jean Paul gives a good precept: "On the whole it is right that everything great—of deep meaning to a rare mind—should be uttered with brevity and (therefore) obscurely so that the paltry mind would rather proclaim it to be nonsense than

> translate it into the realm of his empty-
> headedness. For common minds have an ugly
> ability to perceive in the deepest and richest
> saying nothing but their own every-day
> opinion."[55]

Nietzsche greatly admired both Heraclitus and Schopenhauer. He admired Schopenhauer because it was Schopenhauer who helped Nietzsche discover his passion for philosophy and introduced him to the study. And he admired Heraclitus for (1) his reliance on intuition (rather than logic) for his philosophic thinking, his proclivity to explain things via riddle or parable, and (3), as stated above, for the brevity of his explanations.

At the very least, the above quote should provide some measure of proof that Nietzsche foresaw a need to disqualify common minds and dawdling readers from availing themselves to his writing.

And, as I stated earlier, in the *Will to Power*, he wrote of his belief that Christ made a mistake speaking his teaching to the lower classes of his society.

> The Founder of Christianity had to pay
> dearly for having directed His teaching at the
> lowest classes of Jewish society and
> intelligence. They understood Him only
> according to the limitations of their own
> spirit.[56]

Whether or not Nietzsche is correct that Christ's teaching was misunderstood by the people to whom he spoke is not important. What is important to note is that

Nietzsche saw the possibility of his own eventual teaching being misunderstood, specifically by the error of not carefully choosing an audience.

And there was also this concern:

> Securing a Good Hearing. — It is not sufficient to know how to play well; one must also know how to secure a good hearing. A violin in the hand of the greatest master gives only a little squeak when the place where it is heard is too large; the master may then be mistaken for any bungler.[57]

And there was also his concern that people would read into his work that which they wanted to hear, especially with regard to their own egotistical ends, which he wrote about in *Ecco Homo*.

> He who thought he had understood something in my work, had as a rule adjusted something in it to his own image—not infrequently the very opposite of myself, an "idealist," for instance.[58]

Therefore, given these concerns, Nietzsche took measures to prevent any misunderstandings.

First, he arranged his metaphorical gestures in such a way that they presented the false appearance of a book that proposed to teach a way of living, when, in fact, he proposed a way of thinking. Numerous dithyrambs are entitled in such a way as to present this false appearance, such as the dithyramb entitled Of the State and another entitled Of Marriage and

Children. Neither one is about what their title implies: neither marriage and children nor the state. The dithyramb entitled Of the State is about the state of being that presents itself as both an idea and a sense of Self in the course of its discovery. The problem with the image of Self is that, due to its illusory and accompanying redemptive nature, it beguiles the beholder into a state of enchantment that enfeebles the will, which halts further growth. This dithyramb teaches the actor how not be beguiled by the image of Self as it unfolds to him and to look for a deeper Self. All the dithyrambs teach a way of thinking.

Also, if you remember I told you earlier that, since the will is fundamentally a desire that becomes stronger when it is augmented by this and that mood, be it another desire or drive or urge, then it becomes important how you choose which of those moods you wish to harness to achieve your goal, which is always a greater apprehension of Self. The dithyramb entitled Of Marriage and Children teaches you how to choose. Which mood are you going to harness (or marry) every time it raises itself and how effective will it be in leading you to a higher apprehension of your Self (children)?

The metaphors are also arranged to present the false appearance that Nietzsche is telling a story. In the dithyramb entitled Of the Tree on the Mountainside, it appears that a story is being told about a young man who has been learning from Zarathustra and then suddenly begins to avoid him. Therefore, Zarathustra takes the young men to a tree on a mountainside and begins a narration that supposedly will teach the young man why he is avoiding Zarathustra. Specifically, Zarathustra says that life is like the tree next to where they are standing: "the more it wants to rise into the heights, the more determinedly must its roots dig deeply 'into the darkness, into the depths, into evil.'" Clearly, this appears to tell a story. However, the latter part about the tree digging more deeply into the "darkness, the depths, into evil" makes no sense. And that is because the dithyramb does not tell a story. The dithyramb depicts an inner tension of conscience and passion, suffering and Self, passion and thought. The appearance of a story is entirely contrived and serves nothing more than to encrypt the drama. This false appearance is meant to dissuade the dawdling reader from rendering the gestures and finding the inner tension that is actually being depicted in the dithyramb. So long as you read the dithyramb like you would read a story, it makes no sense. As soon as you begin to look at the text as metaphorical gestures that point to something that exists within yourself — and then begin the work of rendering those metaphors, finding that inner tension within yourself, *and entering into it, through a plausible embodiment* — then the dithyramb becomes meaningful.

If you look more deeply at this dithyramb entitled Of the Tree on the Mountainside, what you will find is that the metaphors point to an inner situation in which, having learned the rudiments of finding one's Self, the actor has begun to ascend upon the steps of his minor victories. And his small victory gives rise to a new desire that impels him to rise even higher. But the actor cannot go another step forward. In order to solve this problem, the dithyramb teaches him (or her) that he must begin to look into his subconscious in order to rise higher, which is what he will do. And that is how the drama continues for the actor who finally renders this dithyramb.

Here is the same insight expressed in only partial metaphor in the *Gay Science*.

> ... we ourselves grow, we change continually,
> we cast off old bark, we still slough every
> spring, we always become younger, higher,
> stronger, as men of the future, we thrust our
> roots always more powerfully into the
> deep—into evil—, while at the same time we
> embrace the heavens ever more lovingly,
> more extensively, and suck in their light ever
> more eagerly with all our branches and
> leaves. We grow like trees—that is difficult
> to understand, like all life! — not in one
> place, but everywhere, not in one direction
> only, but upwards and outwards, as well as
> inwards and downwards. At the same time
> our force shoots forth in stem, branches, and
> roots; we are really no longer free to do
> anything separately, or to be anything
> separately.... Such is our lot, as we have said:
> we grow in *height*; and even should it be our
> calamity—for we dwell ever closer to the
> lightning![59]

The many false appearances that Nietzsche contrived are his defense against any misunderstanding of his book — because there has been nothing but misunderstanding for more than a century since it was published. The many false appearances in Nietzsche's dithyramb are his defense against the desecration of his drama. He has erected a wall through which no ego may pass. On one side of that wall lies the sanctuary of unadulterated poetry, which is the most poignant poetry you will ever read anywhere, in my opinion. And on the other side of that wall lies ferocious and barbaric egotistical motivations that will surely ravage and denigrate that beauty. As we will see later in *The Birth of Tragedy*, this wall is a fundamental part of the structure of the dithyramb.

> *The Question of Intelligibility.* — One not only wants to be understood when one writes, but also — quite as certainly — *not* to be understood. It is by no means an objection to a book when someone finds it unintelligible: perhaps this might just have been the intention of its author, — perhaps he did not want to be understood by "anyone." A distinguished intellect and taste, when it wants to communicate its thoughts, always selects its hearers; by selecting them, it at the same time closes its barriers against "the others." It is there that all the more refined laws of style have their origin: they at the same time keep off, they create distance, they prevent "access" (intelligibility, as we have said,)—while they open the ears of those who are acoustically related to them.[60]

The other defense mechanism Nietzsche used in composing the dithyramb is his use of riddle, the best example of which is the dedication on the front page "For Everyone and No One." Insofar as every human being can find their Self in Nietzsche's dithyrambs, the book is intended for everyone. But because they must check their Ego before entering, the book is for no one. Another way to look at that is that, insofar as the dithyrambs depict inner states of mind that are universally embodiable by everyone, then the book is intended for everyone. But, insofar as none of the dithyrambs depict a particular idiosyncratic Ego beholden to a particular individual, then the book is for no one.

And another example of Nietzsche's use of riddle can be found in the dithyramb entitled Of the Vision and the Riddle, at the very end, the last idiom, which states "My longing for this laughter gnaws at me; oh how can I bear to go on living! And how could I bear to die now!" I am not going to render this idiom for you right now because doing so would take us into a discussion that we are not yet ready to undertake. (You can jump ahead to the exegeses section and read the rendition that explains this riddle, if you wish.) But suffice it to say that Nietzsche had a strong proclivity for using riddle, which would prove very effective to dissuade the dawdling reader from further reading.

Lastly, the structure of the dithyramb compels the reader to engage in a lengthy and very deep introspection in order to render the metaphors, which leads to a phenomenon I call dithyrambic transport. It is always important to remain faithful and trusting to the idea that the dithyramb is an accurate depiction of whatever "inner tension" is being pointed to by the gestures in the text, that the gestures are accurate gestures, and that, if you look hard enough, you will find *precisely* what is being pointed to.

The whole process of introspection leads to an isolation of the passion or the subliminal conflict that is being depicted by the dithyramb, and, upon achieving that isolation, then the actor can act upon it, but not before.

Consider what Nietzsche wrote about learning to love something within yourself.

> *One must Learn to Love.* — This is our experience in music: we must first *learn* in

general to *hear*, to hear fully, and to distinguish a theme or a melody, **we have to isolate and limit it as a life by itself**; then we need to exercise effort and good-will in order *to endure it* in spite of its strangeness we need patience towards its aspect and expression and indulgence towards what is odd in it:—in the end there comes a moment when we are *accustomed* to it, when we expect it, when it dawns upon us that we should miss it if it were lacking; and then it goes on to exercise its spell and charm more and more, and does not cease until we have become its humble and enraptured lovers, who want it, and want it again, and ask for nothing better from the world.—It is thus with us, however, not only in music: it is precisely thus that we have *learned to love everything* that we love. We are always finally recompensed for our good-will, our patience reasonableness and gentleness towards what is unfamiliar, by the unfamiliar slowly throwing off its veil and presenting itself to us as a new, ineffable beauty: — that is its *thanks* for our hospitality. He also who loves himself must have learned it in this way: there is no other way. Love also has to be learned.[61] (emphasis added)

The advantage that love imparts to will becomes more apparent if the above instance is applied to a moment when an emotion to which the actor was previously oblivious then makes its way into consciousness and becomes attributed to a deeper sense of Self. Given that the newly-found dimension of Self was previously in a state of oblivion, it may easily sink back into oblivion. But if the actor learns to "love it," it is less likely to sink back into oblivion because love of something imparts a feeling of missing that something in its absence, which would impel the beholder to retrieve it. And insofar as it is a reflection of a deeper Self, which the actor, in pursuit of his Self, wishes to preserve, in this way love becomes an advantage to will.

This, by the way, is precisely what the dithyramb entitled Of the Spirit of Gravity teaches: that love of any newly-discovered attribute of the aborning deeper Self helps to support that deeper Self and prevent its sinking back into oblivion.

But the point to understand here is that the metaphorical structure of the dithyramb *and its deconstruction* assists in the process of isolation. And isolation is the beginning of the second process of will augmentation.

In another instance, which I cannot find for proper citation, when he talks about learning to break a bad habit, he speaks of doing the same thing: first isolating the inner circumstances of the habit and only then beginning the work of dismantling it.

Deciphering the metaphors in which the dithyramb is composed leads to this isolation because the metaphors accurately depict that inner circumstance and provide the clues that lead the actor down the path to isolation, which is precisely what Nietzsche intended.

> Most people stand so strongly under the influence of their drives that they do not even notice what is happening. I want to state what is happening and call attention to it.[62]

However, despite the early ambition revealed in the above quote, what Nietzsche actually ended up doing was to "state what is happening" in metaphor only and, in doing so, he succeeded to "call attention to it" by transporting the actor himself *into* "what is happening."

And it is important to pay close attention to every single detail of the metaphors in the text because some gestures are very discrete but very significant. For instance, in the dithyramb entitled The Prophet, Zarathustra narrates a dream he had, in which he had become a guardian of dead men's coffins in a cemetery. He described coffins with glass tops, so that he could see into the coffins where the dead men lay. He also said that he carried old and rusty keys that would open these coffins, but that, when he did open the coffins, the deal souls therein cried out that they did not want to be disturbed. But then Zarathustra heard a knocking from within the coffins, as if some soul therein did indeed wish to emerge. And Zarathustra said "Alpa! I cried, who is bearing his ashes to the mountain? Alpa! Alpa! Who is bearing his ashes to the mountain?"

Clearly, this text reads like a story. But now you know that all of the text in which *Thus Spoke Zarathustra* is composed is metaphorical and that these metaphors are intended to act like gestures, just like facial gestures, that point you to some inner tension or circumstance of passion and conscience, just like facial gestures point to the emotions that produce them. Therefore, there is no story here. There are only prompts directing you toward some situation that exists within yourself, and those prompts have been carefully arranged to trick you into missing them.

But note also that the representation is an intricate one as well. For instance, the coffins have glass covers on them, which means that the actor can see into them. In this dithyramb, the actor has come upon his subliminal demons, which were previously hidden away in oblivion. And he can see how his Self is suffering as a result of these demons. But he cannot raise them into consciousness; he is still dismembered from them. Until, finally, he is prompted by the dithyramb to ask "Who is bearing his ashes to the mountain?" In other words, he is prompted to ask "Who is suffering in this moment?" This is a mythopoeic moment. Like the fisherman in our previous example who finds himself in a situation in which he observes things happening and cannot understand why they are happening until he finally posits a ghost as their cause, the actor is prompted to understand precisely *who is suffering these demons* that have finally come to the fore. And when he ruminates on that for some time, he will come to realize that it is his deeper Self that is suffering these demons. And with that epiphany, those demons will burst forth from their glass coffins and into consciousness, along with his deeper Self. Therefore, again, it is very important to pay close attention to the details provided by the metaphors and not to overlook any of them.

Rumination is also an important part of the whole rendering process.

> … the aphoristic form produces difficulty, but this is only because this form is treated *too casually*. An aphorism properly coined and cast into its final mould is far from being "deciphered" as soon as it has been read; on the contrary, it is then that it first requires *to be expounded*—of course for that purpose an art of exposition is necessary. The third essay in this book provides an example of what is

> offered, of what in such cases I call exposition: an aphorism is prefixed to that essay, the essay itself is its commentary. Certainly one *quality* which nowadays has been best forgotten—and that is why it will take some time yet for my writings to become readable—is essential in order to practise reading as an art—a quality for the exercise of which it is necessary to be a cow, and under *no circumstances* a modern man!— *rumination*.[63]

It is necessary to reflect a long time on the metaphors while at the same time searching your inner thoughts and emotions while trying to find a match. Very often, the riddling nature of the metaphors will make them stick in your mind, so that, even though you may not be thinking about them, the fact that they were presented as riddles made them take hold within you like something you would like to shake but cannot. The quandary presented by the riddle will struggle to find its way out of your mind like something stuck between your teeth that you keep coming back to work on. One day, while thinking about this or that dilemma within yourself, quite apart from something you may have read in *Thus Spoke Zarathustra*, the metaphors and the clues they provide will suddenly come to you in a verisimilar analogy to that dilemma. And, when you aren't expecting it, the simile will come to you like an epiphany and you will see exactly how the clues do indeed accurately portray the inner circumstance that you are being prompted to find. And when that happens, then you will have precisely isolated that specific circumstance of thought and passions amidst all the many and sometimes chaotic thoughts and passions within yourself. Then you will come back to read that same dithyramb again, and you will understand it then, having rendered it properly. Rendering the rest of the dithyramb will be much easier, and it will teach you how you are supposed to proceed with that circumstance that you will have finally isolated, whether it be by using that circumstance to augment your desire for Self or by learning to untangle yourself from it, like a bad habit, because it may be taking away from your desire for Self. In every case, with every dithyramb, your desire for Self will increase. And if you do not emerge from a particular dithyramb with a clearer apprehension of Self, then you will have strengthened some emotion or found some idea by which to increase it later in another dithyramb.

And you can see from the above quote about Zarathustra and the coffins, this is a very intricately woven depiction of an inner tension or circumstance. *Therefore, you must pay close attention to all the details in the gestures* and overlook nothing, nor take any of the details for granted, as in a quick or hurried manner, because they contain clues that you need in order to complete the embodiment. And most importantly, when the text poses a question, as above when Zarathustra exclaims "who is bearing his ashes to the mountain," that is a question you must ask yourselves and *you must ask the question from within the particular inner circumstance* that is being depicted in the dithyramb. And on that point, we must now move to understand how dithyrambic music produces ideas. But first, you must understand something about the nature of Nietzsche's thinking.

The breadth and depth to which Nietzsche's percipience took him in life was quite extraordinary. But on what did he focus? Some philosophers wrote about the physical, earthly world and everything on it and above it ("the works" or the physics) and then, after that, they wrote about the inner world of man and everything within it (the "after the works" or the metaphysics). Nietzsche wrote *only* about the inner world, which he viewed as a world unto itself. He wrote virtually *nothing* about the physical world. Therefore, when he says something about the "world," he is *always* talking about the inner world. For instance, when he says that we must learn to accept both the good and the bad as it exists in the world, again, he is talking only about the inner world of man. I have heard scholars wonder how Nietzsche could possibly mean that we must accept all the bad that exists in the world, when they mean the physical, earthly world and he meant the inner world.

If you remember my telling you that a summary of the total experience provided by an undertaking of *Thus Spoke Zarathustra* was revealed in a quote by Nietzsche when he said that he had spent his entire life learning how to plumb the subconscious and then learning to free himself from the grip of the bad conscience therein, then it makes sense that learning to accept everything bad that is found along the course of that journey is going to be a primary and fundamental prerequisite of any success, especially if you also consider the value that derives from the redemption of all the bad (or "evil") that is found along the way. In this sense, it makes perfect sense not only to learn to accept all the bad in "the world" but, in fact, to value it. But it clearly makes no sense that we should learn to embrace and celebrate all the bad and evil that exists here on earth in this life we live amongst all the random and hazardous phenomenon that play out.

Remember that whenever Nietzsche speaks of "the world," he means the inner world of man, in every instance. And if you miss that point, then you miss everything, as I hopefully just clarified for you.

The Use of Metaphor in the New Dithyramb

With Nietzsche's invention of a new art form, which will be called the New Dithyramb, we now have a literary representation of something that has never before been communicated: a state of mind arising out of an inner state of tension, a conflict between conscience and passion, which may have been created by a passion, a belief, an instinct or an urge — or a confluence of all. In every instance, what is always depicted in a dithyramb is something that exists only within the inner world of man, not the outer physical world. Nothing in a dithyramb represents an idea. Everything that is written in the dithyramb is a gesticulative metaphor, a symbol of a mood or state of mind, something that is Dionysian.

> The Theory of the Best Style. — The theory of the best style may at one time be the theory of finding the expression by which we transfer every mood of ours to the reader and the listener.[64]

Insofar as Nietzsche's dithyrambic tragedy is a full representation of the will to power, every representation, every metaphor, is a reference either to some inner movement that teaches the actor how to find his Self or shows him a way through a conflict whose resolution leads to a greater apprehension of Self.

For instance, the metaphors in the dithyramb entitled Of the Vision and the Riddle, specifically the representation of the dead man lying on the ground having choked to death on a snake that has crawled down his throat, is a representation of the actor finally reaching his deepest, truest, and most original Self which has succumbed to some terrible and catastrophic suffering. The resolution of this conflict is represented in the metaphors that call the actor to bite off the head of the snake. So, in one instance, we have a representation in metaphor of a *psychological dilemma*, and, in another instance, we have a representation in metaphor of an instinct that calls the actor to *act* upon that dilemma.

In other instances, the actor is called to render metaphors that teach him how to *find* his Self. Specifically, in the dithyramb entitled Of Reading and Writing, the dithyramb speaks of learning to "write with blood" because blood has spirit. If you keep in mind that every metaphor pertains to something with regard to Self, that narrows done the guessing game, which is the gist of rendition. The next thing to keep in mind is that you must be willing to think in leaps and bounds. Ask yourself, does he mean this? Or this? Or this? And always, whatever he means, he means something that you must find within yourself. And lastly, as the final test that your rendition is correct, ask yourself: "does it work?" Does your rendition bring you closer to your Self *in any way*? If it does, then your rendition is good, spot on, or at least on your way to becoming spot on.

For a very long time, I struggled with the dithyramb, Of Reading and Writing. I was pretty sure I had it right, that when you discover something about your Self (reading) and wish to remember it (writing), if what you discover is real, as opposed to imagined, contrived, wayward or superfluous, then you will certainly remember it. But I wasn't very certain that I had guessed it right, and I wanted to be more certain. Reading somewhere, and I do not remember where, I found a reference to something Nietzsche referred to as a "bloodless abstraction." Then I was certain. This dithyramb teaches, among other things, that you must not look for an abstraction or idea of your Self but rather for an apprehension of your Self, a process of genuine thought that he also references in the first sentence of the *Birth of Tragedy*, when he says that, in order to understand the creative process involved in mythopoeia, what is needed is a direct apprehension rather than a mere determination.

The notion of "direct apprehension" also brings us to the notion of "plausible embodiment." Everything that is represented in dithyrambic metaphor is plausibly embodiable. And in order to understand this more thoroughly, we need to refer back to Nietzsche's thesis in *The Birth of Tragedy* regarding lyrical and epic poetry, or, more specifically, the distinction he finds between epic poetry and "folk" poetry, which may be his own invention. We need to understand what he means by folk poetry because the dithyramb is folk poetry. And by "folk poetry," he means something a little different than its traditional meaning.

He likens folk poetry to lyrical poetry, as opposed to epic poetry. And regarding the lyrical poet, he says this:

> As Dionysian artist he is in the first place become altogether one with the Primordial Unity, its pain and contradiction, and he produces the copy of this Primordial Unity as

> music, granting that music has been correctly
> termed a repetition and a recast of the world;
> but now, under the Apollonian dream-
> inspiration, this music again becomes visible
> to him as in a *symbolic dream-picture.* [65]

Like much of what Nietzsche wrote, this makes little sense if you do not parse it and reassemble it. Specifically, what does he mean by (1) "Dionysian artist," (2) the "Primordial Unity" and becoming identified with it, producing a "copy of this Primordial Unity as music," and that music "becomes visible to him as in a *symbolic dream- picture?*" Simply put, the dithyrambist becomes "altogether one with the Primordial Unity" in the sense that he enjoys an extreme communion with inner human nature as it exists, not as it is imagined or in any manner contrived. The dithyrambist possesses an extraordinary measure of knowledge of true human nature. And for the dithyrambist to compose a true representation of that inner nature is to produce a replica of that inner nature as dithyrambic music. By "dithyrambic music," he means the melodious chain (or series) of naturally occurring inner events out of which mythopoeia arises instinctively. And when the dithyrambic actor embodies the "music" and beholds his Self in it by completing the act of mythopoeia that dithyrambic music attains to, then he beholds his deeper Self. And it is always a deeper Self that he beholds because dithyrambic music always transports the actor into a deeper experience of his emotions. But it is his own emotions that the actor experiences, though they be deeper and previously imperceptible to him, And, upon beholding his deeper Self, he also experiences the deeper emotions that gave rise to it (as myth) *as his own.* In such a way, the music (or emotions) becomes visible to the actor as a dimension of Self, so that there occurs a transcendence of experience from the Dionysian realm into the Apollonian realm.

Continuing with the paragraph that follows the above citation, Nietzsche contrasts the dithyrambic poet with the epic poet.

> The plastic artist, as also the epic poet, who is related to him, is sunk [immersed] in the pure contemplation of pictures [images, visions]. The Dionysian musician is, without any picture, himself just primordial pain and the primordial re-echoing thereof.[66]

To reiterate this, the epic poet crafts his art using literary representations of image and idea, and the beauty of his art derives from the contemplation of those images and ideas. But the dithyrambic poet does not work at all with the representation of image or idea. You will not find a single representation of image, idea, or concept anywhere within a single dithyramb. Instead, the dithyrambist's aim is to transport the actor within himself to the *instincts* out of which an idea or image or concept arises. And instincts arise only out of emotions, specifically emotions stirring within a conflict. Therefore, the dithyrambic poet works only with inner emotional conflicts, and *indirectly* (though with an aim and a purpose) with the images and ideas that arise out of those emotional conflicts. Those images and ideas succeed only if the dithyrambist has accurately depicted the emotional conflict *and* the actor has embodied the represented conflict with enough sufficiency that the embodiment then produces the prerequisite instinct within him. And emotion is all you will find represented in the dithyramb. Images and ideas are totally hidden. In order to see the images and ideas created by the dithyrambic poet, the observer must first experience the emotion. Emotion comes first. And idea comes second, as a production of emotion. And he says the same thing more specifically when he writes:

> *Schiller* has enlightened us concerning his poetic procedure by a psychological observation, inexplicable to himself, yet not apparently open to any objection. He acknowledges that as the preparatory state to the act of poetising he had not perhaps before him or within him a series of pictures with co- ordinate causality of thoughts, but rather a *musical mood* ("The perception with me is at first without a clear and definite object; this forms itself later. A certain musical mood of mind precedes, and only after this does the poetical idea follow with me.")[67]

The next point to consider is that, according to Nietzsche, when the lyricist says "I," he does not mean he himself; he means "all human beings" or human nature.

> ... *[the epic poet]* is guarded against being unified and blending with his figures;—the pictures of the lyrist on the other hand are nothing but *his very* self and, as it were, only different projections of himself, on account of which he as the moving centre of this world is entitled to say "I": only of course this self is not the same as that of the waking, empirically real man, but the only verily

> existent and eternal self resting at the basis of
> things, by means of the images whereof the
> lyric genius sees through even to this basis of
> things.[68]

Epic poetry, in contrast to dithyrambic poetry, is an art which invites contemplation of the images that it presents. And dithyrambic poetry presents emotion, which can only be appreciated via compassion or empathy. In other words, the epic poet uses image and contemplation of image as the craft for his art. But the dithyrambist presents emotion as the craft for his art. Are we then supposed to contemplate these emotions for the purpose of achieving empathy with them? No, the dithyramb presents emotion that is meant to be *embodied,* which is a step further than mere compassion or empathy. Embodiment versus contemplation is the contrast we find in epic poetry and dithyrambic poetry. Plausible embodiment of the passions depicted in the dithyramb is the art involved here. But if plausible embodiment is the trick that makes the dithyramb meaningful, then surely the depiction must be universally applicable. Everyone who reads it must be able to find something in it that truly depicts an emotion they are capable of feeling.

Therefore, when we read at the end of every single dithyramb "Thus spoke Zarathustra," it is not Zarathustra the character who is speaking, it is the ground of being, by which he means reality or human nature, that is speaking. And it speaks to every human being. This is also true of every instance throughout the book when any "character" speaks, and there are numerous types of characters, such as philosophers, poets, afterworlds men, sublime men, the wanderer, the shadow, and higher men. In every instance, it is the ground of being or reality that is speaking and what is said is applicable to anyone. Whether the speaker is a "sublime man" (the tendency of the Ego to repress emotion) or a "higher man" (a deeper sense of Self that raises the actor out of the inner chaos of thought and passion) is merely a metaphorical clue as to exactly what inner force of human nature is being referenced. And it is in this sense that the book is dedicated "For Everyone."

But exactly what speaks to us from the ground of being through the dithyramb? Nietzsche says that, in the dithyramb, language imitates music. It is music that speaks to us. And music manifests itself as the will in human being. And the will that '*Zarathustra* teaches is a will to power. Therefore, insofar as the dithyramb is a representation of the will to power and is meant to be embodied, then dithyrambic music is a new kind of music that is meant to be embodied. We will call this new kind of embodiable music *dramatic music*, as opposed to audible music.

The question we now need to answer is how is the will like music. And in order to explain that, we first need to understand what is the will.

The will to power is comprised of any emotion or idea that moves the actor, either directly or indirectly, toward an apprehension of Self. It may be an urge, an instinct, or a passion. Fundamentally, will is desire and hope. And a desire for Self is a critical prerequisite for undertaking *Thus Spoke Zarathustra*. Insofar as an apprehension of Self dramatically empowers the beholder, the confluence of desires that moves him toward that apprehension is called a will to power. When conflicts of conscience and passion arise, such as an inability to incorporate parts of the subconscious that are unmanageable, then idea arises to illuminate a path for the will out of the conflict.

Will is akin to music in two ways. First, will produces image — in the form of mythical being, or Self. Obviously, if you are going to cultivate and embody the will to power that is represented in *Thus Spoke Zarathustra*, which is a will to Self, then you are going to experience apprehensions of Self, especially if you believe in and pursue the deeper Self instead of settling on the more shallow apprehensions. Therefore, with that, we see long periods of focused willing, by which I mean cultivating a confluence of sensations, that culminate in visions of Being, which is a phenomenon that is also found in music, at least with regard to emotion and image or contemplation of image. That, at least, was Nietzsche's observation and belief when he says (in *The Birth of Tragedy*) that listening to music will prompt the listener to imaginative daydreams. While this is the simplest analogy of music producing image, it goes to the point that music produces images within the listener. Music primarily produces mood within its listener, but it can also produce image, which is a phenomenon that Nietzsche incorporated into dithyrambic music with the psychogenesis of myth.

While *Thus Spoke Zarathustra* is a dithyrambic drama, it can be further qualified as a dithyrambic tragedy, which requires an understanding of proto-tragedy. And proto-tragedy is an ancient, redemptory phenomenon that plays out within the inner world and is entirely distinguishable from the modern notion of a worldly and catastrophic phenomenon.

The point he is going to make in the following quotes from the second (1886) preface to *The Birth of Tragedy* is that tragedy, by which both he and I mean proto-tragedy (always, in every case, and never the morally interpreted modern tragedy), was born out of a condition of supreme and robust health, the very opposite of what you might think. And this point will move on to the very critical point that the tragic myth is what singularly makes life possible, so these are extremely important points to understand.

> ... the "Birth of Tragedy from the Spirit of *Music.*"—From music? Music and Tragedy? Greeks and tragic music? Greeks and the Artwork of pessimism? A race of men, well-fashioned, beautiful, envied, life-inspiring, like no other race hitherto, the Greeks— indeed? The Greeks were *in need* of tragedy? Yea—of art? Wherefore— Greek art?...[69]

Continuing,

> Is pessimism *necessarily* the sign of decline, of decay, of failure, of exhausted and weakened instincts?—as was the case with the Indians, as is, to all appearance, the case with us "modern" men and Europeans? Is there a pessimism of *strength*? An intellectual predilection for what is hard, awful, evil, problematical in existence, owing to well-being, to exuberant health, to *fullness* of existence? Is there perhaps suffering in overfullness itself? A seductive fortitude with the keenest of glances, which *yearns* for the terrible, as for the enemy, the worthy enemy, with whom it may try its strength? from whom it is willing to learn what "fear" is?

What means *tragic* myth to the Greeks of the best, strongest, bravest era?[70]

The major, unspoken point here is that proto-tragedy is singularly and powerfully mythopoeic. It follows directly from the collapse of the Ego, which serves to protect the individual from his subconscious, and the subsequent emergence of the Self. And it is that collapse and subsequent reunion that defines proto-tragedy.

In the above quote, the two points are (1) what is the tragic myth? And (2) how did it come into existence during a period when the ancients enjoyed their greatest and most robust health?

Perhaps I should now speak more guardedly and less eloquently of a psychological question so difficult as the origin of tragedy among the Greeks. A fundamental question is the relation of the Greek to pain, his degree of sensibility, — did this relation remain constant? or did it veer about? — the question, whether his ever-increasing *longing for beauty*, for festivals, gaieties, new cults, did really grow out of want, privation, melancholy, pain? For suppose even this to be true—and Pericles (or Thucydides) intimates as much in the great Funeral Speech:—whence then the opposite longing, which appeared first in the order of time, the *longing for the ugly*, the good, resolute desire of the Old Hellene for pessimism, for tragic myth, for the picture of all that is terrible, evil, enigmatical, destructive, fatal at the

> basis of existence,—whence then must tragedy have sprung? Perhaps from joy, from strength, from exuberant health, from over-fullness.[71]

The answer Nietzsche is proposing is that a condition of excellent and robust health called forth a craving for the ugly and the most frightful. I would elaborate on that and call it a craving as well for the horrifically frightful. And that becomes very significant when we begin talking about the problems that the actor will encounter during his efforts to incorporate the subconscious into the conscious.

Tragedy and Musical Dissonance

All of this wisdom turns to gold when it is incorporated into life, which Nietzsche succeeded in doing in his dithyrambs. If you learn how to read a dithyramb and how to practice dithyrambic drama, then you will learn to embody the will represented in the dithyrambs and begin to live the life that is driven by that will. And when you do that, here is what you discover.

I have repeatedly said that an undertaking of *Thus Spoke Zarathustra* is an undertaking of a long journey toward an apprehension of your Self, by which I mean your deepest, truest, and most original Self. Insofar as the journey proceeds upon belief in and pursuit of the deepest Self, it is obvious that eventually you are going to reach the bottom of the well, or the deepest part of the subconscious, wherein you will make that all-important discovery of Self. And I have also said that this is a very, very difficult journey to achieve. The greatest obstacle in your way will be incorporation of the subconscious, in which resides unmanageable horror and pain.

Now we come to another instance in which will is like music. When Nietzsche says in the title of his essay on the birth of tragedy that tragedy was borne out of the spirit of music, he is talking about musical dissonance.

One of the points Nietzsche makes about the derivation of tragedy is that it came into practice during a time when ancient Greek culture was at its zenith, which, in his opinion, was long before the celebrated Socratic epoch.

If we translate that insight into quotidian life, what we discover is that the ever-increasing apprehension of Self throughout the drama leads to a heightening of the self-empowerment that is inherent in that apprehension of Self. And that heightening *creates a need for more empowerment.* In other words, the apprehension of Self creates a need for the subliminal emotions that reside within the oblivion of the subconscious because they define Self. The empowerment that is imparted by Self *itself* summons the subliminal demons. What we have is a heightening of empowerment followed by a sudden and extreme opposite movement, which is the essence of musical dissonance. It is in this sense that Nietzsche says tragedy was born out of the spirit of music, if you concur that the tragedy he was speaking about was proto-tragedy, the rite of passage in life that re-unites the individual with his higher Self, and not modern theatrical tragedy.

This phenomenon of tragic dissonance proves to be a huge asset in the process of life because incorporation of the subconscious is an absolute necessity in that process. And yet, the incorporation of the subconscious is the most difficult effort the actor will undertake. To know that nature itself has provided assistance in achieving this incorporation (of the subconscious) is a huge comfort. Over time and many attempts, the actor will learn that every successful step forward into the subconscious necessarily leads to a greater apprehension of Self, which, in turn, quite naturally leads to an even deeper fathoming of the subconscious. Indeed, one day the actor will realize (as an epiphany) that the process of life is inherently musical: a deep fathoming of the subconscious, wherein resides very difficult and painful emotion, is followed by exhilarating sparks of imagery as the mythopoeic instinct kicks in to produce a higher and more elevated vision of Self, the supra-Self. And it is for this reason that Nietzsche speaks of the dithyramb as dramatic music, something that drives you toward an apprehension of your Self *in a musical manner*. And to have gained that insight is a rare and glorious achievement because now the actor knows that the exhilaration of self-empowerment is eternally entwined with his suffering. The two are inseparable, like the notes in a melody.

It is also important to note that the myth that arises in the wake of proto-tragedy, which Nietzsche calls the tragic myth, is the newly found and deeper Self *and it* incorporates the subconscious emotions into itself. In such a way, the tragic myth is a reverberation of original pain. But, insofar as the illusion of Self is redemptive, given its illusory nature, then the reverberated pain is also redemptive. In such a way, and only in such a way, does original pain become bearable: when it is lived through the perspective of the higher Self.

The last important point to make about dithyrambic music is that it is not a willy-nilly representation of the will to power but rather a spot-on, precise representation of it. Consider, for instance, the notes in a melody. In order to produce the melody, the individual notes must appear in the correct order, obviously. The preceding note necessarily precedes, and the following note necessarily follows, just as the build-up necessarily precedes the crescendo and the letdown necessarily follows that. And it is the same with dithyrambic music. If the dramatic music is meant to be embodied, first, it must be realistic, not a contrived concoction, not even a slight variant. In a story, anything may be written because all that the reader needs to understand is concept. But in a dithyramb, the reader needs to embody will, which is comprised of desire and other forces of human nature that interact with the desire being represented, which, in the case of *Thus Spoke Zarathustra*, is a desire for Self. More specifically, the forces of human nature that are depicted in the dithyramb are those that lead directly to mythopoeia because that is the art of the dithyramb and dithyrambic drama — the production of mythopoeia. If the reader can succeed in becoming actor, then he must embody those forces of human nature in the representation so that he may then achieve the mythopoeia that the dithyrambist wishes to teach. And every step of success requires that both the representation and that which is represented are spot-on, aside from being contingent as well upon the actor's ability to understand the representation and his ability to embody it.

The dithyrambist must himself already know the specific inner circumstance of hope and desire or the specific inner conflict of passion and conscience *out of which* mythopoeia will necessarily arise. Then, he must choose his metaphors carefully so as to gesture the reader/actor toward an embodiment of that circumstance or tension so that the actor will then experience the mythopoeic event that the dithyrambist intends. Thus, the chronology pertaining to the development of the inner circumstance must be spot-on, but, more importantly, so, too, must the inner circumstance itself be spot-on, which is to say real, embodiable. It cannot be made up the way some stories can be made up. Someone who sits down to write fiction, can make up anything he wishes because he is telling a story. But the dithyrambist is creating myth, and he cannot make up *anything*; he must depict reality. And if what he writes is not reality, then neither will it be embodiable. Both the chronology and the circumstance depicted in each dithyramb must be an accurate instance of reality, an accurate instance of human nature.

Theory of Übermensch

We now need to look at how the dithyramb teaches the actor a new way of thinking.

By putting everything in metaphor, the reader is forced to render the metaphor if he is to understand what is being represented. A dithyramb represents an inner conflict involving conscience and passion, a state of mind or mood. The metaphors are merely clues that are meant to direct the reader within himself to the conflict. By unriddling the riddle, you find and isolate the conflict within yourself, which then enables you to act on it. Thus, the rendition of metaphor effects a transport, which I call dithyrambic transport. Once the reader achieves transport, further reading of the same dithyramb reveals a second inner circumstance of passion and conscience which is meant to serve as a resolution of the first, the conflict, in the form of a new way of thinking. And that is what *Thus Spoke Zarathustra* teaches: a new way of thinking, and specifically a new way of thinking about an inner conflict that has been relegated to the subconscious because no way of thinking would previously resolve it.

Also, the creation of the subconscious is a direct consequence of the individual's inability to endure whatever emotion has overwhelmed him. And it is created via a restrictive redrawing of the limits of perception within the individual, resulting in a loss of consciousness, which is something similar to what happens upon the infliction of unbearable pain that causes the body to lose consciousness. I call this phenomenon dismemberment. If something is too painful to perceive, the limits of perception and consciousness are reigned in, thereby creating an entire realm of the inner world that is very active but entirely beyond the purview of assimilative and actionable consciousness. It is important to remember that sub-individuated man can do absolutely nothing to manage anything within the subconscious, which creates a profound malady. And that malady, in turn, creates a profound need which is satisfied by morale. But, when morale is sublimated and enters into the spirit, then it, too, becomes a problem because its dictates a ban on all suffering because suffering is demoralizing, and that ban precludes any hope of reclaiming the subconscious.

It is also important to remember that whatever overwhelming pain or horror is relegated to the subconscious, those emotions may subside into oblivion but they do not themselves expire. They continue to torment the individual, and they do so beyond his reach and beyond his perception, totally. Consequently, he or she may develop extreme ideas or muster extreme emotions in order to counter the effects of the subconscious.

Once you have rendered the metaphors that comprise a dithyramb, then you have achieved an introspective focus that will enable you to act on whatever it is the dithyramb intends for you to focus on. Sometimes, a dithyramb will bring your focus to a particular conflict and show you a way out of it. Other times, a dithyramb will bring your focus to a particular inner force of nature, be it a tendency, an instinct, an urge, a compulsion, etc., and instruct you to grow it or negate it. In such a way, you align or create a confluence of inner forces, which, overall, comprise a will to power, a will towards your Self. As a result of rendering the metaphors that comprise the various dithyrambs of the drama, you become driven toward your Self.

Keep in mind three things: all of *Thus Spoke Zarathustra* is composed in metaphor; all of the metaphors point to something that exists within yourself; the dithyrambic drama, as a whole, drives you toward your Self. Keep in mind also that the growth of the will to Self is entirely incremental, not sudden. There are sudden insights, epiphanies, but there is no sudden movement.

Many of the dithyrambs teach the actor how to restore his (or her) ability to feel emotion, either by negating inner forces that drive him away from emotion, or by learning how to allow emotion into his realm of consciousness, or by driving him into mythopoeia. And it is critical that you understand how mythopoeia restores your sense of feeling.

As I just said, the development of the will to power, the drive toward your Self, is incremental, not sudden, as is all life. Every instance of life presents itself to any mode of perception as a slow, incremental, and entirely unobservable process of growth. And it is no different with the will to power, the drive toward Self.

The process of restoring the sense of feeling is also incremental, gradual and not sudden. And isn't that a good thing, particularly if the subliminal emotions that await you are titanic? In the process of restoring your sense of feeling, then you begin to incorporate into your consciousness emotions that have been relegated to the subconscious precisely because they were unbearable, un-incorporable. Any sudden incorporation would lead to a very untenable situation. Therefore, it happens only gradually. You get closer and closer, but only incrementally. *But*, with each step forward, a newer and more comprehensive sense of Self emerges, the supra-Self. It is emotion that defines your Self, just as it is phenomena that triggers the mythopoeic instinct and gives rise to myth. Therefore, each un-layering reveals a deeper Self, inasmuch as each un-layering reveals deeper, more pronounced emotions. And the perception of a new Self amidst those deeper emotions constitutes the all-important act of mythopoeia, the creation of which is the creativity, the art, that Nietzsche speaks of when he says in *The Birth of Tragedy* that "art owes its continuous evolution to the Dionysian-Apollonian duality." In other words, mythopoeia, or the creation of myth, owes its continuous evolution to the symbiotic development of the two inner realms of emotion and idea. As emotion arises, conflicts occur and idea is generated. And as idea is generated, the will is freed from that which blocks its advance. As the will is freed and moves forward, the need for continued conflict arises, and more subliminal emotions emerge. And then, and this is sudden, mythopoeia happens. You suddenly grasp a deeper sense of Self. However, though the apprehension of Self through mythopoeia is sudden and happens in one moment, insofar as that epiphany requires courage, the gestation of the epiphany, the myth, may require extensive time. The process of learning to feel again is represented by the metaphor of the camel in the dithyramb entitled Of the Three Metamorphoses, taking the weight of the subconscious upon one's shoulders, into consciousness.

With mythopoeia, a new myth arises, a new idea and sense of Self, a new perspective through which to interpret the inner world. (In many ways, this new sense of Self represents a new beginning, which is represented by the metaphor of the child in the same dithyramb.) But with mythopoeia also comes a brilliant new image, the image of Self, which is beguiling. The introduction of beguiling image presents a huge problem in the development of the will to power, which is fundamentally a process of becoming, of growth. Specifically, it halts the development, the becoming. The dithyramb entitled Of the New Idol teaches the solution to this problem.

> A free life still remains open for great souls. Truly, he who possesses little is so much the less possessed: blessed be moderate poverty!
>
> There, where the state ceases, only there does [life for] the man who is not superfluous begin: there begins the song of the necessary man, the unique and irreplaceable melody.
>
> There, where the state ceases – I pray for you to look there, my fellow seekers. Do you not see it: the rainbow and the bridges to the supra-Self?[72]

This dithyramb would have been more aptly titled if Nietzsche had called it Of the States of Being, but that would have made its rendition much too easy.

Nietzsche's solution to this problem is simply ingenious. With this solution, he has found a way to incorporate being into the process of becoming, which is no small feat.

As the actor learns to restore his sense of feeling and finds a newer and deeper sense of Self, he must learn that the goal in all this growth is not the image of Self that he presently beholds. Rather, *the goal in all this growth is the next Self*, an image of the much deeper Self. And it is this act of looking beyond the image of Self in search of an even deeper Self that constitutes the faithful belief in the supra-Self, the superman, the Übermensch. Always the next Self, never the current Self, is the goal, lest the actor becomes seduced by a beguiling image into an arrested development. And it is for that reason that, in the dithyramb entitled On Self-Overcoming, Zarathustra says:

> 'Whatever I create and however much I love
> it – soon I must oppose it and my love of it:
> that is how my will proceeds.[73]

In other words, however many times the actor brings to life a deeper supra-Self, he must find his way beyond it and move on to the next, even deeper one and, therefore, must oppose his love of the preceding supra-Self and devote his love instead to the subsequent one.

> The assumption of a *single subject* is perhaps not necessary, it may be equally permissible to assume a plurality of subjects, whose interaction and struggle lie at the bottom of our thought and our consciousness in general. A sort of *aristocracy* of "cells" in which the ruling power is vested? Of course an aristocracy of equals, who are accustomed to ruling co-operatively, and understand how to command?
>
> *My hypotheses.* The subject as a plurality.[74]

The supra-Self is Nietzsche's idea of the superman or, as I prefer, the supra-man— because what is really implied with the word "uber" is both beyond and above, not great. The Übermensch is not some blonde, blue-eyed beast who is ready to lead the master race. It is a vision of one's aborning deeper Self in the future, the supra-Self. The Übermensch adds to a way of thinking — a way of thinking about one's suffering and one's Self. And it is a way of thinking that leads to one's deepest and truest Self. Specifically, it is — at the same time — both a gateway myth and a mythical being that enables a mode of thought, which enables a way of becoming that is life itself.

And your next Self, or supra-Self, will not be something you will *conceive*. Rather, your supra-Self is something you will *sense* nearby and then *become*— from deep within the realm of dismembered emotion, or the subconscious, layer by layer. Again, the supra-Self is not conceivable or even imaginable, but it is discoverable and embodiable, piece by piece. Pulling it together, like an artist, is the sense in which Nietzsche urges the reader to "become who you are."

The result of this new way of thinking is that the actor eventually (and always incrementally) achieves an extraordinarily deep sense of Self because more layers of Ego must be swept away in order to assimilate more of the subconscious emotions, which brings me to another very important point.

In the course of rendering this dithyrambic drama, the actor's Ego will collapse, fully and entirely. This is the phenomenon of proto-tragedy, which is an integral rite of passage in Nietzsche's drama. In the end, there will be nothing left of Ego, which will be entirely replaced by Self. And every time there is a reference to Zarathustra's down going or downfall, the reference is to the downfall of the Ego. In the end, after the actor has learned the extraordinary value that inheres in the aborning Self, which only comes as a direct result of the Ego collapsing, the actor will no longer think in terms of the drama being a going down or a downfall. Rather, he will think of it as a redemptive reunion. In this way, in the dithyramb entitled The Convalescent, when Zarathustra says:

> '"The hour has now come when he who is falling shall bless himself. Thus *ends* Zarathustra's downfall!'"[75]

There are many references throughout the drama about Zarathustra going down and Zarathustra's downfall, but there is only one instance in which he speaks of the down-going finally ending, and it is in this dithyramb. So, what is it about this dithyramb, The Convalescent, that prompts a reversal of the longstanding downfall that has been ongoing since the outset of the drama?

The Convalescent is a dithyramb celebrating the actor's restoration of feeling. Here is the representation in metaphor:

> "Up, my most abysmal thought, up from my depth! I am your rooster and morning dawn, you sleeping snake that has slept too long: Up! Up! My voice shall soon crow you awake!
>
> Unchain the fetters on your ears: listen! For I want to hear you! Up! Up! There is thunder enough to make the very graves listen!

And rub the sleep and all that makes you dumb and blind from your eyes! Hear me with your eyes, too: my voice is a cure even for those born blind.

And once you are awake you will stay awake forever. It is not *my* way to awaken great-grandmothers from sleep and then tell them to — go back to sleep!

You move, you stretch, you wheeze? Up! Up! You will not gasp, you will speak to me! Zarathustra calls you, Zarathustra the godless!

I, Zarathustra, the advocate of life, the advocate of suffering, the advocate of the circle — I call you, my most abysmal thought!

Glory is mine! You are coming — I hear you! My abyss *speaks*, I have brought my deepest depth into the light!

Glory is mine! Come on! Give me your hand — ha! let be! Ha, ha! — Disgust, disgust, disgust — woe is mine![76]

This is the moment when the actor willfully summons his most horrific suffering, be it a fear or humiliation, into his consciousness, thereby freeing it from the vaulted subconscious for what surely must have seemed like an eternity. And instead of being destroyed by it, he is restored by it. His sense of feeling is restored as is his sense of Self, full Self. In the process, his Ego which arose in the wake of the destruction of the Self, collapses. And the destruction of the Ego in place of the Self is a very good thing, and it singularly constitutes the proto-tragedy phenomenon. This is the pleasure that the ancients found in the destruction of magnificent individuality. In the course of raising himself up out of the chaos of sub-individuation, the actor himself will achieve great individuality, only to see it destroyed as he uncovers a deeper layer of true Self. The fact that we have reclaimed this precious knowledge, which has been lost for more than two millennia, is a milestone in the history of Western civilization and should not go unnoticed.

A good half of the drama comprised by Nietzsche's dithyrambic drama is finding a way to restore feeling, which also leads to a restoration of Self. The reason for that restoration is something I have yet to make clear, which involves the redemption of suffering. But what to do with the subliminal suffering that comes to the fore along with the restoration of feeling comprises the second half of the drama and is very important. But for now, we need to focus merely on the restoration itself. Many dithyrambs are dedicated to helping you achieve this restoration, which cannot be achieved except with an accompanying collapse of Ego, which is why Nietzsche's dithyrambic drama is quite properly a dithyrambic tragedy.

Returning to the significance of the dithyramb entitled The Convalescent and how it marks the reversal of Zarathustra's downfall, the eventual reunion with the deepest and truest suffering Self is not destructive but rather deeply restorative. While it is true that the restoration brings with it previously sublimated suffering that is now brought into the light of day, with that suffering also comes relief. It goes to the old adage that you always feel better after you cry. And if something is eating away at you from an unreachable remote point of oblivion, bringing it into your consciousness is definitely the first step toward resolving it, except that is not the point in Nietzsche's drama of bringing it into consciousness. As I said, what must be done with subliminal suffering once it is raised represents the entire second half of the drama.

Once the actor succeeds in raising subliminal suffering into his consciousness, his downfall ends in two senses. His Ego collapses, giving way to the aborning Self, so there is nothing left to fall down, to collapse. But, in another sense, the aborning Self deeply empowers the actor, and there is nothing destructive (or down-going) in that rejuvenation. Quite the contrary, it is highly exhilarating. And it is for this reason that the collapse of the actor's Ego, which began at the outset of the drama, ends with the phenomenon depicted in this dithyramb. It is here that the tragedy ends. Thus, does Zarathustra proclaim, *"Now the hour has come when he who is going down shall bless himself"* because, he knows, in going down, he will be reborn, rejuvenated, just like the Phoenix rising out of his own ashes.

In fact, the actor eventually achieves a full reclamation of the exact same sense of Self that he once knew before he experienced whatever catastrophe may have happened to destroy that sense of Self, which means he will also relive that exact same catastrophe. Except that, this time, he will have learned and experienced the *springboard* that Nietzsche found in suffering and teaches in his dithyrambs.

On the Redemption of Human Suffering

Many times, I have wondered at the marvels of Nietzsche's genius in his numerous achievements: the idea of the Übermensch, or supra-Self, which overcame the contradiction of being in becoming, the founding of an entire way of thinking, which included the refutation of ideals that had been erected more than two thousand years earlier by Socrates, Plato, Aristotle, and Zoroaster, and the invention of an entirely new art form, the New Dithyramb, as a means for teaching that new way of thinking. But without a doubt, his most wondrous achievement is his ability to have looked into the abyss within the subconscious and discovered a springboard that raises humankind to a height equal and opposite to that depth, thereby raising the center of gravity above the principium individuationis and eradicating the limits of Self via the redemption of the suffering that inheres in the human abyss. It is that redemption and the eradication of the limits imposed by individuation that provides the foundation of his Übermensch.

I said earlier that Nietzsche's Übermensch is an idea and that it is a place within your heart and soul. I have explained the idea to you. Now I will explain the place. But keep in mind that an explanation of the place does not equate with an experience of it.

The first thing to consider is what does belief in and pursuit of the supra-Self lead to, or rather, *where* does it lead to? It leads to a place within your heart and mind, which means that which is meant by the word Übermensch, or supra-Self, is both an idea (of the next, deeper supra-Self) and a place, which unlike supra-Self is called over-Self. And in order to understand the place that is called over-Self, we need to understand the springboard that inheres in all suffering.

Now, unless you have some experience trying to incorporate the subconscious into the conscious, it may be difficult to understand the instincts that come into play when the will is confronted by the severe and extreme afflictions of the conscience. Every instinct in your body, and they are some of the most powerful instincts, will compel you to stay away from the subconscious. It exists solely by virtue of its ability to keep horror and pain out of consciousness. So, by trying to overcome its protective barrier, you are going against some of the fundaments of sub-individuated human nature. But that is what the will to power requires because suffering is like gold to the will to power, provided you know how to redeem it, which I will now try to explain to you.

There is something I call the fourth dimension, which I must also now explain to you in order to understand how suffering is redeemed and made valuable.

When you look at something, you see it in three dimensions: width, length, and height. But there is another quality that you yourself add to it. Sometimes you add beauty to it, and sometimes you add ugliness to it. For instance, you come upon a meadow during a walk in the forest, and you perceive beauty within the image of the meadow and its physical characteristics. You may say there is beauty within the meadow itself, but there isn't; you add the beauty to it. In other words, you add a fourth dimension to the image. The same can be said of any horror or serenity you see in an image, and the same can be said of any other quality beyond the simple physical characteristics that you may perceive in something. And whence comes these added characteristics, this fourth dimension of things? They come from sensations within yourself that arise quite mystically from deep within you. And when they do, you project them onto the image before you as qualities of those images themselves, which they are not.

When you suffer, these very discrete sensations cease because suffering makes you turn away from any communion with the body and its sensations, since those sensations cause you pain or terror or other insufferable experiences. The magical discrete sensations themselves do not cease, but you cease feeling them. Then when you begin to re-incorporate the subconscious into consciousness and therewith restore a proximate communion with your body, they resume, or rather you resume feeling them. *And those discrete magical sensations are exactly the same as they were before*, when you previously experienced them. All that is new is that you are feeling them again. In most people who suffer dismemberment, the suffering began when they were children, when they were unprotected and innocent to the evil of the world and prone to assault. Therefore, when the individual who succeeds in re-incorporating the subconscious and restoring the feeling communion with his body, and when those discrete magical sensations become part of his consciousness again, the fourth dimension as it was when he was a child comes back into play, and he quite literally feels again as he did when he was a child or before he experienced cataclysmic suffering. In other words, things he sees as images of the outer, physical world take on the same qualities he perceived when he was a child. And I mean precisely the same fourth dimension qualities. This comparison will give rise in the actor's mind that perhaps all things within the inner world recur eternally, and the idea is reinforced by the fact that subliminal emotions that were previously hidden but are now visible are also exactly the same. So, there are two phenomena that bring to the actor's mind the idea that perhaps the inner world recurs eternally. However, the other and much more prominent phenomena that raises the possibility of a recurring world is the resurrection of the exact same sense of Self one possessed so long ago, before dismemberment. And what effect does this possibility have on the actor? If he believes it, then he will eventually also believe that the subliminal emotions within the subconscious, which he is working so hard to raise into consciousness, are going to be that much easier to incorporate once he realizes that they are already existent and already a part of him and simply require his acceptance of those two facts. In other words, the idea of an eternally recurring world serves a religious purpose, if you define religion as providing miraculous assistance in the face of the most extreme adversity. The idea of an eternally recurring world assists life by helping to tear down the wall separating the conscious and subconscious realms. And Nietzsche himself stated specifically that the idea of an eternally recurring world was the religion of the Dionysians.[77]

I want to emphasize again that incorporating the subconscious into the conscious is the most difficult effort you will undertake in this dithyrambic drama. It takes years and years and all your ingenuity and newly found bravery. Anything that can assist you will be a valuable asset, and acceptance of the idea that the world recurs eternally will prove to provide the greatest assistance in this effort.

> Probable results which will follow from its [the idea that the world recurs eternally] being *believed.* (It makes everything [i.e., the subconscious] break open.)[78]

Make no mistake that the idea of an eternally recurring world is a direct reference to the immutability of the inextinguishable suffering that resides within the subconscious. Nowhere in all of *Thus Spoke Zarathustra* does the dithyrambist *explain* the idea of an eternally recurring world (the subconscious). Nor, for that matter, does the dithyrambist explain *any* idea. The dithyramb does not explain ideas. The dithyramb leads its actor into an inner conflict and shows him the way out, but everything that is represented is emotion and passion, not idea. Idea comes to the will as a resolution of that which is blocking the path of the will. But the actor must himself experience the blocking of the will. Only then does idea arise. By embodying the emotion and passion and entering into the conflict that is represented, *instincts* come into play, and it is out of those instincts that the actor finds his way through the conflict. The dithyramb teaches instinct directly, and it teaches idea only indirectly. And when ideas arise within the actor, they arise as a naturally occurring production of conflict and the will to move through the conflict *via those instincts*.

Remember, as I explained earlier, that idea arises as a solution to a conflict in which the will has become entangled. If the dithyrambist has accurately depicted the inner turmoil, according to the theory of dithyrambic music, and if the actor succeeds in embodying that music, by which I mean the passions and the conflict they present, then the idea will arise quite naturally all on its own, provided there is will to move beyond the conflict. That is how the dithyramb teaches idea.

And the theory of an eternally recurring subconscious is an idea. But it is also much more than an idea; it is a myth, specifically a gateway myth, which is different from mythical being. Thus, the dithyramb teaches two kinds of myth. But, like idea, myth is never explained in the drama. Instead, the actor is brought into the situation out of which the mythical idea of an eternally recurring subconscious arises. Specifically, the actor, in the course of pursuing his supra-Self, approaches the gateway to the subconscious numerous times, each time trying to incorporate this and that subliminal demon, and succeeding according to his ingenuity and his courage. Initially, the actor will feel as if he is looking at his demons as if through a glass wall. But eventually, that wall will be reduced to a transparent membrane, through which the actor can sense his deeper Self. When that happens, the idea will occur to him that these demons, with which he is thoroughly familiar, never died, though oblivion had reliably convinced him otherwise. And that is an epiphany. But it is a frightening epiphany that will take time to accept.

The idea of an eternally recurring world also presents an exigency, and that exigency will press the actor into action, which is another way that the idea of eternally recurring world serves a religious purpose. On the one hand, insofar as the actor brings some horrific subliminal fear into his consciousness sufficiently so that it reverberates itself as a dimension of Self, then it becomes reality. But, on the other hand, if the actor has yet to realize — or create — the aborning Self that is prompted by the emergence of that much deeper subliminal emotion, so that he experiences that emerging supra-Self only transiently, then he will not have taken ownership of his suffering so that he cannot "touch" or manage it, and he remains powerless against it. Furthermore, if the actor has not yet found the springboard within that extreme fear or other subliminal emotion that would enable him to redeem it, then there really is no reason to grant it full consciousness anyway. But, until he does find the springboard, at least the actor will know, having experienced the reverberation and the reality of that subliminal emotion, that, deep down inside, he is suffering monumentally. And that knowledge, the knowledge that, deep down inside, he is suffering monumentally, will urge him to a meaningful action against that suffering. Leaving it to repose silently in oblivion will no longer be a viable option. And it is the idea of an eternally recurring world that will compel him forward.

Eventually, as the actor finds the courage and the wherewithal to accept his subliminal suffering (and especially when he finds the springboard), then, as if passing through a gateway, the demons within the vaulted subconscious will begin to leap out into consciousness. The idea of an eternally recurring subconscious breaks open the vaulted subconscious. It cures dismemberment and greatly assists the extremely laborious and complicated effort to incorporate the subconscious. It is for this reason that Nietzsche regarded the theory of an eternally recurring subconscious as a religious idea, given the miraculous assistance it provides.

Though this particular gateway myth can only be truly learned via the dithyrambic drama, there are instances throughout Nietzsche's writing where he references it with illuminative comments. In the *Will To Power*, he wrote:

> A certain emperor always bore the fleeting nature of all things in his mind, in order not to value them too seriously, and to be able to live quietly in their midst. Conversely, everything seems to me much too important for it to be so fleeting, I seek an eternity for everything: ought one to pour the most precious salves and wines into the sea? **My consolation is that everything that has been is eternal: the sea will wash it up again.**[79] (emphasis added)

Make no mistake that the idea of an eternally recurring world is a direct reference to the immutability of the suffering that resides within the subconscious. Nowhere in all of *Thus Spoke Zarathustra* does the dithyrambist *explain* the idea of an eternally recurring world (the subconscious). Nor, for that matter, does the dithyrambist explain *any* idea. The dithyramb does not explain ideas. The dithyramb leads its actor into an inner conflict and shows him the way out, but everything that is represented is emotion and passion, not idea. Idea comes to the will as a resolution of that which is blocking the path of the will. But the actor must himself experience the blocking of the will. Only then does idea arise. By embodying the emotion and passion, and by entering into the conflict that is represented, *instincts* come into play, and it is out of those instincts that the actor finds his way through the conflict. The dithyramb teaches instinct directly, and it teaches idea only indirectly. And when ideas arise within the actor, they arise as a naturally occurring production of conflict and the will to move through the conflict *via those instincts*. Remember, as I explained earlier, that idea arises as a solution to a conflict in which the will has become entangled. If the dithyrambist has accurately depicted the inner turmoil, according to the theory of dithyrambic music, and if the actor succeeds in embodying that music, by which I mean the passions and the conflict they present, then the idea will arise quite naturally all on its own, provided there is a will to move beyond it. That is how the dithyramb teaches idea.

Writing in *Richard Wagner in Bayreuth*, and remember, according to Nietzsche's own admission, that the book is not about Wagner and Wagner's music but rather about Nietzsche and dithyrambic music, he says:

> His writings contain nothing canonical or severe: the canons are to be found in his works as a whole. Their literary side represents his attempts to understand the instinct which urged him to create his works and to get a glimpse of himself through them. If he succeeded in transforming his instincts into terms of knowledge, it was always with the hope that the reverse process might take place in the souls of his readers—it was with this intention that he wrote.[80]

If we reiterate this, then we have "My dithyrambs are an attempt to understand the instinct that impelled me to write the dithyramb in the first place. If I could manage to transform instinct into knowledge via the dithyramb, my hope was that the reverse process would take place within the soul of the reader, so that he would learn the instinct himself. That is the hope out of which [Nietzsche] created the dithyramb."

The words in a dithyramb do not signify or point to a concept, as does all other literature. Rather, the words in a dithyramb point to an instinct. And they point not directly, as all other words do, but with only a gesticulative metaphor that alludes to the instinct. By not pointing directly, the gesture only leads the actor in the general area, thereby requiring him to do the work of isolating within his heart and mind exactly what is being alluded to, so that he may then begin the work of either cultivating the instinct or extirpating it, which cannot begin without first isolating it. In such a way does the will begin to grow.

And let me elaborate on what I mean by instinct. In the course of experiencing things happening around you, there are some perceptions that you articulate in thought and there are some perceptions that never reach the level of thought and are never articulated, usually because the articulation is not necessary to achieve the perception or to produce the appropriate response. But in both instances, you understand and register what is happening, and you react. Let us call that level of interaction that is intuitive and never reaches articulation "instinctive reactivity." Instinctive reactivity is much faster than conceptual thought, and it is the level at which the dithyramb speaks to you. In the course of rendering a dithyramb, you will undoubtedly conceptualize. But, in the very beginning, when you are reading the gestures and trying to reckon them, there will not be any conceptualizing, if you are rendering properly. When Nietzsche says that his dithyrambs require good "listeners," he is saying that his dithyrambs require instinctive reactivity. Now, if the reader fails to render the dithyramb, then there will be no instinctive reactivity but there may be plenty of conceptual thought, as the reader falls back onto a backup effort, having missed the instinct that is being taught. And in some instances, conceptual thought may help you with your rendition. For instance, I had a very difficult time understanding the aphorism "Write with blood and you will find that blood is spirit," which is found in the dithyramb entitled Of Reading and Writing. Instinctively, I had an idea what he meant, but it was totally inarticulable and I was not certain. And I wanted to be certain. Articulation that follows instinctive reactivity is always a good proof of proper rendition. Therefore, I had to look for clues in *The Gay Science* and *Human, All-Too-Human*, which are always the best first place to start looking for clarification of a metaphor. And I found what I needed when I found an instance where Nietzsche referred to a "bloodless abstraction," Then I knew that what he meant was to look for your Self as it reveals itself to you in your senses, rather than looking for your Self according to some abstract idea you may have of it. Therefore, conceptual thought can be helpful with the process of rendition. But the instinctive rendition is always the better rendition. And it is the necessary rendition. You must achieve an instinctive rendition, a rendition that speaks to your instincts. And you will know when you have finally achieved the instinctive rendition because an articulable conceptualization of it will then follow. If it doesn't, you may not have achieved the rendition. Also, after you have found some clues as to the possible meaning of a metaphor, it is always necessary to go back and then look for the instinctive apprehension. You do not want to settle for the conceptual rendition that is absent an instinctual rendition and say "Oh, I've got it." The dithyramb aims to teach instinct, not concept, which is why the dithyramb speaks to its reader on the level of instinct.

And these are instincts that you once knew but lost through a devolution that is initiated by suffering so that, when you find them again, you will recognize them as part of your inner nature. Thus, to relearn these instincts is to restore yourself to nature, proceeding along an upward movement via the reversal of a devolution that was initiated by suffering. Inasmuch as the dithyramb teaches idea and myth as a production of instinct by transporting the actor into the conflict out of which the instinct arises, and inasmuch as the dithyramb depicts reality, the entire drama is steeped in nature, specifically human nature. None of this is made up according to Nietzsche's fanciful or idiosyncratic ideas; it is reality.

Consider, in contrast to the dithyramb, what the writer does when he writes fiction. He uses whatever ideas he wishes to create a story. But the dithyramb aims to create myth. Therefore, it must strictly abide by reality.

> Wagner's *poetic* ability is shown by his thinking in visible and actual facts, and not in ideas; that is to say, he thinks mythically, as the people have always done.[81]

Again, remember that you must read this as a statement about Nietzsche, not Wagner, and about dithyrambic music, not Wagner's music. According to this statement, to think "mythically" is to think in terms of reality, "visible and palpable events," and specifically palpable events of the inner world, but certainly not concepts or the fanciful ideas of a person writing fiction.

In fact, when Nietzsche speaks of his dithyrambs as a form of dithyrambic music, he uses the word "music" to refer specifically to both the quality of reality in his depictions and the natural cohesion that exists between the various events in those depictions. Without that reality and without that cohesion, it is not possible to create myth within the mind of the actor, which is the whole purpose of the dithyramb "music:" to create myth. And the concept of dithyrambic music, as I just defined it for you, is a very important concept that Nietzsche uses repeatedly in his disquisition of the production of myth and proto-tragedy — without ever explicitly explaining what he means by "dithyrambic music." And oftentimes, he will simply use the word "music," when he specifically means dithyrambic music. Indeed, in Nietzsche's writing, ambiguity is as prolific as insight.

Thus, the instincts that the dithyrambist is teaching are natural instincts. In fact, the whole drama leads to a restoration of instincts that have long since subsided into oblivion via suffering and dismemberment. This restoration constitutes a re-naturalization of the spirit and nature of subindividuated man. And Nietzsche spoke of this re-naturalization in his writing about Rousseau, who also advocated a re-naturalization of man, except that Rousseau imagined the ideally naturalized man as an idyllic humane shepherd, which was nothing more than a Christian ideal that had nothing to do with nature. Moreover, Rousseau envisioned a re-naturalization of man as a movement "back to nature." Nietzsche, on the other hand, advocated a naturalization of man via an "upward" track of growth, in other words, out of chaotic oblivion.

> *Progress in my sense.* — I also speak of a "return to nature," although it is not a process of going back but of going up — up into lofty, free and even terrible nature and naturalness; such a nature as can play with great tasks and *may* play with them.... To speak in a *parable*. Napoleon was an

157

> example of a "return to nature," as I
> understand it.[82]

Remember that anything which adds to your apprehension of Self becomes a part of the will to power, insofar as your Self empowers you. Love of Self, about which an entire dithyramb (The Spirit of Gravity) is dedicated in order to show how it becomes a part of the will to power, is not possible so long as your apprehension of Self is merely an idea. But when it becomes a sense of Self, then love of Self becomes possible. In short, a sense of Self is much more pronounced than a mere idea of Self. And when you gain a sense of Self, you will sense the Self you once were in the past, as if reversing along the line of devolution that you proceeded on when your original suffering came to the fore and caused you to redraw and rein in the limits of your consciousness. As you learn to incorporate more and more of the subconscious into the light, those limits are redrawn once again but in reverse order this time, in an expansive rather than a restrictive way. In other words, your Self returns to you. And the same sense of Self you previously possessed also returns to you. As this happens, you literally feel yourself coming back to life, as in a resurrection.

In the beginning of the drama, as you begin to focus intensively on your emotions, especially subliminal emotions, you simultaneously begin to experience mythopoeia but in an incremental way. Once you learn to look beyond the vision of Self that you apprehend via mythopoeia, you also focus on deeper emotions and you experience a deeper apprehension of Self, the supra-Self. In the beginning, as I have said, the Self you begin to experience is merely *an idea*. But as you move beyond that image of Self to a deeper Self, then you begin to experience a *sense* of Self, and the difference is quite noticeable. And then finally, in the last stage of the drama, the actor will find the *voice* of his deepest Self, through which his deepest Self will speak directly to his consciousness. And that final, vocal revelation of Self will directly give rise to the phenomenon depicted in the dithyramb entitled The Cry of Distress.

What is important to understand is that the dithyrambic drama is comprised of a cohesive series of inner events that are to be found along the journey of finding one's Self. Insofar as all the dithyrambs are encrypted in gesticulative metaphor, it is not possible, by and large but not without exception, to render dithyrambs that depict events arising out of previous events without first acting out those previous events. And that is certainly the case with the dithyramb entitled The Cry of Distress. Rendition of that dithyramb is not possible without first finding the voice of one's deepest Self because the dithyramb is all about something that voice says to the actor in the last stage of the drama.

The Meaning of Human Suffering

The next question to consider is what happens as a result of all this hard work trying to incorporate the subconscious into the conscious. Belief in (and striving toward) the supra-Self results in a lifelong sojourn into the very deepest parts of the subconscious.

Keep in mind that landmark (or catastrophic, monumental) emotions that were too painful or frightening to be incorporated into Self when they arose and were subsequently relegated to the subconscious, *do not go away*. You may go away by ignoring them and exiling them, but they themselves do not go away. Therefore, as you begin to extend the limits of Self and re-incorporate sensation into being, you come upon these same monumental or catastrophic emotions. And since it is emotion that defines Self, via the mythopoeic instinct, the Self you once were (prior to its destruction) *reappears*. And that same Self reappears exactly, without any variation or difference. When the time comes, when you incorporate the emotions that killed that Self, you will behold the same Self, precisely the same Self. Even aromas and colors will instigate the appearance of that same Self within your senses. With that, consider yourself reborn. And may I add *that* is a resurrection that is far more powerful (and far more plausible) than what the modern Christians claim, or the ancient Christians, when they say they speak of resurrection.

Please note also that, with the reappearance of the suffering Self, the Ego, which was erected in the wake of the original destruction as a stopgap to prevent the re-emergence of the subconscious, *must die*. In such a way, tragedy always accompanies rebirth. The two always go hand in hand through life. And the extension of the limits of Self via incorporation of the subconscious is, in fact, how life manifests itself within human being. That is the model, the paradigm, that Nietzsche endeavored to find when he sought to understand how life manifests itself within human being just as simply and as explicitly as it does in the plant.

Imagine trying to face and re-live something in your past that was truly horrific. In fact, you can't, which is the point. Now let's add another variable to this situation. Let's imagine that you have successfully and fully integrated your subconscious into your consciousness, which means there is no place to go to escape this horrific fear that literally paralyzes you so that you cannot go in any direction except forward. On top of that, add the newfound belief that the horrific past event you have resurrected will never go away. Think hard about that. How are you going to go forward in the face of paralytic fear when there is no alternative but to go forward? You may have to think about that scenario for a long time before something comes to you. But if you were meant to understand *Thus Spoke Zarathustra*, what will come to you is a rare instinct that compels you to *jump* over that paralytic fear — and it will only come in the gravest of circumstances in which your will to move forward is truly and utterly blocked. This, at least, was precisely my experience, as I recorded it in my diary when Nietzsche's dithyrambs brought me to the precipice.

> This walk went very well. The greatest
> problem I've had in trying to bring my
> subliminal torment into consciousness is that
> when I do, I see no light at the end of the
> tunnel. The suffering seems insurmountable
> to me, which is why I relegated it to the
> subconscious realm in the first place. When I
> confront, I have nowhere to go; my will is
> blocked. But, if you recall, a few days ago,
> when I confronted my worst and most
> paralyzing fear, I thought "this is totally
> insurmountable; there is no way I can get
> around this fear" and then my will said
> "Jump'" and I did, and I flew into a height of
> the mind which I did not know existed.

It is very difficult to describe the "jump" over paralytic fear that I am referencing here, but executing that jump, as I have described it, is precisely the reason for all the work that goes into re-incorporating the subconscious into consciousness.

In the drama, Nietzsche depicts the "jump" in the dithyramb entitled Of the Vision and the Riddle.

> *But there lay a man!* And there! The dog,
> leaping, bristling, whining; now it saw me
> coming – then it howled again, then it
> *screamed* – had I ever heard a dog cry out
> that way for help?

> And truly, what I saw, I had never seen the likes of. I saw a young shepherd writhing, choking, quivering, his face distorted; and with a heavy, black snake hanging out of his mouth.
>
> Had I ever seen so much disgust and pale horror on a face? Had he perhaps gone to sleep? Then had the snake crawled into his throat – and taken a grip with his bite.
>
> My hand pulled at the snake, and pulled – in vain! I could not pull the snake out of his throat. Then a voice cried out of me: 'Bite it! Bite it!
>
> 'Take its head off! Bite it" - so it cried out of me, my horror, my hatred, my disgust, my mercy, all my good and bad cried out of me with one cry. [83]

But it is important to note that, in my opinion, the demon that is being overcome in that particular dithyramb is humiliation, while the demon I experienced and wrote about in the above quote was fear, and the instinctual reaction I experienced was not "bite" but "jump." And my opinion is based upon the fact that the overcoming that is depicted in this dithyramb is accompanied by an exorcism (of the humiliation), on which I will elaborate shortly. It is my theory that humiliation and fear are the two primary demons that give rise to the bad conscience, with emotional pain being the third. This dithyramb depicts the overcoming of humiliation. And there is no dithyramb that depicts the overcoming of fear. As important as it is, insofar as the springboard it provides leads directly to "Zarathustra's cave," Nietzsche never wrote a dithyramb on it.

As I have written, the instinct that came to me in the above-mentioned incident was not "bite" but "jump" because, in the above-mentioned incident, I was confronting fear, not humiliation. And that is because a confrontation with fear and humiliation that has been raised from the subconscious arouses a different instinct and a different result. But in both cases, the fundamental result is an ascension via the ground of being inherent in the principium individuationis shifting from below to above. Remember that when the boundaries of Self are violated, resulting in the bad conscience, be it due to some extraordinary fear, humiliation, or pain, the individual falls from Schopenhauer's rowboat and sinks into the sea of emotion, which results in a state of being and mind that is called sub-individuated being. When the individual succeeds in overcoming the subliminal torment that caused his bad conscience and his subsequent collapse, there is an equal and opposite movement to that fall — as an ascension — in the opposite direction, which is above the principium individuationis. And this is the definition of over-Self or a state of being and mind that is called supra-individuation. Except that, while both phenomena (the overcoming of fear and the overcoming of humiliation) impart an ascension, the overcoming of fear provides more than an ascension. Overcoming fear also imparts an inordinate sense of security and clearness (or calmness) of mind that might be aptly described in metaphor as a "cave." And this is "Zarathustra's cave" that is referenced so many times throughout the drama.

In addition, the overcoming of humiliation is accompanied by a literal exorcism of the humiliation, insofar as the actor feels the humiliation exit his inner being like something that previously "crawled down his throat." That, by the way, is a most profound, life-changing, and very specific exorcism (of humiliation) that I would ask you to compare with the exorcism that the Christians talk about in their literature.

I would point out most emphatically that the overcoming of either fear or humiliation is not accomplished by negating or lessening of the either the fear or the humiliation themselves. In fact, on the contrary, the deeper the actor succeeds in fathoming either demon, to the point of having the most impact upon the will, either by blocking it (in the case of fear) or emasculating it (in the case of humiliation) the more intense will be the opposite effect achieved by overcoming it.

To understand this better, allow yourself to succumb to some fear you harbor. As you feel yourself fall into darkness and fear, with all your might, go the other way. Rise above the fear. Defy the fear. Reach deep into your gut and reverse the movement. And you will find that your fall is halted. But the force of the movement with which you "go the other way" will be inversely proportional to the force of the movement by which you feel yourself being drawn into the abyss. By practicing this willful exercise, the deeper you are able to plumb the fear, that higher will you rise above it — because in reversing the falling movement that inheres in fear, you do not return to normal, you do not return to the principium individuationis, you move far beyond it, high above it, into supra-individuation, into the supra-conscious. Thus, Zarathustra says,

> Not the ascension into the heights; the fall into the abyss is the terrible thing!
>
> The abyss where the look shoots *downward* and the hand grasps *upward*. There the heart grows giddy through its two-way will.
>
> Ah, friends, do you also divine my heart's two-way will?
>
> This, this is *my* abyss and my danger, that my look shoots into the heights and my hand wants to hold on to the depths and rely thereon.
>
> My will clings to man, with chains I bind myself to man (the principium individuationis), because I am pulled upwards to the Superman (above the principium-individuation): for my other will wants to take me there.[84]

As with so many other re-definitions and re-evaluations, suffering, too, is now altered. It becomes meaningful. It becomes gold. Previously, it was the bane of existence. Now it is a gateway into heaven as it exists on earth. And that re-evaluation acts to accelerate the process of incorporating the subconscious into consciousness.

Indeed, many re-evaluations occur as a result of the overcoming and redemption of human suffering and as a result of an ever-deepening supra-Self coming to the fore, which is addressed by a lengthy dithyramb, Of Old and New Law Tables.

In summary, if life manifests itself within human being as an extension of the limits of Self, which itself constitutes the being in human being, via incorporation of the subconscious, then the "jump" over demonic suffering constitutes its meaning, the reason and justification for all the work, its reward. And, in another re-definition of some of life's most fundamental phenomena, this "jump" or "bite" may rightly define the redemption of human suffering because it results in an ascension into the supra-conscious realm of the mind, where profound enlightenment and the absolute eradication of compulsion reside.

And just as the subconscious lies below the principium individuationis, the supra-conscious lies above it, which is the most obvious reason that Nietzsche called this supra-individuated state of human being, which lies beyond the limits of individuated human being, "Übermensch" or "overman" or over-Self. In addition, insofar as the subconscious imparts a sense of being weighed down, the supra-conscious imparts a sense of being weightless, of flying (above the principium individuationis).

Thus does Zarathustra say:

> He who teaches men to fly will defy all boundary stones; he will see all boundaries themselves fly into the air; he will rename the earth – "heaven itself."
>
> The ostrich runs faster than the fastest horse, but when he grows heavy with burden, he plunges his head into the burdensome earth: that is how it is with the man who cannot yet fly. [85]

Lastly, I would point out that the ascension unto supra-individuation is entirely incremental, according to the actor's ability to plumb and then become his deeper supra-Self. As he digs deeper, finds the courage to face himself, and succeeds, then he also achieves a deeper fathoming of his fear or humiliation, which results in an even higher ascension, so that he is continually digging, confronting, and ascending. In such a way, life becomes a highly meaningful exercise in the creation of supra-individuation. And the restoration of meaning to life is a milestone in the history of Occidental civilization, especially in this era in which the divine myth is dying, thus causing nihilism to run rampant. It should not go unnoticed that Nietzsche's New Dithyramb provides the one and only cure for nihilism.

While one half of the dithyrambic drama teaches the actor how to find his Self via incorporation of the sub-conscious, the other half teaches him how to achieve the ascension into the supra-conscious. All exhortations in *Thus Spoke Zarathustra* to become the Übermensch are exhortations to ascend into the supra-conscious via the redemption of suffering.

Now we should think about exactly what it is that you are jumping over when you jump over that horrific fear. Let us begin by allowing me to tell you outright: it is the principium individuationis that you are jumping over when you jump over that paralytic fear.

For a better understanding of the principium individuationis (or PI), I will refer back once again to Nietzsche, who references it at the outset of his essay on *The Birth of Tragedy*:

And so we might apply to Apollo, in an eccentric sense, what Schopenhauer says of the man wrapt in the veil of Mâyâ: *Welt als Wille und Vorstellung,* I. p. 416: "Just as in a stormy sea, unbounded in every direction, rising and falling with howling mountainous waves, a sailor sits in a boat and trusts in his frail barque: so in the midst of a world of sorrows the individual sits quietly supported by and trusting in his *principium individuationis.*" Indeed, we might say of Apollo, that in him the unshaken faith in this *principium* and the quiet sitting of the man wrapt therein have received their sublimest expression; and we might even designate Apollo as the glorious divine image of the *principium individuationis,* from out of the gestures and looks of which all the joy and wisdom of "appearance," together with its beauty, speak to us.[86]

Please take note of the phrase, "supported by and trusting in his *principium individuationis.*

Returning again to a scenario in our imagination, imagine being at peace, within a state of contentment. Then allow some fear deep within you to well up and overcome you. What happens? It is as if you feel yourself fall into darkness. It is as if the ground gives way, opens up and swallows you. There is specifically the sensation of the ground giving way and falling into darkness. That is the collapse of the principium individuationis (PI), which we rely on to quite literally keep us afloat amidst a tumultuous sea of emotions. If you fall out of the PI, then you lose your mind. We rely absolutely on the PI.

Returning now to the question of what happens when we succeed in jumping over a truly paralytic fear, we rise above our reliance on the PI. And the experience is very much like a physical transport, an ascension that is very exhilarating. Indeed, when Zarathustra says "You look up when you desire to be exalted, and I look down because I am exalted," it is this ascension (high above the PI) that he references. And that is the place within the heart and mind of man that Nietzsche refers to when he speaks of the Übermensch. That is the place within us where we are led by believing in the idea of the supra-Self. In other words, this place beyond and above the PI is the meaning, the fruit, of all the work that went into both finding the supra-Self and redeeming the suffering that was confronted along the way, *within each supra-Self.*

Definition of Mysticism

Nietzsche's dithyrambic tragedy constitutes an attempt at a re-evaluation of all values because, in the course of the drama, the actor will learn new values that demonstrably enable life, while, at the same time, un-learning old values that Western culture has held sacred for two millennia.

One of the new values that Nietzsche teaches is mysticism. which has been discredited since the days of Socrates.

> Yes, my friends, believe with me in Dionysian life and in the re-birth of tragedy. The time of the Socratic man is past: crown yourselves with ivy, take in your hands the thyrsus, and do not marvel if tigers and panthers lie down fawning at your feet. Dare now to be tragic men, for ye are to be redeemed! Ye are to accompany the Dionysian festive procession from India to Greece! Equip yourselves for severe conflict, but believe in the wonders of your god![87]

The statement "Ye are to accompany the Dionysian festive procession from India to Greece" is a reference to the banishment of mysticism by Socrates' science, after which it found a home in Indian culture. Thus, it has now become the initiative of Dionysian culture to bring it back into Western culture (i.e., Greece).

It was Nietzsche's view that proto-tragedy and mysticism go hand in hand. Without mysticism, proto-tragedy is not possible. It is not so much the case that one must go out looking for mysticism and then bathe oneself in it. What is important to understand is that events will happen within the heart and mind of the dithyrambic actor during the course of the drama and those events will not necessarily be intelligible or even just logical to him nor will they necessarily happen within his consciousness. *But they must be allowed to happen.* It is in that sense that the actor must value mysticism and allow things that may happen mystically to happen despite the mysticism in which they are cloaked.

One of the values that precludes mysticism is science, which was founded by Socrates. And it is important to understand that it does not matter whether or not you ever read Socrates or whether you consider yourself an artist. The tendency to think scientifically or logically is inherent in every human being. But it was Socrates who raised it to a level wherein it became a high value because that is what philosophers do: they legislate values.

So, let us now try to understand the value called science.

> ... to make existence appear to be comprehensible, and therefore to be justified....[88]

And,

> While in all productive men it is instinct which is the creatively affirmative force,

> consciousness only comporting itself critically and dissuasively; with Socrates it is instinct which becomes critic; it is consciousness which becomes creator—a perfect monstrosity *per defectum!* And we do indeed observe here a monstrous *defectus* of all mystical aptitude, so that Socrates might be designated as the specific *non-mystic,* in whom the logical nature is developed, through a superfoetation, to the same excess as instinctive wisdom is developed in the mystic.[89]

In all things, life must be made intelligible, even in art, according to this scientific mode of thought.

> ... we shall now be able to approach nearer to the character *æsthetic Socratism.* supreme law of which reads about as follows: "to be beautiful everything must be intelligible," as the parallel to the Socratic proposition, "only the knowing is one virtuous."[90]

The practice of dithyrambic drama absolutely requires a heavy reliance of intuition and instinct, both of which are anti-scientific. After all, it is instinct itself that the dithyramb teaches. (See the dithyramb entitled Of the Vision and the Riddle.) And the ability to think and act in leaps and bounds, without the lag of reckoning, is a critical fundament of dithyrambic drama. And to require that every inner phenomenon enter into consciousness and be subjected to the criteria of logic would absolutely go against the process by which myth is created, which is the other aim of dithyrambic drama.

For instance, a great part of the entire drama involves learning to allow repressed or subliminal emotions to come into consciousness or at least to become unfettered by the very strong proclivity of a repressive willfulness. But it is the Self, not consciousness, that makes emotion intelligible and manageable; consciousness merely provides the arena. However, deeper emotions define a deeper Self, the supra-Self, which will not exist when those repressed emotions first rise up. Therefore, trying to make them intelligible through the eyes of the existing shallow Self would defeat the mythopoeic instinct that would trigger the creation of the deeper Self, the supra-Self. Therefore, it is necessary to learn to allow repressed emotion to rise up without understanding it initially. This is what the dithyramb entitled Of Joys and Passions teaches.

In order to render this dithyramb, the first thing to understand is that Dionysia has redefined virtue, which is yet another re-evaluation. A virtue is some manner of behavior that we value for one reason or another. In many instances, those reasons have been rooted in morality, which has made virtues of things like just behavior, prudence, and fortitude. Virtues like faith, hope, and charity are rooted in Christian morality. And the virtue of righteousness is rooted in ancient Persian morality.

It should make sense that an entirely different culture might have entirely different virtues. Although, morality exists in every culture to some extent, so it would be reasonable to expect to find similar moral virtues in different cultures. However, in this Dionysian culture, there are no moral virtues because there is no morality.

In Dionysian culture, anything that rises from within the realm of emotion and assists with the all-important task of finding one's supra-Self and becoming that supra-Self — is a virtue. Love of Self, which greatly assists movement toward one's Self, is a virtue. And love of supra-Self, which is a different thing, is also a virtue, but it is a more noble virtue, for obvious reasons. However, if a repressed emotion comes to the fore and defines Self or supra-Self, that, too, is a virtue, for the same reason. And it could be any emotion; it does not matter. It might be some repressed pain. What matters is the depth from which it rises and its ability to trigger the mythopoeic instinct. It is that ability which makes it a virtue, an asset.

And what does the dithyramb entitled Of Joys and Passions say?

> My brother, if you have a virtue, and it is your own virtue, you have it in common with no one.
>
> To be sure, you want to call it by a name and caress it; you want to pull its ears and amuse yourself with it.
>
> And lo and behold! Now you have its name in common with the people and have become one of the people and the herd with your virtue!
>
> It would be better for you to say: 'Unspeakable is that which is pain and sweetness to my soul and is also the hunger of the belly of my being.'

> Let your virtue be too high for the familiarity of names: and if you must speak of it, do not be ashamed to stammer about it.
>
> Speak thus and stammer: 'This is *my* good, this is what I love, this is how I like it, this is how *I* alone want the good.
>
> 'I do not want it as the law of God, I do not want it as one of man's statutes and need of necessity: let it be no sign-post to heaven and paradises.[91]

This dithyramb says that if something rises from deep within you, and if it defines your Self or your supra-Self, do not try to familiarize it. Do not try to make it intelligible via your current, existing Self. Leave it unintelligible if, at times, it seems unintelligible. Do not pull it down to your level because what you should want instead is to use it to drop down to its depth of emotion and also to rise up to its level of clarity. And do not use it to define your Self absolutely because, as time passes and you work harder and dig deeper, then you will find another supra-Self, and this newly found emotion that defines your current Self may become unsubstantial and insignificant, especially as even deeper, more pronounced, and more definitive emotions arise. At the end of this dithyramb, Zarathustra says "you should love your virtues – for you will perish by them." In other words, learn to love your "virtues," your defining emotions, because they will lead you to your supra-Self, and, in the process, your Ego will come that much closer to its eventual and total collapse.

In my opinion, everything that this dithyramb teaches goes without saying. But for some, perhaps it is not that easy. In any case, the dithyrambist covered it. And many times, it is quite remarkable how thorough he is, which brings me to another point. Many of the aphorisms in each dithyramb all point to the same inner conflict but with a different perspective so that the actor has a multitude of opportunities to find his way. In most instances, it is not necessary to render every single idiom, just one that makes the point.

Another dithyramb, entitled Of Immaculate Perception, teaches a devaluation of the insatiable desire to know all things merely for the sake of knowing, which is another trait inherent in scientific thought.

> Science without thus selecting, without such delicate taste, pounces upon everything knowable, in the blind covetousness to know all at any price.[92]

Knowledge of the inner world merely for the sake of knowing is not going to help the actor move forward to his Self. It is true that he may discover things about his Self that he was not looking for, but to indulge the insatiable thirst of knowledge that characterizes scientific thought would be very wayward. Everything that is discovered within the inner world must be incorporated into the image of supra-Self that is slowly coming to the fore.

> The deeper the roots of a man's inner nature, the better will he take the past into himself; and the greatest and most powerful nature would be known by the absence of limits for the historical sense to overgrow and work

> harm. It would assimilate and digest the past,
> however foreign, and turn it to sap.[93]

Notice the last part of the last sentence in the above quote, "turn it into sap." In the first part of the above quote, Nietzsche is talking about a man's ability to assimilate his past, by which he means the subconscious. And in the latter part, he is talking about assimilating the past and turning it into "sap," by which he means nutrition with which to grow. This insight into the use of this metaphor to allude to nourishment (or life) is strengthened by a different translation in which the word "sap" is translated as "blood."[94]

The actor must learn that the insatiable drive for knowledge merely for the sake of knowledge has no place in the intuitive thought that the dithyrambs teach.

Finally, regarding the substantial role that mysticism plays in Nietzsche's dithyrambic drama, consider that, in the beginning, and for a long way into the drama, regarding the Herculean effort to learn to feel again, the actor will mount this or that difficult subliminal emotion, and that will be a great achievement. Then he will learn to ride a difficult emotion for a short distance, and that will be a great achievement as well. But then, near the end of the drama, the actor will learn to ride the emotion all the way to its end, which will take him deep into the fourth dimension of his Self. But for that to happen, the wall that is erected between the actor and his emotions must be *completely* torn down, which will happen; his Ego will collapse fully and entirely. And when that is about to happen, he will have a dream in which he looks into a mirror and sees his face, and it will be the ugliest thing he has ever seen. An onlooker would be horrified by the ugliness of the appearance, but not the dreamer. He will recognize his Self, and, for a very long time, he will already have known the horror he now faces, so he will not be horrified. But he will be overwhelmingly disgusted. When the actor has this dream, he should take it as an omen that the conflict represented in the dithyramb entitled "Of the Ugliest Man" is near and he should redouble his efforts to render that dithyramb. In such a way, Nietzsche's dithyrambic tragedy is steeped in mysticism, so much so that some insights will first present themselves to him only in his dreams. Indeed, following the dream about the ugliest Self, the actor will later have another dream in which he experiences *for the first time* his Self beyond all suffering, the Übermensch. What does it mean that these virtuous images first appear in dreams? I do not know! That is the nature of mysticism. Or, as Zarathustra puts it,

> The world is deep: and deeper than day [consciousness] can fathom. Not everything should be spoken in the daylight.[95]

The Meaning of Life

When you ask "What is the meaning of life?" you must understand the question you are asking, and, most likely, you do not. If we were to ask the plant "What is the meaning of life?" it would answer "the fruit." In other words, the fruit is the one good thing in this world that the plant produces. The fruit is the reason that the plant undertakes all the hardship of growing and all the turmoil it endures during its growth. The fruit makes life worthwhile.

The fruit that the human species produces is called the genius, by which I mean individuals like Caesar, Beethoven, Napoleon, Shakespeare, da Vinci, and, of course, Nietzsche. These are individuals who possess a vision that sees into the future. Usually, they engender this vision in their youth and then spend their entire lives working to achieve it. And *no one else* sees the vision that the genius sees. The genius is entirely alone in his vision of the future. And their achievement provides an inordinate measure of benefits to humanity, which the combined efforts of generations of people could not match.

There are two obvious reasons that the genius is able to achieve something so extraordinary. One, they are not bound by the limits of thought and action that most other people abide by. For instance, they think and act in leaps and bounds.

And two, their passions are also limitless, not bound by the limits to which most individuals abide. For instance, they are driven by a will that can hold fast for decades, even a lifetime. It is the absence of limits, both in idea and in passion but especially in will, as we see in supra-individuated being, that most characterizes genius.

And the very definition of life as a process of growth is growth beyond the limits of an existing state of being, as in the seed to the seedling to the plant to the tree. And growth beyond the limits of Self, the ability of mind to incorporate unmanageably titanic sensation into itself, is the very definition of life within human being. And that whole process of growth is precisely what Nietzsche's dithyrambic drama teaches *and imparts* to those who undertake it. In other words, Nietzsche dithyrambic drama avails us life and its meaning. In his drama, the individuated human being who has become sub-individuated through suffering then becomes supra-individuated through the redemption of that suffering.

How, then, does supra-individuated human being become incarnate in those individuals we recognize as genius? The answer is heredity, about which we seem to have a false notion.

> Generally speaking, everything *is worth no more and no less than one has paid for it.* This of course does not hold good in the case of an isolated individual; the great capacities of the individual have no relation whatsoever to that which he has done, sacrificed, and suffered for them. But if one should examine the previous history of his race one would be sure to find the record of an extraordinary

> storing up and capitalising of power by means of all kinds of abstinence, struggle, industry, and determination. It is because the great man has cost so much, and not because he stands there as a miracle, as a gift from heaven, or as an accident, that he became great: **"Heredity" is a false notion.** A man's ancestors have always paid the price of what he is.[96] (emphasis added)

Nietzsche believed that genius was an accumulation of power through the generations. He believed that this accumulation grew increasingly more potential, until, for whatever capricious reason, the accumulation was triggered and released and thereby resulted in the birth of one very extraordinary human being: a Napoleon, a Caesar, a Mozart, et cetera.

> I teach that there are higher and lower men, and that a single individual may under certain circumstances justify whole millenniums of existence —that is to say, a wealthier, more gifted, greater, and more complete man, as compared with innumerable imperfect and fragmentary men.[97]

Thus, Nietzsche's focus was not on raising the lot of the masses but rather on raising individuals.

> The problem that I set here is … what type of man must be *bred*, must be *willed*, as being the most valuable, the most worthy of life, the most secure guarantee of the future. This

> more valuable type [the genius, e.g., Beethoven, Mozart, Shakespeare] has appeared often enough in the past: but always as a happy accident, as an exception, never as deliberately *willed*. Very often it has been precisely the most feared [e.g., Napoleon, Caesar]; hitherto it has been almost *the* terror of terrors....[98]

And,

> Mankind surely does *not* represent an evolution toward a better or stronger or higher level, as progress is now understood. This "progress" is merely a modern idea, which is to say, a false idea. The European of today, in his essential worth, falls far below the European of the Renaissance; the process of evolution does *not* necessarily mean elevation, enhancement, strengthening.
>
> True enough, it succeeds in isolated and individual cases in various parts of the earth and under the most widely different cultures, and in these cases a *higher* type certainly manifests itself; something which, compared to mankind in the mass, appears as a sort of superman. Such happy strokes of high success have always been possible, and will remain possible, perhaps, for all time to come. Even whole races, tribes and nations may occasionally represent such lucky accidents.[99]

In any case, the point to be taken here is that the creation of great individuals is the goal, not the elevation of the masses.

> The *fundamental errors* of the biologists who have lived hitherto: it is not a matter of the species, but of rearing stronger individuals (the many are only a means).[100]

> *Fundamental errors*: to regard the *herd* as an aim instead of the individual! The herd is only a means and nothing *more*! But nowadays people are trying to understand *the herd* as they would an individual, and to confer higher rights upon it than upon isolated personalities. Terrible mistake! ![101]

Also, at the end of The *Will to Power*, he wrote "Not 'mankind,' but overman is the goal!" And by "overman," make no mistake that he means the incarnation of the effort to rise above the principium individuationis, the transcendence of the limits of individuated human being.

And finally, regarding the extreme difficulty of reading *Thus Spoke Zarathustra*, as evidenced by the widespread failure by many to make any sense of it for more than a century, it should be plainly evident that it was not Nietzsche's intent to be understood by the masses. Rather, it was his intent to be understood by only a few, those whom he hoped he could lead.

> *The order of rank*: he who *determines* values and leads the will of millenniums, and does

187

> this by leading the highest natures—he is *the highest man.*[102]

Nietzsche predicted that whichever people adopted his philosophy, learned his new way of thinking, and acted it out generation after generation would come to rule the world. I wish to endorse that prediction with another prediction of my own. This culture, which will be called Dionysia, will, in time, produce within its people a progeny of geniuses the likes of which the world has never known, exceeding even the magnitude that the ancient Greeks achieved. And it is through that progeny that such people will indeed rule the world.

Re-Evaluation of Values

As I have said repeatedly and throughout, it is no easy task to undertake this drama. Plus, it takes a long time to complete, if you stay with it. In my case, it took a lifetime. I started as a teenager, and I didn't reach the end until I was an old man. Nietzsche, however, was a mere thirty-seven years old when he finished. Personally, I do not believe it would require a lifetime for most people. I think my circumstances were particularly egregious and difficult to overcome. In addition to the years spent, there is also the necessity of having time to work on the drama, so, unless you have some wealth, be prepared to live with the utmost frugality in order to make that time. But beyond all those temporal concerns, there is also the difficulty of undertaking a life of continuous change, and I mean change at the most fundamental level: mind altering change. Remember that reality is founded upon the mythical Self, and, in the course of this drama, you will grow through a long lineage of supra-Selves, each time assuming a new enter of gravity with ever increasing depth and intensity of emotion and mind. The words of Zarathustra, "My today refutes my yesterday," best describe how your values will change repeatedly and unendingly.

Beyond those difficulties, there is the difficulty of achieving a revaluation of values that have been fundamental up until now.

Let us begin a review of those changes with the concept of will. The common, most widespread understanding of will is what we call will power: to concentrate on something intensively and to disallow any distraction that would take away from our intense concentration. The will to power that *Thus Spoke Zarathustra* teaches is much more sophisticated, although the kind of "rude willing" I just described does have its place in the will to power.

At its simplest, to will something is to want something and then to look for and promote the passions, volitions, and beliefs that will help you achieve your goal, which requires that the fundamental desire be sufficiently strong to endure through different and changing conditions. Sometimes willing means undoing or unlearning something that is preventing you from reaching your goal. In such a way, willing is not always a matter of going forward, and it is not always a hands-on activity. Sometimes it requires preparation of better circumstances, and sometimes you must go in a direction other than forward. In short, sometimes it requires a refrain rather than an exertion and a circuitous route rather than a straight line. But in every case, willing requires an accumulation of the various forces of human nature, such as the force of a desire or a wish or a hope as well as the confluence that those forces comprise together.

With regard to the will to power, the fundamental desire is for Self. Thus, to want to find your Self is the primary prerequisite for an undertaking of *Thus Spoke Zarathustra*. The will to power desires Self because the image of being empowers its beholder. Therefore, whatever helps to increase the apprehension of Self constitutes the will to power. But what helps to increase the apprehension of Self? The answer to this question is extremely important to a seed that has forgotten how to grow. One can only hope that one day a special seed will come along that succeeds in re-learning how to grow and then share that know-how with the others. Nietzsche is that special seed, and *Thus Spoke Zarathustra* teaches everything that helps to increase the apprehension of Self, how to grow, as well as everything that must be unlearned if it is a detriment to the process of growth. Specifically, each dithyramb presents in metaphor either something that must be learned or something that must be unlearned.

And exactly what does it mean to learn everything that increases the apprehension of Self? It means to embody the will that is being taught in the dithyrambs. The dithyramb is a metaphorical representation of some aspect of the will to power, and that representation is a plausible embodiment. The dithyrambic drama must be lived. *Thus Spoke Zarathustra* is not a book like all other books that requires nothing more than a mere reading to be understood. This book must be lived. And if you live out the drama, then you become an object of the drama. And what does one become at the end of this drama? You become a work of art yourself. Reading *'Zarathustra* will lead you to your Self as well as the demons that reside within. Once there, the book will teach you how to free your Self from the grip of your demons. If you succeed, then you will ascend to a state of enlightenment wherein all your suffering will be redeemed *and made worthwhile.* That is what this book will do for you.

Insofar as you are continually trying to apprehend your supra-Self, a more vivid and more comprehensive vision of Self than what exists in the present, then you must plumb ever more deeply into your feelings because it is feeling that defines Self, according to the theory of mythopoeia, which states that a vision of being arises from the phenomenon of sensation. So, the more pronounced that emotion becomes, the more pronounced does the vision of Self also become. Eventually, by pursuing the supra-Self, you reach the bottom of the well, where emotion is immediately intuitable, without the intervention of thought, and Self achieves a state of brilliant percipience. It is in this sense that Zarathustra says "Become what you are." And it is in this sense that Zarathustra says "Live dangerously, and you will be redeemed." To live dangerously is to live without guarding yourself against whatever monsters dwell within the subconscious. Eventually, you do lower your guard toward your feelings, and, as you do, the most sublime and most imperceptible emotions rise to the surface.

Many of the dithyrambs in *Thus Spoke Zarathustra* teach the actor how to incorporate the subconscious into the conscious while, at the same time, restoring those emotions that reside within the subconscious to a full and intense capacity so that they become clear and articulate movements instead of mere rumblings.

Keep in mind that what you are doing throughout this drama, in search of your Self, is you are altering reality, your reality. The alteration is toward an improvement, specifically an improvement in percipience, but, still, you are altering reality. And that is no easy task. In fact, it is an extremely difficult task.

There is a good reason that difficult emotions are relegated to the subconscious: they are unmanageable. And this is especially true of horror, which arouses intractable fear. And fear is unsurmountable. It is by definition the feeling that erupts in the absence of will at a moment when the will is needed. Thus, fear represents a frontier, the limits of the individual will.

And every instinct in the body and mind repels any attempt to incorporate horrific fear into consciousness just as every instinct in the body repels any attempt to walk into a burning house. Tremendous resistance will be met by any effort to incorporate into consciousness an horrific experience that has been relegated to the subconscious. But there are dithyrambs that teach the actor how to do it. And one way to do it is to allow the sense of Self from which the resisting instincts arise, which is really the Ego, to "give way" or to die. In the wake of this collapse, difficult emotions are then allowed to come to the fore, and it is only then that redemption and salvation become possible. This collapse is the Dionysiac definition of tragedy. This collapse is what is meant by the word "tragedy." And this definition is a re-evaluation.

There are many re-evaluations to be found in a Dionysian way of thinking, particularly with regard to major life events that have been highlighted by Christian theology, specifically the ideas of death, resurrection, eternal life, and an ascension unto a better place. Whereas Christian theology teaches that these events are mostly other-worldly, the Dionysian view of these events is more practical.

Resurrection refers to the resurrection of the old Self that succumbed with the relegation of the emotions that define that wounded Self to the subconscious. And it really is a whole new person (though entirely familiar) that emerges from the collapse of the old, protective Self via proto-tragedy. A whole new sense of Self comes into being, through which one feels more whole, more alive, more perceptive, and more willful. Of course, keep in mind that insofar as the actor will proceed in life through many Selves, there will be many resurrections. Also, every resurrection is preceded by the disintegration of the previous Self. Thus, proto-tragedy precedes resurrection, in every instance.

Eternal life is another major accomplishment in life. In order to explain this phenomenon, it is necessary to understand that a proximity to Self is the most precious possession a human being can obtain. There is nothing more valuable in life than this one possession. But it is a very difficult possession to obtain and even harder to keep simply because there is so much within us that drives us away from our Self and even bigger obstacles that keep us from reaching our Self. I'm talking about suffering. A man or woman who was the victim of a crime, for instance, and harbors horrific memories of that crime and its effect on him or her must first overcome that horror to apprehend his or her Self *just once*, to say nothing of maintaining that proximity. And that is no easy task. The odds of failure are much higher than the odds of success. But even if he or she should succeed, there is much to prevent the maintenance of that proximity because there are so many wild passions and superfluous beliefs tempting us to their indulgence, which would constitute a major distraction from Self. But what if a man or woman who spent enough time at it eventually succeeded in overcoming true and genuine horror and, in the process, also learned sufficient respect for Self that he allowed *nothing* to distract him from his vision once he achieved it? Then there would a constant proximity. And that constant proximity with Self is the Dionysian view of eternal life.

And what about the quality of mind within an individual who has undertaken this process of inner growth and succeeded in overcoming the horror that once ruled over his being in every aspect of his existence? I can tell you from personal experience, as one who has undertaken this process and succeeded, that the transformation is profound and deeply redemptive. I will speak later and extensively of what one becomes as a result of pursuing and attaining one's supra-Self. But suffice it to say that it is a state of overwhelming enlightenment, far beyond the limits of individuated being, where happiness and bliss are overflowing and therefore present themselves as a condition that constitutes a malady, not a justification, for life, which says much about the age-old belief that happiness is the goal of life. For a Dionysian, achievement of this enlightened state of supra-individuated being is like an ascension unto heaven or paradise regained. It is not something we are promised in an after-life; it is something we are promised in this life. And it is not something we are promised through a grant based on the merits of our contribution in the battle between good and evil, as the Christians teach. Rather, it is something that we are meant to achieve, through hard work, and specifically through our efforts to overcome horror and transform that horror into an inner serenity. That is heaven for the Dionysian, and it is achievable in this lifetime. Thus, for a Dionysian, the most important thing to seek in life is not happiness and God but work and Self. The most enlightened man is not he who has found God; it is he who has found his Self. Indeed, he who has found his Self has been saved.

Lastly, I'd like to talk about exorcism, which is a deeply religious and meaningful experience that Christianity has turned into a burlesque. A Dionysian exorcism occurs in the dithyramb entitled Of the Vision and the Riddle. The metaphorical scenes that depicts that exorcism are that of Zarathustra coming upon a man lying on the ground and choking on a snake that has crawled down his throat and taken a hold on him deep inside. In my experience, this turned out to be humiliation. Humiliation is a very insidious demon. It does, in fact, seem like a snake that has crawled down your throat and taken a hold insofar as it is not easily expelled and, when it is finally expelled, it does indeed feel as if something is exiting from deep within your being as if through your throat. This is the Dionysian experience of an exorcism. And this exorcism is profoundly transformative and meaningful. Imagine living your whole life with a deep-reaching, intractable sense of profound humiliation and then suddenly it is gone and you are free! That is an exorcism.

Thus, to summarize, some of life's most profoundly transformative and meaningful achievements — resurrection, eternal life, paradise regained, salvation, and exorcism — all occur within the Dionysian interpretation of life but as very practical, very achievable and truly transformative experiences, in this lifetime.

Part II: Exegeses

Zarathustra's Prologue

On Initiation into the Drama Via an Evaluation of Cerebral Self and Mythical Self

Please note that what follows here are demonstrative exegeses. You will experience no dithyrambic transport whatsoever from reading my renditions of *Thus Spoke Zarathustra*. That will come only from your own renditions. Remember that the entire process of rendering a dithyramb requires the lengthy process of introspection, wherein you isolate the particular inner state of mind that is being depicted so that you may then act upon it, which will then necessarily lead you to the next conflict because that is the nature of dramatic music; it depicts a melos, and the melos is not of sounds but of inner events. My only hope by providing you these demonstrative renditions is to show you a cohesion of content from one rendition to the next, namely the pursuit of an apprehension of supra-Self, the whole of which is an inner sojourn driven by a will to power. At the least, I hope to show you that the dithyrambs of *Thus Spoke Zarathustra* are rich with meaning but that their wealth must be mined.

Simply put, the Prologue initiates the actor into the drama, and without initiation it is not possible to begin an undertaking of the drama.

The Prologue directs the actor's will away from the Platonic ideal of Self as a contemplative image of being that is assimilable via one or another intensely focused determination and onto the emotions. Nietzsche achieves this *devaluation* by showing the actor the futility and absence of meaning in his numerous attempts to become assimilated into the ideal, which the actor will have already undertaken numerous times. Plato may have memorialized the Self as an assimilable ideal but he did not invent it. It occurs as a most natural inclination in any individual who seeks his Self.

Nietzsche also offers a dialectical argument in *Philosophy in the Tragic Age of the Greeks* in which he refutes Parmenides' Theory of the Identity of Thought and Being, upon which Plato's ideal is founded. I will present that argument in its entirety, but it is provided only for the most astute philosophers as a proof. It is extremely difficult to follow, and it is not necessary for the student to understand it in order to achieve the devaluation. I did not understand it when I achieved my devaluation and found it only afterwards as a proof for my exegeses of the Prologue.

It is perhaps a phenomenon unique to philosophy that just a few individuals, whose lives are separated by hundreds or, in this case, thousands of years, will undertake a common inquiry and expend their entire lives on a contribution to that inquiry. "Is the world driven by a process of Becoming or does it derive from a singular state of Being?" Thales initiated the inquiry with a proclamation that came to him, according to Nietzsche, as a mystical intuition rather than an inferential concept. "*All is water*," Thales said, by which he meant that the world derives from one thing. From this came many questions. "Is the one thing a state of Being", as Parmenides argued, or "is the one thing a process of Becoming, a process by which Being grows or deteriorates into another Being, as Heraclitus argued?"

Practically speaking, the two questions being asked are "Does Self, by which I mean human being, exist eternally and in an unchanging state?" and "or is human being, by which I mean more specifically an idea and sense of Self, an illusory construction of time and space that does not exist at all, leaving only the process of growth as the one thing?" That first question is tantamount to the original ancient question, "Is the one thing a state of Being?" If the one thing is Being, which means the Self is eternal and unchanging, then any degradation of Self, as we see in suffering man where Self devolves into Ego, is merely apparent, not real, insofar as the original Self has not changed at all. According to this dogma, through suffering, man falls from the state of being constituted by Self, and all the lesser gradations of being, including the Ego, which appear along the way of this devolution, are also mere appearance. Moreover, as Parmenides argues (and, later, Plato will argue the same thing), the key to life would lie in avoiding this semblance and finding one's Self within the mind, focusing on it, and attaining to it via thought and contemplation, and especially pure contemplation. [See the dithyramb, Of Immaculate Perception.]

In Philosophy in the Tragic Age of the Greeks, Nietzsche followed this great converse with the arguments proffered by Anaximander and Anaxagoras as well, recitations of which would deflect from our examination of the Prologue. However, Nietzsche's refutation of Parmenides' doctrine of being bears enormous significance for Western thinkers because they adopted and developed it, and so I will recite that doctrine fully, as Nietzsche understood it.

Originally, like Heraclitus, Parmenides also ascribed to a theory of becoming, which he himself developed. Summarizing Nietzsche, and sometimes verbatim, he says that Parmenides categorizes all the opposites into two realms, existent and non-existent, according to whether they are respectively positive or negative, and thereby creates a duality. Becoming is driven by the attraction between opposites. Desire unifies contradictory elements and effects growth. And when the desire is satiated, inherent contradiction drives the same opposites apart and causes deterioration. In such a way, Becoming requires both good and bad elements. Thus, while there is a duality in Parmenides theory of Becoming, there is also a unity. However, Parmenides than faulted his theory of Becoming. By creating a dichotomy within the qualities, both positive and negative, and then, taking the dichotomy to the extreme, creating two realms, existent and non-existent, such as we might see in a comparison of hot and cold (a quality characterized by the absence of heat), he tripped himself up. Again, according to Nietzsche, that which is — is, and that which is not — is not. Therefore, there are no negative, non-existent qualities, and there is no duality. There is only Being and no Becoming, according to the conclusions that follow from the argument put forth by Parmenides.

What follows next is *my* summary of the argument put forth by Nietzsche that both cites Parmenides theory of the Identity of Thought and Being and refutes it.

Being is indivisible because it is the only thing that exists. Nothing else exists that could divide it. Therefore, Being exists in the absence of space because space would be a second existent. And the presence of two existents requires a third which would separate them, and so on. But there is only one existent and that is Being.

Being exists in the absence of motion because it is the only thing that exists. Nothing exists to which it could move, nor does any thing exist that could cause it to move.

Therefore, all that exists is also an eternal unity. Anything which declares otherwise is an illusion and those illusions are created by your senses. The senses cause you to mistakenly believe that Becoming possesses Being.

Parmenides' doctrine of Being was created out of a need to find peace — and especially certainty — in Being, and it is characterized by schematics and abstraction.

Parmenides' argued the existence of peaceful and certain Being because he was able to think it. Thus, his conclusion postulating its existence...

> ... rests upon the supposition that we have an organ of knowledge which reaches into the nature of things and is independent of experience. The material of our thinking according to Parmenides does not exist in perception at all but is brought in from somewhere else, from an extra-material world to which by thinking we have a direct access."[103]

The point regarding the identity of thought and Being is crucial here. According to Nietzsche, Parmenides is saying that there exists within us a state of Being from which we have descended as a result of suffering, that life is a process of struggle by which one attempts an ascension unto that being, and that the attempt proceeds upon a process of thought and contemplation. Suffering man worships this concept of a higher being, his higher Self, in the same way that the pious worships his god, and he attains to an ascension unto it via thought and contemplation. But it does not exist.

It is important to understand that this phenomenon of seeking out an ideal, already existing, higher Self is not merely a dialectical argument carried on by the ancient philosophers. In fact, it is a naturally occurring phenomenon that plays out within an individual who is looking for his Self. He mistakenly believes that there exists an identity of thought and being, that he can find his Self through thought and contemplation and a ruthlessly focused effort to capture it like some elusive butterfly. And, by one way or another, he must bring himself to see the error in this thought, although this documentation here of the argument is unlikely to provide that final, definitive resolution, which will more likely come from the individual's own extended introspection via Zarathustra's Prologue. However, the entire phenomenon — and its refutation — is memorialized in this famous ancient argument that was argued for several generations by some of history's most celebrated philosophers.

Continuing with the argument, then, how could Parmenides have erred so gravely? Because he employed dialectic as his mode of inquiry, though there were other reasons as well. For Nietzsche, dialectic is sophomoric and inadequate, and intuition is far more superior. Consider what he says about Heraclitus, who employed intuition for his inquiry and whom Nietzsche admired perhaps more than any other philosopher. For Heraclitus and Nietzsche, intuitive thought was far superior to conceptual thought and logic. In the following passage, Nietzsche argues that time is easily experienced via intuition but does not exist via logic. Now, I, too, would argue that time does not exist, that it is simply a perception of change that is affected by the wax and wane of the powers that be, that where the power is greatest, there is no change and no sense of time. But the fact is that we do experience time, or change, and the experience does not require any labor of thought whatsoever. However, if we rely on logical thought, rather than intuitable experience, to obtain an understanding of time, we fail. And the difference in the two modes of thought should be considered, especially with regard to the efficacy of philosophical inquiry. The difference, as it turns out, according to the following account provided by Nietzsche, is that there are two distinct realms of interpretability in the world. On the one hand, there is actuality, and, on the other hand, there is reality. The question put to the student is "which realm is most worthy of study?" And the answer Nietzsche provides is that actuality, not reality, is most worthy of our study. And it is intuition that understands actuality, but it is logic that understands reality. In all likelihood, the student will deem reality the far superior realm. And that is a mistake. The better realm for study is actuality.

I will now cite in its entirety the account provided by Nietzsche in which he says what I just reiterated above. It is here for your processing, but I strongly recommend that you skip it, given its extreme complexity, and rely instead on the above reiteration.

> Heraclitus has as his royal property the highest power of intuitive conception, whereas towards the other mode of conception which is consummated by ideas and logical combinations, that is towards reason, he shows himself cool, apathetic, even hostile, and he seems to derive a pleasure when he is able to contradict reason by means of a truth gained intuitively, and this he does in such propositions as: "Everything has always its opposite within itself," so fearlessly that Aristotle before the tribunal of Reason accuses him of the highest crime, of having sinned against the law of opposition. Intuitive representation however embraces two things: firstly, the present,

motley, changing world, pressing on us in all experiences, secondly, the conditions by means of which alone any experience of this world becomes possible: time and space. For these are able to be intuitively apprehended, purely in themselves and independent of any experience; *i.e.,* they can be perceived, although they are without definite contents. If now Heraclitus considered time in this fashion, dissociated from all experiences, he had in it the most instructive monogram of all that which falls within the realm of intuitive conception. Just as he conceived of time, so also for instance did Schopenhauer, who repeatedly says of it: that in it every instant exists only in so far as it has annihilated the preceding one, its father, in order to be itself effaced equally quickly; that past and future are as unreal as any dream; that the present is only the dimensionless and unstable boundary between the two; that however, like time, so space, and again like the latter, so also everything that is simultaneously in space and time, has only a relative existence, only through and for the sake of a something else, of the same kind as itself, *i.e.,* existing only under the same limitations. This truth is in the highest degree self- evident, accessible to everyone, and just for that very reason, abstractly and rationally, it is only attained with great difficulty. Whoever has this truth before his eyes must however also proceed at once to the next Heraclitean consequence and say that the whole essence of actuality is in fact activity, and that for actuality there is no other kind of existence and reality, as Schopenhauer has likewise expounded ("The World As Will And Idea," Vol. I., Bk. I, sec. 4): "Only as active does it fill space and time: its action upon the immediate object determines the perception in which alone it exists: the effect of the action of any material object upon any other, is known only in so far as the latter acts upon the immediate object in a different way from that in which it acted before; it consists in this alone. Cause and effect thus constitute the whole nature of matter; its true being *is* its action. The totality of everything material is therefore very appropriately called in German *Wirklichkeit* (actuality)—a word which is far more expressive than *Realität* (reality). That upon which actuality acts is always matter; actuality's whole 'Being' and essence therefore consist only in the orderly change, which *one* part of it causes in another, and is therefore wholly relative, according to a relation which is valid only within the boundary of actuality, as in the case of time and space."[104]

Parmenides, it must be noted, subscribed to reality over actuality. And out of that subscription, contrived purely out of conceptual thought, arose his Identity of Thought and Being. In the next passage, Nietzsche uses the example of a flying arrow to show even further the absurdity of Parmenides' subscription to reality and specifically his Identity of Thought and Being, which I now also cite in its entirety.

> At any instant of its flight it has a position; in this position it rests. Now would the sum of the infinite positions of rest be identical with motion? Would now the Resting, infinitely often repeated, be Motion, therefore its own opposite? The Infinite is here used as the *aqua fortis* of reality, through it the latter is dissolved. If however the Ideas are fixed, eternal and entitative—and for Parmenides "Being" and Thinking coincide—if therefore the Infinite can never be perfect, if Rest can never become Motion, then in fact the arrow has not flown at all; it never left its place and resting position; no moment of time has passed. Or expressed in another way: in this so-called yet only alleged Actuality there exists neither time, nor space, nor motion. Finally the arrow itself is only an illusion; for it originates out of the Plurality, out of the phantasmagoria of the "Non-One" produced by the senses. Suppose the arrow had a "Being," then it would be immovable, timeless, increate, rigid and eternal—an impossible conception! Supposing that Motion was truly real, then there would be no rest, therefore no position for the arrow, therefore no space—an impossible conception! Supposing that time were real, then it could not be of an infinite divisibility; the time which the arrow needed, would have

to consist of a limited number of time-moments, each of these moments would have to be an *Atomon*—an impossible conception! All our conceptions, as soon as their empirically-given content, drawn out of this concrete world, is taken as a *Veritas æterna,* lead to contradictions. If there is absolute motion, then there is no space; if there is absolute space then there is no motion; if there is absolute "Being," then there is no Plurality; if there is an absolute Plurality, then there is no Unity. It should at least become clear to *us* how little we touch the heart of things or untie the knot of reality with such ideas, whereas Parmenides and Zeno inversely hold fast to the truth and omnivalidity of ideas and condemn the perceptible world as the opposite of the true and omnivalid ideas, as an objectivation of the illogical and contradictory. With all their proofs they start from the wholly undemonstrable, yea improbable assumption that in that apprehensive faculty we possess the decisive, highest criterion of "Being" and "Not-Being," *i.e.,* of objective reality and its opposite; those ideas are not to prove themselves true, to correct themselves by Actuality, as they are after all really derived from it, but on the contrary they are to measure and to judge Actuality, and in case of a contradiction with logic, even to condemn. In order to concede to them this judicial competence Parmenides had to ascribe to them the same "Being," which alone he allowed in general as *the* "Being"; Thinking and that one increate perfect ball of the "Existent" were now no longer to be conceived as two different kinds of "Being," since there was not permitted a duality of "Being." Thus the over-risky flash of fancy had become necessary to declare Thinking and "Being" identical. ... *[The fact that this notion of the identity between thought and being denies sensation any place in the world guarantees better than anything else]* ... that such an identity is not borrowed from the senses.[105]

Finally, using one argument based on the mobility of reason and another based on the origin of semblance, Nietzsche refutes Parmenides' doctrine of Being, specifically his identity of thought and being and his contemptuous and absolute separation of ideation and sensation.

Firstly, if the Thinking of Reason in ideas is real, then also Plurality and Motion must have reality, for rational Thinking is mobile; and more precisely, it is a motion from idea to idea, therefore within a plurality of realities.[106]

Secondly, if only fraud and illusion come from the senses, and if in reality there exists only the real identity of "Being" and Thinking, what then are the senses themselves? They too are certainly Appearance only since they do not coincide with the Thinking, and their product, the world of senses, does not coincide with "Being." If however the senses themselves are Appearance to whom then are they Appearance? How can they, being unreal, still deceive? The "Non-Existent" cannot even deceive. Therefore the Whence? of deception and Appearance remains an enigma, yea, a contradiction. We call these *argumenta ad hominem:* The Objection Of The Mobile Reason and that of The Origin Of Appearance. From the first would result the reality of Motion and of Plurality, from the second the impossibility of the Parmenidean Appearance, assuming that the chief-doctrine of Parmenides on the "Being" were accepted as true.[107] (Here is where Nietzsche snagged Parmenides.)

In summa, the enigma posed by the origin of semblance as it arises within Parmenides' argument itself — refutes Parmenides' argument, twenty-five hundred years later. And Parmenides' argument is further refuted by the mobility of reason.

Upon devaluing the Platonic ideal of Self, the actor is then directed toward his feelings, not his ideas or images or concepts, as the place to begin looking for his Self. It is common knowledge that one's Self is discoverable in one's feelings. Psychiatry teaches this. However, it is also a natural inclination, which happened to be memorialized by Plato, to look for one's Self in a conceived image, quite separate from emotion, that commands a contemplative piety in much the same way that one who is looking for God would be seduced into a contemplative piety of his concept of God. And the word "God" is a metaphorical gesture that Nietzsche uses to point the actor to his adoration of the Platonic ideal of Self. But do not take my word for it. Begin looking for your own rendition and find the analogy yourself. I am confident, however, that you will find the same rendition and the same analogy that I found because, remember, the metaphors used in Nietzsche's dithyrambic drama comprise dramatic "music," or an accurate depiction of reality or, more precisely, *actuality*.

There are ten parts to Zarathustra's Prologue. In the first part, the text to be noted is Zarathustra's declaration that:

> When Zarathustra was thirty years old, he left his home and the lake of his home and went into the mountains. There, he enjoyed his spirit and solitude, and for ten years did not weary of it. But at last his heart changed....[108]

To my reading, this is written from the perspective of someone who has already ascended above the principium individuationis (PI) and into the supra-conscious, a supra-individuated state of being, and remained there for some extended period of time. That fact is validated by Nietzsche's own statement in his writing in *Dawn*, after he had spent his life plumbing the depths of his subconscious and redeeming all the suffering he found there, when he wrote, as I cited at the beginning of this essay, that he had finished his sojourn and that he would begin telling what he had found "whensoever" he decided to become man again, by which he meant to descend from the supra-individuated state of being that he had achieved. It is in the very first few aphorisms of the first part of the Prologue that the dithyrambist writes "Behold! This cup wants to be empty again, and Zarathustra wants to be man again." Therefore, all of *Thus Spoke Zarathustra* is written from the perspective of someone who has already plumbed the depths of his subconscious, redeemed all the suffering therein, and ascended into a state of supra-individuated being, which makes sense because how else would the dithyrambist be able to represent the journey.

The next thing to note in the first part of Zarathustra's Prologue is Zarathustra's declaration that "I must *go down.*" Moving away from the perspective of someone who is descending from supra-individuation to the perspective of someone wishing to achieve the opposite, an ascension unto supra-individuation, in every instance, when we render a dithyramb, our perspective will be the latter.

When we suffer, we lose our sense of Self. In its place, we develop an Ego, which is still a Self, but it is a more impoverished Self. For the sake of discussion, we will call the original, wholesome, fully individuated sense of being "Self," and we will call the suffering and sub-individuated sense of being "Ego." The Ego exists as stopgap, a barrier between the individual and his vaulted subconscious, in which reside the demons that have sunk into oblivion. The relegation of conscious suffering to the subconscious is necessary in order to continue living. But keep in mind that those demons do not go away. They may subside with regard to their intensity, but they do not die. They continue to torment you.

In the course of undertaking this dithyrambic drama, you will learn how to redeem suffering, by which I mean you will learn how to transform your demons into angels. And if you think that is not possible, I assure you that is what will happen. And that is yet another example of the difference between psychiatry as we presently know it and psychiatry as Nietzsche re-chartered it. Modern psychiatry will make you whole, but Dionysian psychiatry will transform you into a work of art. And the only thing better than that is the fact that becoming this work of art entails an entirely new way of thinking that, quite naturally, is deeply meaningful and rewarding.

But, in order to redeem suffering, you must first raise the demons from the subconscious, which you will also learn to do by undertaking this drama. Since the Ego is a stopgap between you and the subconscious, the Ego must undergo a process of disintegration. The Ego must be eliminated. It is for that reason that Zarathustra says at the beginning of the drama, in the second part of Zarathustra's Prologue, that he must go down. It is the Ego that must "go down." And, in fact, the going down does not end until you reach the point in the drama that is memorialized by the dithyramb entitled "Of the Convalescent." We need to look at what happens in that dithyramb.

> "Up, my most abysmal thought, up from my depth! I am your rooster and morning dawn, you sleeping snake that has slept too long: Up! Up! My voice shall soon crow you awake!
>
> Unchain the fetters on your ears and listen to my command because I want to hear you! Up! Up! I have enough thunder to make the very graves listen!
>
> And rub the sleep from your eyes and all that makes you dumb and blind! Hear me with your eyes, too: my voice is a cure even for those born blind.
>
> And once you are awake you will stay awake forever. It is not *my* way to awaken great-

grandmothers from sleep and then tell them to — go back to sleep!

You move, you stretch, you wheeze? Up! Up! You will not gasp, you will speak to me! Zarathustra calls you, Zarathustra the godless!

I, Zarathustra, the advocate of life, the advocate of suffering, the advocate of the idea that everything that goes away also comes back — I call you, my most abysmal thought!

Glory is mine! You are coming — I hear you! My abyss *speaks*, I have brought my deepest depth into the light!

Glory is mine! Come here! Give me your hand — ha! Leave me be! Ha, ha! — Disgust, disgust, disgust — woe is mine!"[109]

This is when the actor, who has been undertaking the drama for quite an extended time and has learned *and developed* much of the will to power, summons a demon from the subconscious and into his consciousness — willfully, on command. It will take a long time to summon the courage to do this and to develop the conditions that will even make it possible, but the time will come one day, and you will do it. When it happens, you will be reunited with your true, original Self, and the Ego in you will become nullified. You will rejoice in this reunion, and, in fact, that is the pleasure that the ancient Greeks found in proto-tragedy, which is what this phenomenon is — a tragedy, but it is certainly not a moral tragedy

Immediately following this summoning and arousal, Zarathustra then says "The hour has now come when he who is falling shall bless himself. Thus *ends* Zarathustra's downfall!"[110]

That is the only part in the entire drama, after Zarathustra begins his down-going, that he says the down-going ends, and it occurs in the latter part of the third part of the book, which means that there is much to learn before you will finally be reunited with your Self.

Keep in mind that what I am trying to explain here is the text in the first part of Zarathustra's Prologue that says "Thus began Zarathustra's downfall."[111] Insofar as there is only one declaration in the entire drama that references that "downfall" as having ended, and that the reference occurs at a point when the actor finally summons a demon from the subconscious, I am saying that the downfall that is mentioned at the outset of the drama is the disintegration and death of the Ego, which will result in a reunion with original Self. Insofar as *Thus Spoke Zarathustra* is a dithyrambic drama, which must be acted out, it would be more specific to say that it is a dithyrambic tragedy, which will result in any actor who undertakes it being reunited with his original Self via a tragic collapse of his Ego. And that is what will happen to you.

Continuing now with the rest of the drama. In the second part of Zarathustra's Prologue, he comes upon a hermit. The hermit is the great thinker in all of us who avoids passion, unless the passion adds to his focused determination for Self. More specifically, it is the great thinker in all of us who believes that original Self is a concept into which one may pass via extremely focused thinking. In fact, the Self is not a concept; it is a myth.

Here, in the second part of Zarathustra's Prologue, the metaphor of the hermit who worships his God in the forest points to the individual who seeks his Self in a single thought via a pious contemplation. The metaphor of the "forest" points perhaps to a desire for knowledge *absent passion* (except the passion for knowledge, because passion distracts the thinker) as an accompaniment to the adulatory passion for the Platonic Self. The fact that Zarathustra passes by the hermit seeking God (who is really the great thinker seeking Self as concept) without a substantive exchange of words is because there is nothing you can do to extirpate this drive toward conceived Self. You can only ignore it, and the easiest way to ignore it is to devalue it, which is achieved in the sixth part of the Prologue.

In the next, third part of Zarathustra's Prologue, he comes into a town called the Pied Cow, which is that place within your mind into which you settle after falling into a sub-individuated state after suffering. In other words, it is that place within your heart and mind where you have found a complacent ease in the face of subliminal demons. Everything that rises from the subconscious immediately subsides back into oblivion without having any effect on your easy and complacent state of mind.

> Consider the herds that are feeding yonder: they know not the meaning of yesterday or to-day, they graze and ruminate, move or rest, from morning to night, from day to day, taken up with their little loves and hates, at the mercy of the moment, feeling neither melancholy nor satiety. Man cannot see them without regret, for even in the pride of his humanity he looks enviously on the beast's

happiness. He wishes simply to live without satiety or pain, like the beast; yet it is all in vain, for he will not change places with it. He may ask the beast—"Why do you look at me and not speak to me of your happiness?" The beast wants to answer—"Because I always forget what I wished to say": but he forgets this answer too, and is silent; and the man is left to wonder.

He wonders also about himself, that he cannot learn to forget, but hangs on the past: however far or fast he run, that chain runs with him. It is matter for wonder: the moment, that is here and gone, that was nothing before and nothing after, returns like a spectre to trouble the quiet of a later moment. A leaf is continually dropping out of the volume of time and fluttering away— and suddenly it flutters back into the man's lap. Then he says, "I remember...," and envies the beast, that forgets at once, and sees every moment really die, sink into night and mist, extinguished forever.[112]

Obviously, this particular state of mind presents a huge problem to any effort to raise the subconscious for the purpose of redeeming the demons within it. And the very long journey from oblivious complacency to engaged enlightenment begins here, in the town called the Pied Cow.

The Ego, which exists solely as a stopgap, preventing the subconscious from rising into consciousness and disturbing one's easy complacency, is responsible for the development of the state of mind to which Nietzsche refers in the third part of Zarathustra's Prologue, the town called the Pied Cow. *And this is the state of mind* the individual, who has only just undertaken this dithyrambic drama and resolved to find his Self within it, will appeal to begin his undertaking when he speaks to the "people." Needless to say, his appeal will fall on deaf ears, surely. Notwithstanding this futility, the actor will proceed with his appeal by resolving in his heart to achieve supra-individuation, whatever that may be (and he will not have a clue whatever that may be; that is, his instincts will have no clue) by rendering these dithyrambs and practicing the dithyrambic drama they present.

And this is how the dithyramb teaches him to appeal to that undertaking. He says "Behold, I teach you the Übermensch." Like me, when I first read this, you will not have any idea what that means. I can tell you, as I did in the first part of the hermeneutics that the Übermensch is the supra-Self. In other words, while it is your Self that you seek, what you will learn by living out this dithyrambic tragedy is that you never settle on the Self you find. Rather, it is always the next Self you want to find. But you must learn that yourself. And until you do learn it, or rather apprehend it, instinctively, you will not understand it. You may be able to ascertain what I mean, but you will not fully understand it until you see the supra-Self within you, through your own efforts. Suffice it to say, any appeal you make to yourself about the Übermensch will go unheeded, until you learn where the will to power begins — in a particular hope and a particular desire, not via a general appeal to *all* the passions, which is the metaphor that represents Zarathustra's appeal to the people.

But he goes on with the appeal, which you should do also. And he says:

What is the greatest thing you can experience? It is the hour of the great contempt. The hour in which even your happiness becomes loathsome to you, and your reason and your virtue also.

The hour when you say: 'What good is my happiness? It is impoverished and unclean and wretched self-complacency. But my happiness should justify existence itself!'

The hour when you say: 'What good is my reason? Does it long for knowledge as the lion for its food? It is impoverished and unclean and wretched self-complacency!'

The hour when you say: 'What good is my virtue? So far it has not moved me to a frenzy. How weary I am of my good and my bad. It is all impoverished and unclean and wretched self-complacency!

The hour when you say: "What good is my justice! I do not see that I am ashes and fire. But the just man is ashes and fire!"

The hour when you say: 'What good is my pity? Is not pity the cross upon which he who loves man is nailed? But my pity is no crucifixion!'

Have you ever spoken thus? Have you ever cried out like that? Oh, I've heard you crying out like that!

> It is not your sin — it is your impoverished passion that cries out to heaven, your very dispassion in sinning cries out to heaven!
>
> Where is the lightning to lick you with its tongue? Where is the passion to break your mold and move you?
>
> Take heed, I teach you the supra-Self: he is that lightning, he is that passion![113]

He's talking about the Ego. And he says the greatest thing you can experience is the moment when you experience contempt for your Ego. And remember, when I speak of the Ego in the exegeses, I mean the impoverished sense of Self that has risen up in the wake of the original Self that deteriorated through suffering. In your pursuit of your supra-Self, you will experience incremental and minor collapses of your Ego. But as you progress in the drama, there will come a moment when your Ego collapses *fully*. And it will be a joyful moment because it will result in a reunification with your original Self. This is the moment he references in the above quote.

The "lightening" he speaks of is the mystical experience you will have when you sense your supra-Self in the depths of your subconscious and then realize that your being runs much more deeply than you had previously thought. There are dithyrambs written about this experience and we will discuss them later.

Moving on to the fourth part of Zarathustra's Prologue, but keep in mind that the dithyrambist is depicting what will happen when you first begin to appeal to yourself toward an undertaking of the supra-Self, he says that the people who have gathered in some marketplace believe that Zarathustra is talking about some tightrope walker when he speaks of the Übermensch.

The tightrope walker is a metaphor that speaks to the Platonic ideal, which is also a naturally occurring phenomenon within sub-individuated man, that Self is a conception which one may pass into through some severely focused mode of thought. If only you could think hard enough, you would find your Self and assimilate it, so says the Platonic ideal.

Prior to undertaking this drama, pursuit of the Platonic conception of Self via a mode of thought is probably the best effort you know. Therefore, at the outset of the drama, as you begin to learn, you will try to apply what you learn to improve that effort. This, too, is an exercise in futility, which you must come to see. And when you do see the futility in this, then you will abandon it and pursue it no more.

Continuing with the fourth part of Zarathustra's Prologue, he says "Man is a rope, fastened between animal and Superman — a rope over an abyss," which means that the suffering Self is a bridge between sub-individuation and supra-individuation — a bridge that traverses a very deep abyss.

> What is great in man is that he is a bridge and not a goal; what can be loved in man is that he is a *going upward* and a *going under*.[114]

In the course of the drama, you will expend tremendous effort on trying to raise the subconscious into consciousness. But the purpose of this enlightenment is not to unravel the knot in which your conscience has become mired but rather to find the springboard within the tension that inheres in the knot so that you may use it to raise yourself above the principium individuationis (PI) into the supra-conscious. And as you traverse the numerous layers of Self into the depths of your being, what is great about your journey is your ability to tragically shed those layers to reveal deeper layers, not your discovery of Self because, though it may be a long time before you realize it, when you reach the deepest supra-Self, the highest supra-Self, you will transcend that also and ascend unto supra-individuation, beyond the limits of individuated being.

None of this appeal to the supra-Self will invigorate your desire for its undertaking because you do not yet understand what the supra-Self is nor will you until you move along in the drama and find your first supra-Self, which will speak directly to your instincts, not your mind.

In the fifth part of Zarathustra's Prologue, the dithyrambist prompts the actor to consider a very mediocre alternative to the supra-Self, which is the Best Man, to become like the "cows grazing before you," who desire oblivious complacency, which he writes about in *Use and Abuse of History*, as I previously quoted.

> Behold! I shall show you the *Ultimate Man*.
>
> 'What is love? What is creation? What is longing? What is a star?' so asks the Ultimate Man and blinks.[115]

What is love of Self? What is mythopoeia? What is a longing for "the other side," which is supra-individuation? What is the supra-Self? These are primary elements of the will to power. And they all require effort. Within sub-individuated man, there is a strong inclination to avoid any effort with regard to difficult emotions. Keep everything at a level playing field. Let nothing rise to the surface that would cause a disturbance.

> The earth has become small, and upon it hops the Ultimate Man, who makes everything

> small. His race is as ineradicable as the flea;
> the best man lives longest.
>
> 'We have discovered happiness,' say the
> Ultimate Men, who then blink.[116]

It would be utterly useless to try and convert this strong inclination toward an easy complacency into an undertaking of the pursuit of the supra-Self, but, not knowing any better, that is precisely what the young actor will do. And there is a danger that he (or she) will convert the plea to battle and then rise above his suffering into a plea to settle or mitigate his suffering, again, into an easy complacency.

> 'Give us this Ultimate Man, Zarathustra' —
> they called out — make us into these
> Ultimate Men! Then we will give you the
> Supra-man as a gift,'[117]

Rendition of the sixth part of Zarathustra's Prologue, in which the tightrope walker falls to his death is, without doubt, the most important rendition. It is also the most difficult to achieve.

Presuming that the reader and potential actor has been pursuing his Self for some time before he began reading *Thus Spoke Zarathustra*, it is highly likely that he is familiar with the Platonic ideal of Self as a contemplative image and that he had previously been honing a focused and determined mode of thought as a way to achieve assimilation of that image. Nietzsche categorically refutes both the notion of Self as a conception and any mode of thought as a means of achieving it. He says as much outright in the Second Preface of the Birth of Tragedy.

"And shall not I, by mightiest desire, In living shape that precious form acquire? [i.e., the Platonic, conceptual Self]" (SWANWICK, trans. of *Faust.*)

"Would it not be *necessary*?" ... No, thrice no! ye young romanticists: it would *not* be necessary! But it is very probable, that things may *end* thus, that *ye* may end thus, namely "comforted," as it is written, in spite of all self-discipline to earnestness and terror; metaphysically comforted....[118]

In Wagner in Bayreuth, he says:

No particular thought lies at the bottom of a myth, as the children of an artificial culture would have us believe; but it is in itself a [mode of] thought: it conveys an idea of the world, but through the medium of a chain of events, actions, and pains.[119]

But the uninitiated proselyte firmly believes that his Self exists in a single thought that is driven by a single passion, which, if he can only find and then mount the correct singular passion or cerebral determination, will carry him to his Self. This is the particular inner state of mind that is represented in the metaphor of the tightrope walker who appears in the marketplace (where he looks for the particular passion or cerebral thought amongst all his passions and thoughts for the one that will transport him into the Platonic Self) to traverse the abyss in front of the people who have assembled to watch below him.

Then, however, something happened that muted every mouth and focused every eye. In the meantime, of course, the tightrope walker had commenced his performance: he had emerged from a little door and was going along the rope that was stretched between two towers so that it hung above the people and the market square. When he was midway across, the little door opened again and a gaudily-dressed fellow like a buffoon sprang out and quickly approached the tightrope walker. Go on, lame foot!' cried his frightful voice, go on lazy-bones, interloper, paleface! — lest I tickle you with my heel! What are you doing here between towers? You belong in the tower, you should be locked up, you are blocking the way of a better man than you!' — And with every word he came nearer and nearer to the tightrope walker. When he was only a single step behind him, however, something frightful happened that muted every mouth and focused every eye: he uttered a scream like a devil and jumped over the tightrope walker who was in his way. The latter, however, when he saw his rival thus triumph, at the same time lost his head and his footing on the rope; he threw his pole away and plunged downward, faster even than it, like a whirlpool of legs and arms, into the depth. The marketplace and the people were like the sea when a storm brews: they all flew apart in disorder, especially where the body was about to fall.[120]

The marketplace is that place within yourself where you go to evaluate all the thoughts and passions to find the particular one on which to mount your hope to ride to your Self, if you are under the spell of this false hope. And you have done this over and over again, always failing, always falling back to the same point where you began, to begin anew. And when you begin anew, you will again assemble all the potential passions and thought on which to make your re-evaluation yet again to make another attempt.

There are two critical revelations that these metaphors in the sixth discourse teach. One is that this hope to find one's Self in a single thought or upon a single passion *is meaningless*, in the sense that it lacks continuity. When the effort fails, as it has already done many times, you don't fall back to the next lowest step before the moment of failure; you fall back to the very beginning of the effort, to the marketplace. Secondly, the smallest distraction can kill your focused determination and force you back to the beginning. If your climbing was meaningful, whatever distraction came into play would have some meaning in your pursuit, be it simple or complex; it wouldn't just completely destroy your effort — if the effort was meaningful. But it is not meaningful, and the smallest distraction of thought or passion will destroy it.

The other critical revelation in the metaphors is that this concept of Self you so mightily pursue and worship, as if it was like God himself, worthy of your most pious adoration, *is dead* in the sense that it lacks emotion. It is a concept! It lacks animation, vitality, life. It is an entirely cerebral image devoid of emotion. It is worthless!

Once you grasp the meaning of these metaphors, you will devalue the pursuit of a conceived Self and begin to look elsewhere. But where?

This entire devaluation — and the revelations that result from it — is articulated by Nietzsche, outside of any dithyramb, in *Twilight of the Idols*, which I now quote.

> ## HOW THE "TRUE WORLD"
> ## ULTIMATELY BECAME A FABLE
>
> ### THE HISTORY OF AN ERROR
>
> 1. The true world, attainable to the sage, the pious man and the man of virtue, — he lives in it, *he is it.*
>
> (The most ancient form of the idea was relatively clever, simple, convincing. It was a paraphrase of the proposition "I, Plato, am the truth.")
>
> 2. The true world which is unattainable for the moment, is promised to the sage, to the pious man and to the man of virtue ("to the sinner who repents").
>
> (Progress of the idea: it becomes more subtle, more insidious, more evasive, — It *becomes a woman,* it becomes Christian.)
>
> 3. The true world is unattainable, it cannot be proved, it cannot promise anything; but even as a thought, alone, it is a comfort, an obligation, a command.
>
> (At bottom this is still the old sun; but seen through mist and scepticism: the idea has

become sublime, pale, northern, Königsbergian.)

4. The true world — is it unattainable? At all events it is unattained. And as unattained it is also *unknown.* Consequently it no longer comforts, nor saves, nor constrains: what could something unknown constrain us to?

(The grey of dawn. Reason stretches itself and yawns for the first time. The cock-crow of positivism.)

5. The "true world" — an idea that no longer serves any purpose, that no longer constrains one to anything, — a useless idea that has become quite superfluous, consequently an exploded idea: let us abolish it!

(Bright daylight; breakfast; the return of common sense and of cheerfulness; Plato blushes for shame and all free- spirits kick up a shindy.)

6. We have suppressed the true world: what world survives? the apparent world perhaps?... Certainly not! *In abolishing the true world we have also abolished the world of appearance!*

> (Noon; the moment of the shortest shadows;
> the end of the longest error; mankind's zenith;
> *Incipit Zarathustra*.)[121]

Notice in his point number six that he asks "What world survives?" When the actor devalues Self as a conceived being, where should he begin to look for Self instead? The remaining part of Zarathustra's Prologue suggests an answer to this question, which is yet another critical revelation.

> A light has dawned upon me: I need companions — living ones, not dead companions and corpses that I carry with me where I will.
>
> But I need living companions who will follow me because they want to follow themselves — and to the place where I will.[122]

After living with his newfound devaluation for some time, the actor will turn to his feelings to find his Self, especially his hope and his desire to find his Self, which are prerequisites for undertaking the drama and which are analogous to "living companions, insofar as they are alive with emotion rather than mere cerebral concepts.

> A light has dawned for me: Zarathustra will not speak to the people but to companions![123]

And the actor will no longer appeal to "the people," to his passions — in a general way. He will appeal only to specific thoughts and passions, namely those that will assist his hope and desire to find his Self. And he will develop those particular thoughts and passions so that they become stronger.

> To lure many from the herd — that is why I have come. The people and the herd must be angry with me: the herdsmen will call Zarathustra a robber.[124]
>
> This is what Zarathustra said to his heart when the sun stood at noon-tide ....[125]

Throughout the drama, there are many references to "noontide," and there is even an entire dithyramb dedicated to the phenomenon. "Noontide" is that moment when your supra-Self becomes clearest to you. And there is not just one noontide; there are many, as you go deeper and deeper into your feelings and uncover more and more layers of your deeper Self. At that moment when your newly found Self becomes apparent to you, that is when you should look for a stronger desire for Self, as it continues to grow with every discovery, at every noontide.

> Then he looked inquiringly above — for he heard above him the sharp call of a bird. And lo and behold! An eagle swept through the air in wide circles, and on it hung a serpent, not like a prey but like a friend: for it kept itself coiled around the eagle's neck.
>
> 'They are my animals!' said Zarathustra and rejoiced in his heart.[126]

And as you discover layers of your deeper Self, you will also discover that your desire for Self grows stronger as well. This ever-increasing desire for Self is referenced in metaphor as one of Zarathustra's animals, specifically the eagle, which flies above the chaos of thought and passion within you to seek out true Self amidst all that superfluity and wilderness. And there is always coiled around the eagle's neck a serpent, which is a metaphor for knowledge of your higher Self because knowledge of your higher Self is a direct result of your ever-growing desire for your higher Self.

And when you get lost amidst the chaotic maelstrom of thought and passion within you, look for your desire for Self to carry you out of that chaos. Your desire for your higher Self and your knowledge of your higher Self do not require a reason to live; they are passions (i.e., animals), and they will come to you like a yearning.

In short, Zarathustra's Prologue teaches the actor that the way to his Self is through his emotions. But that is not news. Psychiatry already teaches this wisdom. However, psychiatry does not teach that a devaluation of the Platonic ideal of Self is necessary, which is very specific. And more importantly, while it is an easy concept to look for Self in one's emotions, a concept is not an apprehension, which is much more compelling.

In the dithyramb, reading the metaphors are like a child reading the gestures on his mother's face in order to understand the meaning of certain emotions. As he interprets the gestures, he experiences the associated emotion himself. And as the actor reads the gestures presented by the metaphors in a dithyramb, he, too, experiences the emotions associated with those metaphors *so that he becomes transported into the conflict* that is represented in the dithyramb. And in that way, he struggles with the dilemma, which necessarily leads to its solution as well. That solution is an experience, an apprehension, not just a concept, which enters into the realm of instinct. And that is the power of the dithyramb.

Lastly, I would refer you back to the History of an Error above. The last line reads "Incipit Zarathustra." The Prologue initiates the actor into the drama by teaching him that Self is a myth and not a concept. The whole of Zarathustra is about finding your Self through mythopoeia, by which I mean the creation of Self as myth out of the mythopoeic instinct that itself is triggered by the perception of emotion. And as you learn to experience your emotions more deeply, the whole realm of sensation will become more vibrant and animated within you, as the sensations reverberate within myth, while, at the same time, the image of being within you will become more and more brilliant, according to the theory that "art" (or the creation of mythical Self) is dependent upon the evolution of the "Apollonian" (or ideational) and the "Dionysian (or sensational) duality. In such a way, the dithyrambs will teach you to look beyond your discovery of Self to an even deeper Self (the supra-Self) while at the same time enabling that process of discovery via proto-tragedy or the incremental collapse of Ego.

If you fail to grasp that Self is a myth and not a concept, then you cannot begin the drama. Moreover, all the experiences that are presented in metaphor in all the dithyrambs point you to experiences that are related to the creation of Self as myth. And each experience is dependent upon a successful embodiment and resolution of the previous dithyrambs and the conflicts they depict. You simply will never render a metaphor that points to an experience in the fourth part of the drama without having successfully undertaken all the experiences that preceded it in the first three parts of the drama. In other words, the dithyramb can only be understood by its initiates because myth arises out of a series of inner events. Rendition of Zarathustra's Prologue provides that initiation.

The Academic Chairs of Virtue

On the Presiding (or Prevalent) and Erroneous Value of Virtue

Within subindividuated human nature, there is a strong proclivity to maintain a monotone rhythm within the emotions, a comfortable ease.

Without Melody.—There are persons to whom a constant repose in themselves and the harmonious ordering of all their capacities is so natural that every definite activity is repugnant to them. They resemble music which consists of nothing but prolonged, harmonious accords, without even the tendency to an organised and animated melody showing itself. All external movement serves only to restore to the boat its equilibrium on the sea of harmonious euphony. Modern men usually become excessively impatient when they meet such natures, who *will never be anything in* the world, only it is not allowable to say of them

> that they *are nothing*. But in certain moods
> the sight of them raises the unusual question:
> "Why should there be melody at all? Why
> should it not suffice us when life mirrors
> itself peacefully in a deep lake?"[127]

Any work that subindividuated man does within himself is meant to achieve a comfortable ease, so he believes. Any willful activity that succeeds in coming to the fore is meant to be followed by a quiet repose, not a process of change that is a direct result of that willful activity.

> Sleeping is no small art: it requires staying
> awake all day.
>
> You must overcome yourself ten times a day:
> that causes a wholesome weariness and is
> poppy to the soul.
>
> You must reconcile with yourself ten times:
> for overcoming is bitterness and the
> unreconciled man sleeps badly.
>
> You must find ten truths during the day:
> otherwise you will seek truth during the
> night, because your soul will be hungry.[128]

That is about to change. Going forward, the actor will learn that any work he does on himself will lead to changes and that is because he is embarking on a journey by which to raise subliminal emotion from deep within oblivion. There will be periods of frequent and protracted willful efforts that will be followed by periods of satiated rest, during which the actor will wait for his appetite to return.

> Intercourse With the Higher Self.— Every one has his good day, when he finds his higher self; and true humanity demands that a person shall be estimated according to this state and not according to his work-days of constraint and bondage. A painter, for instance, should be appraised and honoured according to the most exalted vision he could see and represent. But men themselves commune very differently with this their higher self, and are frequently their own play actors, in so far as they repeatedly imitate what they are in those moments. Some stand in awe and humility before their ideal, and would fain deny it; they are afraid of their higher self because, when it speaks, it speaks pretentiously. Besides, it has a ghost-like freedom of coming and staying away just as it pleases; on that account it is often called a gift of the gods, while in fact everything else is a gift of the gods (of chance); this, however, is the man himself.[129]

As I have said repeatedly, discovery of the supra-Self proceeds upon a desire for Self. And that desire is not constant. It comes and goes, like a mood. Therefore, the actor must learn to wait for the mood to return before he can attempt further self-discovery. It is for this reason that, in the dithyramb entitled Of the Spirit of Gravity, Zarathustra says "Truly, I have learned to wait also, and I have learned it well, —

but only to wait for myself."[130] Also, when Nietzsche says that people "imitate" that which they discovered about their higher Self after a communion with it, this is the same sense in which Zarathustra says "Once you were apes, and even still, man is more of an ape than any ape."[131] His uses the word "ape" as a metaphor for imitation, play-acting, posturing.

During periods of rest, when the actor is waiting for his desire for Self to return, though he will not know it, changes will be occurring within him, so that, when he returns to work, he will find himself in a place that is different from when he began his work. That is the nature of willful growth. This dithyramb teaches the actor to unlearn the tendency to sink back into restful oblivion after every willful effort and instead learn to anticipate deep results from his willful efforts. And eventually, the rhythmically monotone state of his emotions will be replaced by a very lively state with emotions of varying tone and rhythm, which is the more natural state of feeling, just as it was before suffering and dismemberment set in.

The Three Metamorphoses

The Three Stages of Growth

> I name you three metamorphoses of the
> spirit: how the spirit becomes a camel, and
> the camel becomes a lion, and finally the lion
> becomes a child.[132]

As the actor begins to learn to feel again, he will begin to incorporate more and more of the subconscious into his consciousness, and his spirit will become heavy like a burdened camel as he begins to carry the weight of that suffering. But then he will learn to rise above that suffering as his spirit begins to revolt against the burden of his suffering. It is in this sense that his spirit will become like a lion. In his ascension, his spirit will become exalted as he finds the springboard that inheres in his suffering and uses it to rise above the principium individuations, and he will feel as if flying. This exaltation will create a need for him to dig even deeper into the subconscious, according to the theory of dissonance that inheres in tragedy. When he digs deeper, then he will discover his supra-Self, which will be like a new beginning. And it is in this sense that his spirit will become like a child. Upon becoming like a child, the whole process of three metamorphoses begins anew, as he goes deeper and deeper and higher and higher. Eventually, the entire subconscious becomes incorporated into the conscious. And as he learns to redeem what he finds in the subconscious, all the while he is increasing the realm of the supra-conscious as well. The process of digging deeper, redeeming, rising above the suffering, and beginning anew is the process of life. And the subsequent creation of the supra-conscious through this process is its meaning. In such a way, the supra-Self becomes the meaning of life.

Backworldsmen

On Those Who Seek Comfort in the Metaphysical World

This dithyramb speaks to the mode of thought that gave rise to a conception of Self as a state of being attainable via a severe form of contemplation, as devalued in the Prologue.

Consider the difference between a concept and an apprehension. A concept is something you "believe in" and understand via thought. And apprehension is something you actually grasp or "touch" with intuition and instinct. In my experience, with regard to the inner world at least, what I conceive is rarely the same as what I eventually apprehend. For example, I had a concept of Self as a state of being that was independently existent and something into which I could find passage through a mode of intense contemplation. This is what Plato taught. And before Plato, Parmenides taught the same thing with his theory of the Identity of Thought and Being. The fact that Plato and Parmenides enunciated this philosophy of Self as Being via Contemplation does not mean that they invented it. Rather, it is a penchant of the human condition that Plato and Parmenides celebrated and memorialized. And it is a penchant that originates from a thought process that has been divorced from the reality of emotion, and that divorce itself derives from dismemberment.

As it turns out, the theory of the Identity of Thought and Being is fallacious. And the penchant is deeply misleading, which is the first lesson that Nietzsche's dithyrambic drama teaches.

Regarding another matter, one of the most important lessons to be learned in general, from many dithyrambs, is how to incorporate the subconscious into consciousness, how to learn to feel again. For a long time, I had a concept of how this would happen. I believed that, if I could just bring one major emotion out of oblivion and into my consciousness, then my sense of feeling would be suddenly and totally restored. That was my concept of what I expected, and that is what I worked toward. But that is not how it happens in the inner world. What actually happened was that I could bring subliminal emotions out of oblivion and into consciousness little by little, incrementally, which led to my apprehension of the supra-Self. Do you see how the idea of the supra-Self came to me as a result of my experience as opposed to coming to me as a purely cerebral concept absent any meaningful or contextual footing in reality. *That is how Nietzsche teaches idea via the dithyramb*. Without ever explicitly articulating any idea, he simply leads you into the tensive experience out of which the idea instinctively rises.

So that is the difference between purely cerebral concept and intuitive apprehension that is rooted in experience. This dithyramb teaches you to devalue and cast aside all purely cerebral concepts of what you expect to find within the inner world of man and heed instead what you actually experience in the world.

There are many fallacious "realities" that arise from a mode of thought that has been divorced from emotion. As the actor undertakes this drama, he will learn a new mode of thought that is rooted in intuition and apprehension, and he should heed that new mode of thought more intently than the cerebral mode of thought he has previously known for so long.

It is also important to note that cerebral thought, which is divorced from the wisdom that derives from emotion and experience, is a problem arising from dismemberment (or subliminal suffering) and the inability or weakness to incorporate that subliminal suffering into consciousness.

Looking specifically at the metaphors used in this dithyramb, I have already shown that the metaphor "God" is used to indicate the Self as conceived being that commands a pious worship and a belief that it exists independently and eternally and is attainable via an extreme mode of focused contemplation. Of that fallacy, the dithyrambist says the following:

> Ah, brothers, this God whom I created was human work and human madness, like all gods!

> He was human, and only a poor fragment of man and Ego: this phantom came to me from my own fire and ashes. Truly, it did not come to me from the hereafter![133]

The metaphor "fire and ashes" is a metaphor for human suffering. Thus, the dithyrambist says that this fallacy arose within the mind of the actor as a result of his suffering, and I say that it derives specifically from dismemberment.

> What happened, my brothers? I, the sufferer, overcame myself, I carried my own ashes to the mountains, I created for myself a brighter

> flame. And lo and behold! With that, the phantom *left* me!
>
> Now, to me, the convalescent, it would be suffering and torment to believe in such phantoms: it would be suffering to me now and humiliation. That is what I say to those who seek comfort in the metaphysical worlds.
>
> It was suffering and futility — that created all metaphysical worlds; and that brief madness of happiness that only the greatest sufferer experiences.[134]

If you read my rendition of the dithyramb entitled "The Convalescent," you will understand that the convalescent is someone who has achieved a measure of success with the grand effort of incorporating the subconscious into consciousness, which is a profoundly transformative experience. After achieving convalescence and experiencing that transformation, the actor will subsequently clearly see the fallacy of his belief in Self as Being via extreme contemplation because a more vivid and more animated image of Self, which is myth, will appear to him as a direct result of incorporating subliminal emotion into consciousness. However, until the actor learns to achieve this incorporation, which, in part, requires him to find strength and carry the burden of his suffering, he must learn to disregard the weakened and fallacious mode of thought that derives from his affliction.

> Weariness, which wants to attain the ultimate with a single leap, with a death-leap, an

> impoverished ignorant weariness, unwilling
> to will any longer: that created all gods and
> metaphysical worlds.
>
> Believe me, my brothers! it was the body that
> despaired of the body – that sought the
> ultimate walls with the fingers of its
> bewitched spirit.
>
> Believe me, my brothers! It was the body that
> despaired of the earth — and it heard the
> belly of being speaking to itself.
>
> And then it wanted to get through the
> ultimate walls with its head— and not only
> with its head — into the "other world"[135]

The metaphor "Self" in this dithyramb is used to indicate a mode of thought. While the "Ego" or mode of thought that derives from dismemberment is wayward, a new "Self" or mode of thought that derives from proto-tragedy (or the destruction of dismembered thought in the wake of thought that arises from incorporation of the subconscious into consciousness) is much wiser and more "true to the earth and the body" and must be heeded. Speaking of the "Self," the dithyrambist says that thought is a good leader and should be trusted, provided it is the Self that is rooted in emotion.

> Yes, this Self, with its contradiction and
> confusion, still speaks most honestly of its
> being—this creating, willing, evaluating Self,
> which is the measure and worth of things.

And this most honest being, the Self — it speaks of the body, and still wants the body, even when it poeticizes and romanticizes and flutters with broken wings.

Always more honestly it learns to speak, the Self; and the more it learns, the more it find words and honors for the body and the earth.

My Self taught me a new pride, which I teach to men: no longer to bury one's head in the sand of heavenly things, but to carry it freely, an earthly head, which gives meaning to the earth!

I teach men a new will: to want this path than man has walked blindly, and to call it good and no longer to shirk it, like the sick and dying![136]

Learn to heed the mode of thought that derives from the Self that is rooted in your emotions.

Heed rather, my brothers, to the voice of the healthy body: this is a purer voice and a more honest voice.

The healthy body speaks more honestly and purer, the perfect and robust body: and it speaks of the meaning of the earth.[137]

The Despisers of the Body

On the Tendency to Harbor a Profound Antipathy for One's Feelings

While the Ego constitutes a way of thinking, it also imparts an idea of being, as Descartes so famously memorialized in his "I think, therefore I am" axiom. However, feelings also impart an idea of being, as well as a sense of being, which we call the Self. And the Self is a far more powerful idea of being than the Ego. In fact, what the Self feels is what the Ego thinks about. Therefore, if you value your thoughts more than your feelings, you have lost your way. As a result of dismemberment and the resultant aversion to pain and suffering, there is also within sub-individuated man an antipathy toward emotion. That antipathy must be devalued. And eventually, through tragedy, it must be overcome, which is what will happen.

This dithyramb does not teach a way out of a conflict. Rather, it teaches that the low regard that the thoughtful man who suffers has for the entire sensate realm does not contribute to the will to power.

Your Self can no longer do what it most wants to do: to create beyond itself. That is what it most wants, that is its whole ardor.

247

> But now it is too late: — so your Self wants to perish, you despisers of the body.
>
> To perish — that is what your Self wants; and therefore, you have become despisers of the body! For you are no longer able to create beyond yourselves.
>
> And therefore, you are now angry with life and with the earth. An unconscious envy is in the sidelong glance of your contempt.
>
> I do not go your way, you despisers of the body! You are not bridges for me to the Supra-man![138]

What this dithyramb *does not* say is that any sub-individuated man or woman who despises the sensate realm has no hope of ever achieving supra-individuation. It does not say that. It only says that nothing good will come of your contempt or antipathy for the sensate realm.

Joys and Passions

On the Articulation of Feelings Emerging from the Subconscious

Another translator has translated the title of this dithyramb as "On the Passions of Pleasure and Pain." To my mind, knowing as I do the meaning of this dithyramb, the latter translation is more informative and less confusing.

As you slowly learn to incorporate subliminal emotion into consciousness, it will be the first time that these emotions have "spoken to you." Do not try to understand them through the perspective of your current self. Rather, look for your supra-Self in them, an as yet unknown myth. Emotion defines Self. And as new emotions come to the fore, you must look for the new myth that is defined by them. If you try to understand these new emotions in terms of your current Self, you will gain no life from them. Within human being, life is the incremental growth of the limits of Self, which is achieved via the postulation of the supra-Self. This is the art, the creativity, that Nietzsche speaks of when he says that art owes its continuous evolution to the Apollonian-Dionysian duality (or the ideation-sensation duality).

Let me also say at this point, having just clarified the creative process in the postulation of supra-Self, that every mention of the metaphor "creator" in *Thus Spoke Zarathustra* is meant to indicate this creative process (mythopoeia) whereby the supra-Self is created.

Throughout this dithyramb, there is frequent use of the metaphor "virtue." The word is not just a metaphor. In some ways, virtue has been redefined by Dionysia. Previously, "virtue" was a word applied to attributes that were deemed morally upright. But morality has been completely devalued by Nietzsche's legislation of new values, as taught within this dithyrambic drama. While the word is still used to indicate good attributes, what is good has been redefined by the will to power. In this dithyramb, the word virtue is meant to indicate attributes that contribute to the will to power. In the course of trying to incorporate the subconscious into consciousness, which is a fundamental process in the grander process of life (i.e., expansion of the limits of Self), success brings forth into consciousness previously sublimated (repressed) emotions that now define the supra-Self (the aborning Self). These emotions are very good insofar as they define the supra-Self. Thus, they are virtues.

> My brother, if you have a virtue, and it is your own virtue, you have it in common with no one.
>
> To be sure, you want to call it by a name and caress it; you want to pull its ears and amuse yourself with it.
>
> And lo and behold! Now you have its name in common with the people and have become one of the people and the herd with your virtue!

It would be better for you to say: 'Unspeakable is that which is pain and sweetness to my soul and is also the hunger of the belly of my being.'

Let your virtue be too high for the familiarity of names: and if you must speak of it, do not be ashamed to stammer about it.[139]

The Socratic school of thought would have you work hard to understand everything that happens within you. But in this case, if some repressed emotion within you is struggling to come to the fore, and if you struggle to understand it, then you must understand it through the perspective of your current Self, which will preclude mythopoeia. What is important in such an instance is not to understand exactly what is trying to come to the fore but rather simply allowing it and prodding it to come to the fore, which is actually the more difficult task. Let it come into your consciousness and you will discover a deeper and much more comprehensive Self. Concentrate your efforts on bringing it to the fore, not trying to understand *what* is coming to the fore.

This is a good opportunity to explain the dithyrambist's use of the metaphors "people" and "rabble" throughout the drama. The creation of the supra-Self via mythopoeia and the emergence of repressed emotion into consciousness is an elevating experience, which should be obvious. It actually silences superfluous thought and superfluous emotion. The metaphor "people" is meant to indicate superfluous thought and emotion, in contrast to specific "virtuous" thoughts and emotions that augment the will to power, in much the same way that the "people in the marketplace," which is mentioned in Zarathustra's Prologue, is used to indicate the randomly selected and multitudinous emotions and thoughts that sub-individuated man uses to muster an extreme focus that he believes will assist his contemplative passage into an independent and eternally existent conception of Self. These superfluous thoughts and emotions have no cohesion within the context of either an existing mythical Self or an aborning mythical Self (the supra-Self). Outside of mythical Self (not conceived, cerebral Self), where emotion and thought present as a dimension of Self, superfluous emotion and thought present as "rabble."

> Thus speak and stammer: "That is *my* good, that I do love, as such does it please me entirely, only as such do *I* desire the good.
>
> I do not want it as the law of God, not as a human law or a human need do I desire it; it is not to be a guide-post for me to super-earths and paradises.
>
> It is an earthly virtue that I love: there is little wisdom in it, and least of all common wisdom.
>
> But this bird built its nest with me: therefore, I love and cherish it— and now it sits with me on its golden eggs."[140]

And do not make what comes to the fore a "law of God" by saying "this defines my Self and this must be preserved at all cost" because what is coming to the fore is only the beginning of much more that will eventually emerge. If you struggle to preserve an instance of Self-enlightenment, then you halt further Self-enlightenment.

> Once you had passions and called them evil.
> But now you have only your virtues: they
> grew out of your passions.
>
> You placed your highest aim into the heart of
> these passions: then they became your virtues
> and joys.
>
> And though you came from the race of the
> hot-tempered or of the voluptuous or of the
> fanatical or of the vindictive:
>
> In the end, all your passions became virtues
> and all your devils angels.[141]

Subliminal emotion that has been repressed because you do not have the strength to incorporate it into consciousness is suffering. In this sense, those subliminal emotions are "evil." But after you allow them to come forward and you discover your supra-Self in them, then they become your virtues, as re-defined by Dionysia.

> Once you had wild dogs in your cellar: but
> they changed at last into birds and charming
> female singers.
>
> From your poison you brewed your balsam
> for yourself; your cow, affliction, milked
> you, now you drink the sweet milk of her
> udder.[142]

But, once you achieve an enactment of the dithyramb entitled "The Convalescent," you will understand that bringing subliminal and repressed suffering into consciousness provides tremendous relief and also provides the very moving comfort that is provided by the phenomena whereby your soul seems as if to sing to you with the great pleasure that derives from momentarily enduring great pain (the fourth dimension comes alive), inasmuch as it becomes "shared" pain that is brought into the light imparted by the consciousness and beauty of illusory Self as opposed to remaining a mere haunting, distant, and foreign rumbling. It is within the nature of human being that an experience with great inner pain is followed by an experience with great inner pleasure. That is not a contrivance of mine or Nietzsche's; it is the way of human nature.

> Man is something that must be overcome:
> and therefore, you shall love your virtues —
> for you will perish by them.[143]

You must learn to love as virtues whatever repressed subliminal suffering you bring to the fore because (1) there is will in love (i.e., movement toward a goal) and (2) that suffering will lead you deeper into the well, wherein you will find a deeper and much more comprehensive Self. In doing so, the Self you previously knew, prior to that deeper perception, will collapse via proto-tragedy.

The Pale Criminal

I have always found this dithyramb to be exceedingly difficult to render. Finding a passage in *Twilight of the Idols*, entitled Of the Pale Criminal, did not help. Still, for the benefit of the reader, I will cite the passage in its entirety here.

> *The criminal and his like.* — The criminal type is the type of the strong man amid unfavourable conditions, a strong man made sick. He lacks the wild and savage state, a form of nature and existence which is freer and more dangerous, in which everything that constitutes the shield and the sword in the instinct of the strong man, takes a place by right. Society puts a ban upon his virtues; the most spirited instincts inherent in him immediately become involved with the depressing passions, with suspicion, fear and dishonour. But this is almost the recipe for physiological degeneration. When a man has to do that which he is best suited to do, which he is most fond of doing, not only clandestinely, but also with long suspense, caution and ruse, he becomes anæmic; and

inasmuch as he is always having to pay for his instincts in the form of danger, persecution and fatalities, even his feelings begin to turn against these instincts — he begins to regard them as fatal. It is society, our tame, mediocre, castrated society, in which an untutored son of nature who comes to us from his mountains or from his adventures at sea, must necessarily degenerate into a criminal. Or almost necessarily: for there are cases in which such a man shows himself to be stronger than society: the Corsican Napoleon is the most celebrated case of this. Concerning the problem before us, Dostoiewsky's testimony is of importance — Dostoiewsky who, incidentally, was the only psychologist from whom I had anything to learn: he belongs to the happiest windfalls of my life, happier even than the discovery of Stendhal. This profound man, who was right ten times over in esteeming the superficial Germans low, found the Siberian convicts among whom he lived for many years,—those thoroughly hopeless criminals for whom no road back to society stood open—very different from what even he had expected,—that is to say carved from about the best, hardest and most valuable material that grows on Russian soil. Let us generalise the case of the criminal; let us imagine creatures who for some reason or other fail to meet with public approval, who know that they are regarded neither as beneficent nor useful,—the feeling of the Chandala, who are aware that they are not looked upon as equal, but as proscribed, unworthy, polluted. The thoughts and actions of all such natures are tainted with a subterranean mouldiness; everything in them is of a paler hue than in those on whose existence the sun shines. But almost all those creatures whom, nowadays, we honour and respect, formerly lived in this semi-sepulchral atmosphere: the man of science, the artist, the genius, the free spirit, the actor, the business man, and the great explorer. As long as the *priest* represented the highest type of man, every valuable kind of man was depreciated.... The time is coming—this I guarantee—when he will pass as the *lowest* type, as our Chandala, as the falsest and most disreputable kind of man.... I call your attention to the fact that even now, under the sway of the mildest customs and usages which have ever ruled on earth or at least in Europe, every form of standing aside, every kind of prolonged, excessively prolonged concealment, every unaccustomed and obscure form of existence tends to approximate to that type which the criminal exemplifies to perfection. All pioneers of the spirit have, for a while, the grey and fatalistic mark of the Chandala on their brows: *not* because they are regarded as Chandala, but

> because they themselves feel the terrible
> chasm which separates them from all that is
> traditional and honourable. Almost every
> genius knows the "Catilinarian life" as one of
> the stages in his development, a feeling of
> hate, revenge and revolt against everything
> that exists, that has ceased to evolve....
> Catiline—the early stage of every Cæsar. [144]

These statements go back to the theory of the origin of the bad conscience, which is enunciated in *The Genealogy of Morals*. But if it is going to make any sense as a dithyramb, as presented in this dithyramb with the same title as the cited passage, we have to find analogous examples of the "terrible beast" turned "criminal" or outcast within the soul. And all I see are terrific desires or terrific hopes that are inconsonant with the miserable ease or monotone rhythm of sensations that subindividuated man endeavors to maintain. Inasmuch as subindividuated man places the highest priority on this maintenance, any passion that might disturb it might rightly be devalued as perhaps "criminal." These circumstances are addressed in other dithyrambs. Therefore, I do not believe that is what is being addressed here in this dithyramb.

However, if the overbearing passions arise from within subindividuated man as a result of the chaos that inheres in him, say as a compulsion, for instance, instead of as an overbearing desire for the supra-Self, that would constitute a different circumstance entirely, and I believe that is what is being addressed here in this dithyramb.

When you find fault with yourself, whether it be due to folly or error or excess, do not condemn yourself. Presently, as sub-individuated man, that is what you do. Unlearn this manner of self-condemnation. That is what this dithyramb teaches. It is one thing to grow contempt for your Ego out of love for our supra-Self. Under those circumstances, contempt for your Ego would augment your will to power by prodding your Ego to eventually collapse so that you can pass over to your Self without your Ego holding you back. But it is another thing to condemn your Ego and therewith to heap scorn upon yourself. You do not want to heap scorn on yourself. You do not want to create a bad conscience for yourself or weigh yourself down unnecessarily simply because you did something stupid.

> 'My Ego is something that should be overcome: my Ego is to me the great contempt of man': that is what this eye says.
>
> When he judged himself - that was his supreme moment: do not let the exalted one relapse again into his low estate![145]

And,

> You should say 'enemy', but not 'villain; you should say 'invalid', but not 'wretch; you should say 'fool', but not 'sinner'. [146]

And just observe someone who is more individuated (wholesome) than subindividuated (unwholesome) when they catch themselves looking foolish. Sometimes, they will laugh at themselves. That is the better reaction, according to this dithyramb.

Reading and Writing

On Reading One's Feelings and Finding One's Self in Them

> Of all that is written, I love only that which
> one writes with one's own blood. Write with
> blood: and you will learn that blood is
> spirit.[147]

This dithyramb teaches about "reading" your Self and imprinting what you learn to memory. By blood, he means the opposite of a "bloodless" abstraction. The Self is perceptible both as an idea and as a sense. However, at the outset of the drama and for a long time into it, your sense of Self may be elusive. But your idea of Self will come to you quickly, which will cause a problem because the idea (or image) of being induces contemplation, and contemplation stifles the will. There is a dithyramb entitled Of the New Idol that teaches you how to deal with this problem, whose resolution leads directly to an apprehension of the supra-Self.

Given the nature of idea, it is easy to confuse an abstract idea of Self with a more tangible, living, animated idea of Self, which is the better form. You must learn to look for "blood" in your idea of Self, lest you succumb to a mere concept of it. And when you find it, you want to remember it in such a way that you are brought back to it at a later time. If what you find within the inner chaos of thought and passion is truly your Self, it should enter into your spirit, which will leave a deep, lasting, and recurrent imprint, and that spirit will bring you back to your Self when it becomes elusive. And it becomes much easier to learn to love your Self once you have discovered a sense of it. In short, what you discover about your true Self, should then bring that Self to life.

> It is not easy to understand unfamiliar blood:
> I hate the idlers who read.
>
> He who knows the reader, does nothing more for the reader. Another century of readers – and spirit itself will stink.
>
> Allowing everyone to learn to read will ruin in the long run not only writing, but thinking too.
>
> Once the spirit was God, then it became man, and now it is even becoming mob.
>
> He who writes in blood and aphorisms does not want to be read, but to be learned by heart.
>
> In the mountains the shortest way is from peak to peak, but for that you must have long legs. Aphorisms should be peaks, and those to whom they are spoken should be big and tall.[148]

When your supra-Self reveals itself and speaks to you, it will not be a familiar appearance or a familiar voice, but, if you look for "blood" in your thoughts and emotions, you will recognize it immediately, and that is when you should pay heed. But if you are a "reading idler" who looks for nothing in his thoughts and emotions, then you will recognize nothing. You must be on the lookout for your supra-Self, so that you are ready to listen when it finally speaks. And if you heed its voice and plumb the emotions that define it, then it will be easy to traverse from one proximate and older supra-Self to a more distant and newer supra-Self, because, indeed, in the mountains, the shortest route is from peak to peak, but you must have long legs to do it.

The Tree on the Hill

On the First Discovery of the Subconscious and Its Role in Life

As you begin to delineate your Self amidst the chaos within you, you will become exalted as you begin to rise above that chaos. And then all growth will cease — inexplicably. And you will have a difficult time trying to figure out why the growth has ended. This dithyramb teaches you how to resolve the crisis.

> Zarathustra came to understand that a youth was avoiding him. And as he was walking alone one evening upon the mountains surrounding the town called "the Motley Cow" [of many boisterous and discordant appearances]," lo and behold, he found the youth sitting and leaning against a tree and gazing with a wearied look into the valley. [149]

The young man is the actor who has only recently learned how to grow. Thus, he is young, a novice. The mountains surrounding the town called the Pied Cow are the exaltations of his spirit upon the steps of his delineation of Self. The fact that these "mountains" are in close proximity to the town called the Pied Cow are further indication that his minimal ascension is only recent.

> The more he wants to rise up into the heights and the light, the more his roots vigorously struggle earthward, downward, into the dark and deep, into the evil.'[150]

The more you wish to rise into the heights by finding your Self and lifting yourself up out of the chaos within you, the more you must reach into the subconscious to find your demons. It is an extraordinary revelation about the nature of life, the nature of the will to power, and it is the first of many that will come to you in the course of this drama. Please note that these revelations will only come to you after you enter into the conflict of which those revelations are a solution. Without a need, nothing new comes into the world.

> 'This tree stands lonely here by the mountains; it has grown up high above man and beast.
>
> 'And if it wanted to speak, it would have no one who could understand it: so high has it grown.
>
> 'Now it waits and waits - for what does it wait? It dwells too close to the seat of the clouds: is it waiting, perhaps, for the first lightening?'[151]

The lightening is the knowledge of a deeper Self that will come to you only upon the heights of Self delineation, upon the "mountains," which follows the theory that proto-tragedy derives from dissonance. Lifting yourself up out of the chaos of thought and passion that constitutes sub-individuation is a manifestation of the will to power. And every increase in power creates a need for more power. A high note creates the need for a low note, which will come to you quite naturally. But it would help if, upon reaching the high note, you had some anticipation for the low note to come afterward. This dithyramb teaches that anticipation. And if you follow that anticipation, it will lead you to your first mystical experience, which you will find in the dithyramb entitled Of Great Events.

The Preachers of Death

Weary Thoughts and Cowardly Thoughts that Avert the Growth of the Will

If life is a process of growth that is driven by the will to power, as it is, and the will to power is driven by a desire to find one's Self, as it is, then "death" is a process of deterioration of will that proceeds upon an aversion of the will to find one's Self.

This dithyramb points the actor to three reasons that leads to a deterioration of will.

> The earth is full of the superfluous, life is spoiled by the many-too- many. May they be lured by 'eternal life' out of this life![152]

If there exists a passionate desire for Self that is strong enough to dominate other passions, then, clearly, life will prevail. But if there exists a majority of superfluous and extraneous passions, as is usually the case at the outset of the drama, then a ruling passionate desire for Self will become diluted and weak.

> "The yellow ones": this is how the preachers of death are called, or "the black ones." But I

> want to show them to you in different
> colors.[153]

Moreover, if a sentiment of doom and gloom ("black ones") exists deep down inside, then passions and beliefs will arise out of that sentiment and will weaken the will to life via the Spirit of Gravity.

Lastly, if the actor lacks courage ("yellow ones") to face the difficult demons that define the supra-Self, then that lack of courage will stifle life.

> But I want to show them to you in different
> colors.[154]

Lack of courage and a sentiment of doom and gloom are the obvious aversions to life (black ones), but there are also more insidious forms.

> There are the dreadful ones who carry the
> beast of prey within themselves and have no
> choice but to indulge in lust or self-
> destruction. And even their lust is still self-
> mutilation.[155]

By beast of prey, perhaps he means a solitary consciousness of a ferocious inner torment whose suffering leaves its victim in a state of continual ferocity towards himself, resulting in frequent self-mortification or extreme self-indulgence. Where would a desire for Self stand in proximity to that state of mind?

> 'Giving birth is troublesome – say others –
> 'why give birth? You only give birth to the

unhappy!' And they too are preachers of death.[156]

When you uncover your supra-Self within your subliminal emotions and immediately think "What is the good of all this work when all I uncover is suffering," that is a mode of wayward thought that must be averted.

> If you believed more in life, then you would devote yourselves less to the moment. But you don't have enough patience for waiting – nor to be lazy![157]

Instead, you must continually look ahead with an eye toward eventually redeeming the suffering you uncover. But for that, you must have some measure of experience with redemption in order to know what to look forward to, and, until you achieve that first experience with redemption, you will not have any faith in your work or the future. And you certainly will not have any capacity to wait until you are able to uncover your suffering sufficiently to strain the bow and find the springboard.

Learn to brand and recognize these aversive passions and beliefs as anti-life. And learn to keep them separate from the will to power that you are endeavoring to grow within yourself so that the aversion they constitute does not itself have the liberty to grow. Do not allow them to avail themselves to life. At the very least, understand in your mind that these aversions are not a part of life.

In the beginning, when you will have had little experience with life so that it is not easily recognizable to you, it will be difficult to make a distinction between that which assists life and that which stifles it. But later, after you have had some practice, the distinction will be much easier for you. And this distinction that is delineated here will assist you because you will grow a bad conscience toward that which you know does not assist life, thereby dampening its effect on your will.

The New Idol

On the Beguiling Image of Self and Its Interference with
the First Discovery of the Supra-Self

> Somewhere, there are still peoples and flocks,
> but not with us, my brothers: there are states.
>
> A state? What is that? Well! Now open your
> ears to me, because now I will tell you what I
> know about the death of peoples.
>
> State is the name of the coldest of all cold
> monsters. It also lies coldly; and this lie
> creeps from its mouth: 'I, the state. am the
> people.'[158]

First of all, he is not talking about the State, though it
clearly looks like he is. Rather, he is talking about the state of
being. Art, by which I mean the creation of Self (or
mythopoeia), according to Nietzsche, proceeds upon an
antagonistic relationship between the Apollonian (or ideational)
realm and the Dionysiac (or sensational) realm. Sensation
begets image, and image begets sensation, which is what we see
happening to the actor in the few dithyrambs we have examined
thus far. By learning to seek his Self out within the chaos within

him, he finds his Self and becomes exalted upon the steps of his ascending delineation. And then, wanting to rise even higher, he learns that he must also descend into the subconscious, wherein he will find much stronger sensations, emotions, in which his idea and sense of Self will become even more defined. If he stops at any stage within the process, the process itself ceases. The problem is that the Apollonian realm, which is an image of being, of Self, induces contemplation. And contemplation can be very beguiling. It can halt the process. And it will. The actor will become mesmerized by his images of Self, especially as it gets brighter and more vivid. This dithyramb teaches him to look beyond the image of Self.

> There, where the state ends, only there does
> the man who is not superfluous begin: there
> begins the song of the necessary ones, the
> single and irreplaceable melody.[159]

Only where complacent contemplation of the image of being ends will you find the deeper Self to which is tied a deeper fate.

> There, where the state *ends* - look there, my
> brothers. Can you not see it: the rainbow and
> the bridges of the Supra-man?[160]

You will not gain any apprehension of the supra-Self from what I am about to tell you, from my rendition, though you might conceptualize it, which is very different from an apprehension, but still valuable. This dithyramb teaches you that the supra-Self, your deeper Self, always lies beyond the complacent contemplation of image. And I will tell you that you cannot imagine or conceive of just how deeply your Self runs. It is beyond your power to see that because, as I have said before, life only reveals itself in the process. Rather, it is something in which you must have faith and actively pursue. Whenever you find yourself contemplating the most brilliant image of Self, which you yourself have uncovered through your own had work, always remember that there is indeed an even deeper Self to be found. Always keep that faith because that faith will take you very far. Do not be beguiled by the brilliance and beauty of illusory being, and it is an illusion. There will be many images of Self. But until you reach the Higher Man, which is another dithyramb that is found in the later stages of the drama, all those images are mere shallow images of Self.

This dithyramb teaches you to look beyond the image of Self for more life. And you will grasp that lesson, and you will move on to the subconscious and look for a deeper Self. It also teaches you the supra-Self, that you must *always* look beyond your Self. Every time you find a deeper Self, you must look beyond it for an ever deeper, higher Self. But you will not grasp that easily, not yet. Not until you have been living the drama for quite some time will you finally grasp the meaning of the supra-Self and believe in it as a way of thinking and growing, a way of thinking about life. But it will come to you, most surely.

And pay most attention to the instinctual exclamation that the image of Self is the end all of life, its goal, or that this image is the rule by which all life must proceed.

> 'There is nothing greater on earth than I: I am the regulating finger of God' – thus the monster roars. And not only the long-eared and short-sighted fall upon their knees![161]

First, note that "God" is always a metaphor for the pious adulation of Self in the dithyrambs. Eventually, when you move beyond the image of Self to a deeper apprehension of Self, you will learn the value of the supra-Self as a gateway myth, and you will easily disregard the instinctual exclamation that is depicted in the above aphorism, which, if heeded, halts the process of life because the illusoriness and beauty of Self stifles the will by continuously satiating it.

Eventually you will behold a very brilliant and animated vision of your Self, and it will take a hold of you that will be difficult to break, so bright and commanding will the image seem. But if you are unable to break its grip on you, life will cease at that point. So, it is necessary to find a way to move beyond the beguiling temptation to become wholly enchanted by the image of Self.

The Flies in the Marketplace

Everyone has moments when they obsessively recall one or another little injustice that was done to them. This dithyramb refers to that manner of annoying thought and points out the great distraction it causes. But it is also a great distraction when you have inflated thoughts about oneself that are intrinsically egotistical. They, too, are a great distraction from finding one one's true Self.

> Flee, my friend, into your solitude! I see you deafened by the noise of the great men and stung all over by the stings of the little ones.
>
> Forest and rock are admirable for knowing how to be silent with you. Be like the tree you love, the wide-branching tree: silent and attentive it hangs out over the sea.[162]

This dithyramb teaches the actor that the best way to avoid the distraction caused by petty and inflated thought is to flee into the solace of the image of being. That is the avenue to take when distracted by these thoughts. Learn to seek out your Self more diligently and seek repose from this manner of distractive thought in the presence of your true Self. And quite remarkably, as the actor succeeds in finding his Self and maintaining that image through all the accidents that might befall him, then petty and egotistical thought does, indeed, subside. That is the entire gist of this dithyramb.

But then the dithyrambist goes on to give many examples of petty and inflated thought and the manner of the numerous distractions they cause. And that is typical of all his dithyrambs. If one vantage point does not work to make a point, there are numerous others that might succeed. It is not necessary to render every single aphorism. And since they are all encrypted, that is something to consider. However, keep in mind that you may not recognize some of your thoughts as inflated or petty, and the numerous other aphorisms, beyond those that teach the resolution to a problem, will likely illuminate for you the petty or excessively egotistical nature in some of them so that you may then recognize them for that they are, namely, wayward.

For instance, in the second aphorism, he writes "Forest and rock know well how to be silent with you. Be like the tree again, the wide-branching tree that you love: calmly and attentively it leans out over the sea." By "forest," I believe he means trees, and by "trees," I believe he means knowledge of life because he frequently uses the metaphor of a tree to symbolize knowledge of life as will to power, as he does in the dithyramb entitled Of the Tree on the Mountainside. And when he writes about "the sea," he always means the sea of emotion. By "rock," I believe he means the inner circumstance in which the will to move forward with life hits a sever obstacle. In both instances, when the actor enters into a state of mind in which he is immersed in concentrated movement forward in the life process and, in the other instance, when he is confronted by a severe obstacle in his path, he is intensely concentrated on going forward. In both instances, all manner of distraction is absent.

But, "where solitude ceases, there the market-place begins; and where the market-place begins, there begins the uproar of the great actors and the buzzing of the poisonous flies."[163] In other words, as soon as the actor leaves or otherwise loses either of the above-mentioned inner circumstances, as soon as he loses sight of his Self, he enters into a contrary state of mind that the dithyrambist calls "the marketplace." Remember that the "marketplace" refers to a state of mind that was referenced in the Prologue as a place within his heart and mind where the actor would go back in the day when he believed in and sought after the Platonic ideal of Self, when he believed he could mount a single thought or passion and ride it to a ruthless assimilation of that ideal. It is a place where life is undefined and every thought and passion is deemed potentially valuable for one ulterior motive or another but not for the will to power, the will to Self.

In the pursuit of Self, while it is successful, there is no question of what is valuable and there is peace of mind. But outside of it, all values are questionable and there is distraction everywhere. Therefore, expend your efforts only on the former. In other words, "flee into your solitude," the calm determination and clarity of vision that inheres in a proximity to Self.

Chastity

Sexual behavior is significantly shaped by the subconscious, the bad conscience. As you delve deeper and deeper into the subconscious and redeem what you find inside, your conscience will be cleansed and your sexual behavior will change. As it changes, that which you previously desired will become undesirable, and there will be an interim period when you will become chaste, uninterested in anything sexual. Do not let this become a law of your existence, to remain chaste. A sexual appetite will return to you but it will present in a very different way, in a more normal state, purer, particularly as you begin to overcome subliminal humiliation. The chastity that results from cleaning your conscience is a temporary condition. Do not attempt to make it a permanent condition.

But it is not just sexual behavior that this dithyramb addresses. It also addresses sensuality, which creeps into the interactivity between the will and the passions. There is the matter of a preference for cerebral and eremitical thought over passionate willing.

> I love the forest. It is bad to live in cities:
> there are too many of the lustful there.

> Is it not better to fall into the hands of a
> murderer than into the dreams of a lustful
> woman?[164]

Do not allow chastity to drive you away from your
passions because all life proceeds upon the passions. But if you
find yourself immersed in contemplation, do not be
concerned and let it play out to its end. Just be careful not to
allow your will to become entangled and addled by a passion that
provides warmth in the face of an "icy" and steeled
communion with your aborning supra-Self.

And there is the matter of the actor seeking pleasure
through the exercise of will. Happiness is not the aim of life. The
aim of life is bringing the supra-Self into creation, which
often requires arduous and painful work. It is the work that
is important, not happiness, though happiness will surely follow
as a result of that work. And be careful as well about imposing
chastity upon yourself because chastity that does not come from
the heart will result in sensuality entering the spirit, which will
then distract your will.

> Do I counsel you to chastity? Chastity is a
> virtue with some, but with many it is almost a
> vice.
>
> They may abstain, it is true: but the bitch
> Sensuality looks enviously out of all they do.
>
> With its discord, this creature follows them
> even into the heights of their virtue and the
> depths of their cold spirit.

> And how discretely the bitch Sensuality
> knows how to beg for a piece of spirit, when
> it is denied a piece of flesh![165]

You do not want to look for chastity nor yearn for it, but, if it comes to you, welcome it and let it stay. And when it leaves, do not try to lure it back.

> 'Is chastity not folly? But this folly came to
> us and not we to it.
>
> 'We offered this guest shelter and heart: now
> it lives with us – let it stay as long as it
> will!'[166]

The Thousand and One Goals

On Finding the Over-Self as the Goal of the Numerous Overcomings

There will come a time in the course of undertaking this drama when you will realize the goal in every obstacle, and it will always be the same goal, namely, to rise above the PI in every instance where the PI has become heavily weighed down. When you reach that understanding, then you will have come to understand the meaning of all suffering and the meaning of life itself. But, starting out, you will be a long way from that discovery and that understanding.

Second to the goal of finding the springboard in all suffering by which to ascend above the PI is the goal of finding one's supra-Self in all suffering which is a more easily attained apprehension. And that should be the actor's goal until he finds the voice of his highest Self, after which the former or more primary goal will become visible to him, although he will experience that ascension long before he finds that voice.

> Zarathustra saw many lands and many peoples: thus he has discovered the good and the bad of many peoples. Zarathustra has

> found no greater power on earth than good
> and bad.[167]

By "people," the dithyrambist means nothing more than a confluence of passions, hopes, and desires that have come together under a common interest, namely, a will to a supra-Self. That which the confluence senses as a good influence on that will is "good," and that which the confluence senses as a hindrance, or more specifically subliminal suffering, is "evil."

> No people could live without first evaluating;
> but if it wants to maintain itself it must not
> evaluate as its neighbor evaluates.[168]

Without an evaluation of something that is sensed being either a good influence or a bad influence, then there is no confluence of hope and desire or other passions. In fact, it is precisely upon that evaluation that a confluence arises. In such a way, evaluation is essential to life. And if something else is later sensed as a better influence or hindrance, such as will come from deeper emotions, a new evaluation will arise and the older evaluation and its confluence will fall away.

> Much that was good to this people was called
> mockery and disgrace to another: thus I
> found. I found many things called bad here
> and there decorated with purple honors.[169]

Without an evaluation of what can augment the will to power, subliminal suffering will be deemed as nothing more than suffering. But if one finds one's supra-Self in that subliminal suffering, then that suffering will be deemed as golden.

> One neighbor never understood the other: his soul always wondered at the neighbor's madness and malice.[170]

There will gather within the actor many different confluences of hope and desires, all of which will be based around a sense of something of a supra-Self, perhaps a supra-Self of different depths and perhaps arising out of different circumstances or hindrances. And there will be no common understanding and no common goal amongst these many confluences.

> A table of values hangs over each people. Lo and behold, it is the table of its conquests; take heed, it is the voice of its will to power.[171]

But there is something common in all these differing confluences of hopes and desires. They all share a will to attain to a supra-Self; they all share a will to power.

> That which is difficult to it is praiseworthy; what is indispensable and difficult is called good, and that which frees iy from the greatest need, the rare, the most difficult, — that it praises holy.[172]

That which is hard to bear, such as subliminal suffering or the ability to keep focused on a goal, is deemed worthy by the will to power. That which directly augments the will to power is deemed better. And that which raises the actor's center of gravity above the principium individuationis is deemed the greatest good by the will to power.

> That which makes it reign and triumph and shine, to the horror and envy of its neighbor, that it deems as the highest, the foremost, the measure and meaning of all things.[173]

And when the supra-Self is finally realized and comes into creation, that which brought the supra-Self into existence, for instance, a newfound depth of feeling, is deemed the meaning of all the efforts that preceded it.

> Truly, my brother, if you only knew the distress and land and heaven and neighbor, you could divine the law of its overcoming, and why it rises to its hope on this ladder.[174]

If you knew what was lacking to bring the supra-Self into existence, and if you also knew what limits were preventing that from happening and what lay beyond the aborning supra-Self, such as a deeper supra-Self, and if you knew what existing hopes and desires would assist bringing the supra-Self into existence, then you would understand entirely the life, the process of growth, by which the supra-Self could come into existence.

> 'Always be the first and foremost to command to others: your jealous soul must love no one except a friend' — that made the soul of a Greek tremble: and he followed his path to greatness. [175]

If you are going to love your hopes and passions, learn to love only those that will provide assistance in some manner to your will to power, your will to attain to your supra-Self.

> "Speaking the truth and doing well with bow and arrow" - so it seemed to the people from whom my name comes, a name that is both dear and heavy to me.[176]

Always deal with your Self and your supra-Self with the highest integrity, so that you are always honest with and about them. And, when your integrity leads to discoveries of Self and supra-Self, then learn to set goals based upon the truth you have uncovered and abide faithfully by an effort to achieve those goals.

> 'Honor father and mother and to do their will down to the very the roots of your soul': this table of overcoming hung over another people and they became powerful and eternal with it.[177]

When reaching for your aborning supra-Self, remember when you came into the previous supra-Self. Specifically, remember the circumstances out of which that previous Self arose, such as the need to look beyond the limits of Self to the next Self, and abide by what you learned.

> 'To have loyalty and for the sake of loyalty to risk honor and blood even in evil and dangerous things: by so teaching itself, another people mastered itself, and thus

> mastering itself, became pregnant and heavy
> with great hopes.[178]

Be loyal to your Self, and, when you face a difficult obstacle or even if you fear your destruction in some instance of subliminal suffering (if you allow it to come to the fore, for instance), take the risk and assume the danger, for the sake of your Self.

> Truly, people have given themselves all their
> good and bad. Truly, they did not take it, they
> did not find it, it did not fall to them as a
> voice from heaven.
>
> Man first placed values into things to
> preserve himself – he first created meaning
> for things, a human meaning! That is why he
> calls himself: 'man', that is: the one who
> evaluates.[179]

When you discover an aborning supra-Self and then endeavor to bring it into creation, that which you sense as helpful to your efforts is entirely a judgement you must make. Without your own judgement, there is no other way to make your way forward.

> Evaluation is creation: hear it, you creative
> ones! Evaluation is itself the treasure and
> jewel of the valued things.
>
> Only through evaluation is there value: and
> without evaluation the nut of existence would
> be hollow. Hear it, you creative ones![180]

Indeed, the very act of judging what amongst your hopes and passions will assist you is the very step forward that enables a process of growth. Without that evaluation, there will be no growth.

> A change in values – that means a change in the creating ones. He who has to be a creator always has to destroy.[181]

When you finally succeed in bringing your aborning supra-Self forward so that it then becomes your existing Self, and then when you look beyond it for the next, deeper supra-Self, then all your evaluations about what will assist you will change. And that is because life reveals itself in the process. And as you sense your next supra-Self, then you must learn to love it because love greatly augments the will to power. But, in order to love the next supra-Self, then you must stop loving the old supra-Self, your existing Self. And you must be willing to allow the old supra-Self to fall away, to die, so that the new supra-Self may emerge.

> The creating ones were the first among peoples; only later were there individuals. Truly, the individual himself is still the latest creation.[182]

At the outset of the drama, all the actor had was a hope and desire to find his Self. But he had no Self. That came later.

> Peoples once hung a table of values over themselves. Love that wants to rule and love

> that wants to obey created such tables
> together.[183]

And after the Self was found in parts, the parts came together as a whole only after there developed a will founded on both setting a goal to bring the Self forward and efforts that abided that goal.

> Pleasure in the herd is older than joy in the
> Ego: and as long as the good conscience is
> called herd, only the bad conscience says:
> I.[184]

The passions have always provided a place for indulgence. But the aborning Self requires discipline, which is far from indulgence. Thus, the passions and their indulgences are sometimes easier and preferred.

> Truly, the cunning, unloving Ego, that seeks
> its advantage in the advantage of the many –
> that is not the origin of the herd, but its
> ruin.[185]

The aborning Self does not indulge the passions; it seeks its definition and revelations of itself in the passions. And as a result of such seeking, it will grow. And as it grows, the passions will become a dimension of Self and become anchored in Self, where self-control will preclude indulgence.

> It was always loving ones and creating ones
> who created good and bad. Fire of love glows
> in the names of all virtues, and fire of
> wrath.[186]

The goal of finding and raising one's Self from oblivion creates many judgements about what helps to attain that goal and what hinders it.

> Zarathustra has seen many lands and many peoples: Zarathustra has found no greater power on earth than the creations of the loving ones: these creations are called 'good' and 'bad'.[187]

And so long as the aborning supra-Self exists only in parts and has not yet become whole, then there will be many scattered and incongruent judgements about what helps and what hinders.

> Truly, the power of this praise and blame is a monster. Tell me, who will vanquish it for me, brothers? Tell me, who will throw the shackles over the thousand necks of this animal? [188]

> Hitherto, there have been a thousand goals, for there have been a thousand peoples. Only shackle for the thousand necks is still missing, the one goal is missing. Humanity still has no goal. [189]

The actor must learn to look for what grand whole Self all these evaluations of help and hindrances point to.

> But tell me, my brothers: if mankind still lacks a goal, is not humanity itself still missing?[190]

And only when the actor sees his whole, nascent Self in all the scattered efforts that attain to it will he then find a cohesion in those parts and understand the meaning of the growth he has undertaken. And only then will his Self emerge from oblivion, not in parts but as a whole.

And to see the meaning in all the scattered efforts by which you attain to your aborning Self — or, to see your aborning Self emerging through all those scattered parts — is to create a myth, specifically a gateway myth, which will invigorate and drive your will forward. Thus, the dithyramb moves the actor toward another myth.

Or perhaps the myth it teaches is not the aborning Self. If the actor has learned "laughter" in the face of suffering, if he has learned to rise above the principium individuationis, then he might see a different myth in all his efforts to raise his subliminal suffering out of oblivion and into the light. Perhaps he will see the meaning in all his suffering as not a way toward his Self, which it certainly is, but rather as a way to supra-individuation, which it also is, and that would be another gateway myth. And that would be a more far reaching gateway myth.

Neighbor-Love

On Loving the Feelings that Are Near (in Consciousness)
and Those that Are Far (in the Subconscious)

> You crowd around your neighbor and have
> fine words for it. But I say to you: your love
> of your neighbor is your bad love of
> yourselves.
>
> You flee to your neighbor away from
> yourselves and would fain to make a virtue of
> it: but I fathom your 'unselfishness'.
>
> The 'You' is older than the 'I'; the 'You' has
> been consecrated, but not yet the 'I': so man
> presses near to his neighbor.[191]

Man is drawn within himself to his comforting emotions as
a way of maintaining a comfortable ease. He is comfortable
with those emotions that come to him on a regular basis,
day in and day out. Amongst the emotions, familiarity breeds
love. And that which is unfamiliar gets less love. But love is a
powerful augmentation to the will to power, the will to Self.
And subliminal emotions coming to the fore are unfamiliar,
but they define the aborning supra-Self. Therefore, it is

necessary to learn to love that which is a dimension of Self but which may be unfamiliar due to its newness. Insofar as emerging emotions will help the actor find his way to his Self, in a sense, they are his friend.

> I teach you not the neighbor but the friend.
> May the friend be to you a festival of the
> earth and a foretaste of the Supra-man.[192]

It is important to learn to love those emerging subliminal emotions that define Self.

> My brothers, I exhort you not to love of your
> neighbor: I exhort you to love of that which is
> most distant, of the future, of the aborning.[193]

The Bite of the Adder

This dithyramb speaks similarly to that which is spoken about in the dithyramb entitled Of the Flies of the Marketplace, namely the bite of conscience. However, in the previous dithyramb, what is taught is to seek refuge in the nascent supra-Self from annoying memories of small injustices that continually wear down the conscience amd the will. This dithyramb teaches a solution to the greater injustices that afflict the actor in everyday life.

In order to understand the solution this dithyramb teaches, it is necessary first to think of the will as a series of melodies (for instance, a series of pleasures and displeasures or a series of waxing and waning emotions) that, in turn, comprise a rhythm. Rhythm is an important element of the nature of the will to power. For instance, a series of pleasurable moments would not strengthen or augment the will to power, just as a series of displeasures would neither. But a mix of the two would, and a rhythmic mix certainly would. This dithyramb teaches how to create that strengthening rhythm.

> When, however, you have an enemy, do not repay his evil with good: for that would make him ashamed. But prove that he has done you good.[194]

This aphorism says that, when something strikes against your will, do not let that strike deflate your will. Instead, look for something good that has come about as a result of the strike, and take that good to heart.

For instance, when you extend a helping hand to someone and they respond rudely to you so that you are hurt, are you able to feel the hurt or do you become embittered? If you are able to feel the hurt, then something good has happened to you because you are struggling to incorporate the subliminal into consciousness, to learn to feel again, and this moment proves that you are succeeding. Plus, there is no bitterness in pain that is felt as a dimension of Self because the vision of Self, due to its illusory nature, heals. On this point, the dithyramb says:

> Did you ever know this? Shared injustice is half justice. And he who can bear it should take the injustice upon himself.[195]

This aphorism seems to be saying that pain is best relieved by causing pain to others. And there are people who hold this belief to be true. But that rendition is incorrect, and its suggestion from the literal text is merely a deliberate distraction. The second half of the aphorism, "he who can bear it..." clarifies the first half, "shared injustice is half justice." If you suffer an injustice, learn to experience it through the eyes of your deeper Self, not your shallow Self. And if you can experience the pain through the eyes of your deepest Self or, at least, your aborning Self, that is the best scenario.

However, if something happens that is much worse than someone merely being rude to you and causing your feelings to be hurt, if you experience an injustice that causes endless and obsessive thought, then you should "kill" that eremitical obsession with ruthless and "rude" will power, lest it take an inordinate measure of focus away from your efforts to find your Self.

> Finally, my brothers, beware of doing wrong to all the hermits! How could a hermit forget? How could he repay?
>
> A hermit is like a deep well. It is easy to throw a stone into it; but if it should sink to the bottom, tell me, who will bring it out again?
>
> Be careful not to offend the hermit! But if you do, well then, kill him too![196]

Child and Marriage

You must choose wisely which passions, hopes, and desires you decide to "marry" to your will in your attempts to find your Self. Keep in mind that the whole process of growth by which you endeavor to incorporate subliminal emotions into consciousness is always accompanied by the epiphenomenal mythopoeia that leads to your Self. And in a sense, this creative process is analogous to birthing a child, especially when you consider that the aborning Self that is brought forward truly represents a new beginning.

There are many circumstances under which various passions, hopes, and desires are "wedded" to the will, and some of those unions are not helpful with regard to bringing one's Self forward.

> You are young and want a child and marriage. But I ask you: are you a man who can wish for a child?
>
> Are you the victorious one, the self-conqueror, the master of your senses, the lord of your virtues? So I ask you.
>
> Or do the animal and need speak out of your wish? Or isolation? Or strife within you?

> I want your victory and your freedom to yearn for a child. You should build living monuments to your victory and your liberation.[197]

When you succeed with even one small step forward, that is the moment to look around for something that will assist you further. Do not look at a time when you are disconsolate or frustrated with your stalled growth, and do not look at a time when you are afflicted; look at a time when you are victorious.

The best "marriage" is between a will and a passion or hope or belief that aims directly toward your supra-Self.

> Thirst in the creating one and an arrow and longing for the Supra-man: speak, my brother, is this your will to marriage?
>
> I call holy such a will and such a marriage.[198]

Voluntary Death

On Properly Reposing the Moods that Move the Will
Toward the Supra-Self

Learn not to push your efforts to the point of exhaustion. If
you come upon an obstacle, such as a particularly difficult
subliminal emotion that will not surface, rather than pushing the
effort until your will is exhausted and it simply withers away,
step back, and, in doing so, make a promise to yourself that the
next time you undertake the same effort, you will go a little
further, perhaps by being more brave, for instance. In such a
way, that vow will return to you when you undertake the
same effort again, and, the next time, whatever vow you
made in the previous attempt will then augment your will. In
such a way do you learn to grow your will.

> Many die too late and some die too early.
> Still the doctrine sounds strange: 'Die at the
> right time.'
>
> Die at the right time: thus Zarathustra
> teaches.[199]

And,

> I show you the triumphant death, which becomes a thorn and a vow to the living.
>
> The man achieving his life's work dies his death triumphantly, surrounded by those who hope and promise.
>
> Thus one should learn to die; and there should be no festival at which such a dying man does not consecrate oaths to the living![200]

As I said in the exegesis of The Chairs of Virtue, in the quote about "Traffic with one's higher Self," the desire to find one's Self proceeds upon a mood, as represented by the metaphor of the eagle, which is one of only two of Zarathustra's companions, the other being the serpent around the eagle's neck. And the mood comes and goes. When the will to Self is satiated, it is as if it then goes to sleep, and the actor must wait for it to awaken. It is for this reason that Zarathustra values the ability of waiting for oneself rather than expending any effort or frustration absent that mood. If there is anything you could do to lessen the wait time, that would be helpful. And whetting one's appetite by making a vow to overcome an obstacle that becomes apparent at the point of exhaustion, at the point of satiation, would be helpful.

Also, it is important to sense when is the best time to quit one's efforts.

> I commend to you my sort of death, voluntary death that comes to me because *I* want it.

> And when shall I want it? – He who has a
> goal and an heir wants death at the right time
> for the goal and the heir.[201]

But most importantly, do not forestall the moment that is most appropriate to quit your effort, to refrain from further willing, simply because you prefer to wallow in the pleasure of a minor victory or because you lack the courage needed to eventually approach the next goal that you know will surely present itself in the next effort.

> Many never become sweet, they rot even in
> the summer. It is cowardice that holds him to
> his branch.[202]

The Bestowing Virtue

As I said earlier in the exegesis of the dithyramb entitled Of Joys and Passions, Dionysia, as a way of thinking, has redefined virtue as a joy in supra-Self or a painful or otherwise afflictive passion of which the supra-Self is suffering. Either quality defines the joy or the passion as a virtue because it augments the will, the desire, to bring the supra-Self into existence, which is the work and the meaning of life: creation of the supra-Self.

When you find your Self, it will present as an image, a vision, in contrast to a passion, though there will also be passions aroused by the vision, such as the joy of Self-discovery (empowerment) and the passion or suffering that the Self is suffering and that originally caused its demise, its repression. Most likely, you will also experience fear because, as the principium individuationis shifts to a greater depth, the ground will seem to give way under you, which is the proto-tragic phenomenon, but also because it will take some time to find the will (the lion) arising out of the newly discovered Self. And fear is the feeling that exists in the absence of will. But, most importantly, you will "see" a vision of Self.

> Take heed, my brothers, to every moment when your spirit speaks in similes: there is the origin of your virtue.[203]

As I said, the image of Self upon discovery will enchant you as it lifts you up out of the chaotic maelstrom of superfluous thought and compulsive emotion. But it will also present a new ruling idea, which rules in the sense that further discovery dictates a certain obedience to the image you suddenly behold, in contrast to indulgence in wayward emotions. The question, "Is my Self in this thought or that emotion," for instance, would be a ruling idea.

> Then your body is elevated and raised up; it enraptures the spirit with its delight, so that it becomes creator and evaluator and lover and benefactor of all things.[204]

Upon discovery of Self, you will also experience an exhilaration arising out of the freedom you sense in your discovery because one of the ways that Self-discovery empowers its beholder is by nullifying the Spirit of Gravity.

> When your heart is wide and full like the river, a blessing and a danger to those around you: there is the origin of your virtue.[205]

And when you find your "ruling idea" and resolve to abide by it, you will proceed upon a love for Self toward your goal, the next supra-Self, not a ruthless abhorrence for your vices.

> When you are exalted above praise and blame, and your will would command all things as the will of a loving one: there is the origin of your virtue.[206]

And, insofar as you will have come to understand that your Self and your supra-Self can only be found in that which afflicts you, your demons, you will learn to "love your enemies" and you will learn the value of your affliction and the value of stoicism.

> When you despise the soft bed and the pleasant and cannot make your bed far enough from the soft one: there is the origin of your virtue.[207]

This dithyramb speaks of the apprehension of Self and supra-Self as a "bestowing" virtue because it bestows freedom and empowerment to its beholder.

> Truly, it is a new good and bad! Truly, a new sound from the depths and the source of a new voice![208]

This dithyramb also teaches the value in learning to trust the instincts that *Thus Spoke Zarathustra* is teaching you *as your own instincts* — because, in fact, they are your own instincts that you are learning; it is only that the instincts were lost and are now being found again.

> I now go alone, my disciples! You too now go away and be alone! So I will have it. … It is hard to repay a teacher if you remain the pupil.[209]

And,

> You say you believe in Zarathustra? But of what account is Zarathustra? You are my

> believers: but of what account are all
> believers?
>
> You had not yet sought yourselves: then you
> found me. Thus do all believers; therefore all
> belief is of so little account.
>
> Now I bid you lose me and find yourselves;
> and only when you have all denied me will I
> return to you.
>
> Truly, with other eyes, my brothers, I shall
> then seek my lost ones; with another love I
> shall then love you.[210]

Lastly, there is something called "the noontide," which is mentioned often throughout many dithyrambs. The noontide is that moment when the actor comes upon a deeper supra-Self for the first time. It is when the image of Self is clearest and brightest. At that moment, the actor stands between that which he once was, a chaotic maelstrom of wayward thought and compulsive emotion (the animal) and that which he is becoming (a state of enlightened being that is enhanced by the empowerment of Self).

Invariably, that bright vision of the supra-Self will fade like a setting sun into a state of mind that might rightly be alluded to as "the night." But something happens at "night" about which the actor has no organ for perception, that which happens beyond the pale of consciousness, deep within a state of mysticism. And then finally, when the actor's appetite to seek out his Self returns from its satiated state, and he returns again to the same vision to which he was last beholden, things will be different. Perhaps the will arising out of that new supra-Self will have begun to emerge and that new will have become a dimension of the actor's being. In any case, the state of mind existing at the time of discovery will have matured, and the actor will experience the previously unfamiliar and aborning supra-Self as an existing Self, with a much deeper center of gravity, a much deeper scope of perception. And that matured state of being will constitute a new beginning for the actor. In a sense, it will be very much like a child.

> And this is the great noon: it is when man stands at the middle of his course between animal and Supra-man and celebrates his way to the evening as his highest hope: for it is the way to a new morning.
>
> Then the one going under will bless himself; for he will be going over; and the sun of his knowledge will stand at noontide.[211]

And most importantly, at that glorious moment of noontide when your Self is clearest and most brilliant, which is a moment that is the fruit of all your labor, that is the moment when you should make a vow to find the next supra-Self, always the next supra-Self. What awaits you is a measure of freedom that can be found only in heaven on earth — and it exists only beyond the bounds of individuation, in supra-individuation. Do not become beguiled by the beauty of Self. There will be many noontides, not just one, and not even just a few.

> '*All gods are dead: now we want the Supra-man to live*' – let this be our final will one day at the great noontide![212]

The Sublime Ones

On the Tendency to Repress the Subconscious

The subconscious can appear to be very still, so much so that most people are not even aware of its existence, except in concept that maybe they read about. It is well-hidden. Yet it is teeming with subliminal emotions.

> Quiet is the bottom of my sea: who could guess that it hides playful monsters![213]

There are within you very strong forces specifically directed against any emotion attempting to rise into your consciousness. It would be very helpful if you could learn to weaken those forces. This dithyramb focuses on that tendency to sublimate and teaches you how to lessen its grip on you.

> Today I saw a sublime one, a solemn one, a penitent of the spirit: oh, how my soul laughed at his ugliness!
>
> With upraised breast and like those who draw in their breath: thus did he stand, the sublime one, and in silence.

> Draped with ugly truths, his booty, and rich
> in torn clothes; many thorns also hung on him
> - but I saw no rose.
>
> He has not yet learned laughter and beauty.
> This hunter returned gloomily from the forest
> of knowledge.
>
> He returned home from the fight with wild
> beasts: but a wild beast still gazes out of his
> seriousness – an insuperable one!
>
> He stands there like a tiger about to spring;
> but I do not like these tense souls, my taste is
> against all these withdrawn ones.[214]

There are instances, as in the dithyramb entitled The Stillest Hour, when forces within us act against the progress of life and those forces can be nullified, as we will see in the exegesis of that dithyramb. But the strong tendency to repress the subconscious cannot be nullified. However, it can be lessened.

As you progress with life and with this drama, you will discover the beauty and the goodness that results from allowing the subconscious into the conscious, and that sentiment will lessen the grip of "the sublime men."

> He must also unlearn his heroic will: he
> should be an exalted one to me and not just
> an exalted one - the ether itself should raise
> him, the willless one!

He has conquered monsters, he solved riddles: but he should also redeem his monsters and riddles, he should transform them into heavenly children.

His knowledge has not yet learned to smile and to be without jealousy; his gushing passion has not yet become still in beauty.

Truly, his desire should not be silent and submerged in satiety but in beauty! Grace belongs to the magnanimity of the great-minded.

With his arm over his head: this is how the hero should rest, this is also how he should overcome his rest.

But for the hero in particular, *beauty* is the hardest of all things. Beauty is unattainable to all fierce wills.

A little more, a little less: that is a lot here, that is the most here.

To stand with relaxed muscles and detached will: that is the hardest thing for all of you, you sublime ones!

When power becomes gracious and descends into the visible: I call that descent beauty.

> And I want beauty from no one as much as I
> want it from you, powerful one: let your
> goodness be your final self-conquest.[215]

Specifically, as you grow more tragic, embracing the subconscious with all its horror and ugliness, which you will do only when you learn to redeem it as well so that your demons become angels, only then will you realize that there is much more greatness and goodness in freeing the subconscious than there is in subduing and defeating it. And you will learn that. And when you do, the tendency to subdue your demons will be ameliorated by a willingness to free them and bring them into the light.

> You should strive after the virtue of pillar: the
> more it rises, the more beautiful and more
> tender does it become, but harder and more
> sustaining inside.
>
> Yes, you sublime one, one day you shall be
> beautiful and hold up the mirror to your own
> beauty.
>
> Then your soul will shudder with divine
> desires; and there will be adoration even in
> your vanity!
>
> For this is the secret of the soul: only when
> the hero has left it does there approach you in
> a dream — the supra-hero.[216]

The "supra-hero" is the effort to free the repressed demons, not the heroic Ego that struggles to repress them.

Immaculate Perception

On Merely Seeing the Subconscious and Actively Raising It

There is within subindividuated man a strong proclivity to obtain knowledge for no other reason than to accumulate knowledge, as if driven by a lust for knowledge, even if nothing can be done with the knowledge obtained. This proclivity, which is also called an insatiable drive for knowledge, is celebrated in science. Whatever knowledge about your Self that you uncover must be useful to your effort to raise your aborning supra-Self. Otherwise, that knowledge is superfluous and not meaningful.

According to this dithyramb, if the insatiable desire for knowledge could speak, this is what it would say:

"That would be the highest thing for me" — so your lying spirit speaks to itself — to look at life without desire and not like a dog with a hanging tongue::

'To be happy in gazing, with dead will, free from the grip and greed of selfishness – cold and ashen grey all over the body, but with intoxicated moon-eyes!

> "That would be the dearest thing to me" — so the seduced one seduces himself — to love the earth as the moon loves it, and to feel its beauty with the eye only."

> 'And this do I call *immaculate* perception of all things: that I want nothing from things, except that I can lie down before them like a mirror with a hundred eyes.'[217]

And this sentiment, this belief in the value of all knowledge, regardless of its usefulness, is corrected with the following new value:

> And this *I* call knowledge: all that is deep shall rise up – to my height![218]

In other words, to know one's subliminal emotions is to raise them up into the Self, into consciousness. Otherwise, knowledge does not serve life. And this is true not only of the insatiable desire for knowledge that is science but also for any gathering of knowledge that does not assist life, for instance, knowledge that is gained through superfluous or haphazard efforts.

Great Events

On the Manner of Passing into the Subconscious and the False Fear of Doing Entering

> There is an island in the sea – not far from the Blissful Islands of Zarathustra on which a mountain of fire is smoking constantly; the people, and especially the old women among the people, say that it is placed like a boulder before the gate of the underworld, but that the narrow downward path to the gate of the underworld leads through the mountain of fire itself.[219]

Eventually, you will come upon a place within your heart and mind which we shall call a gateway to the subconscious. It is a myth, specifically a gateway myth, unlike a mythical being like Self. This dithyramb depicts that moment, that gateway, what happens when you approach it, and how to deal with the problems that inhere in that approach.

> Now at the time Zarathustra was staying on the Blissful Islands it happened that a ship dropped anchor at the island upon which the smoking mountain stands; and its crew went

> ashore to shoot rabbits. Towards noon, however, when the captain and his men were together again, they suddenly saw a man coming through the air towards them, and a voice said clearly: 'It is time! It is high time!' But when figure was closest to them – it flew quickly past, however, like a shadow, in the direction of the mountain of fire — then they recognized, with the greatest perplexity, that it was Zarathustra....[220]

This is a mystical experience. It is very real, but you will not understand what is happening, and you will most certainly resist it.

Following the novice actor's new-found ability to delineate his Self from within his true feelings, it will occur to him that perhaps he must search for deeper emotions in order to continue his delineation. And that realization will most likely come to him after he has successfully rendered the dithyramb Of the Tree on the Mountainside.

And he will look around within himself and ask "but where are these emotions to be found?" And it is at that point that he will realize that perhaps there are deeper emotions within him to which he has turned a blind eye. And he will ask himself "is there really a subconscious within me?" Then, sometime later, when he is not expecting it, he will have a mystical experience, during which a thought will suddenly race through his mind toward a depth that was previously unknown to him, as if with a "sucking" sensation, as if he is being sucked into some unknown depth within himself. And he will feel an instinct arise from within this experience. And that instinct will speak to him as if to say "It is time." It is necessary for the actor to attempt to understand the meaning of that instinct which says "It is time" so that he understands for what, precisely, is it time.

Unfortunately, the experience will be a little frightening, and the actor is unlikely to take the time to answer that important question. But as he eventually learns to search for his supra-Self, the same experience will recur as he digs deeper and, eventually, he will be able to answer the question when he realizes "it is time to allow his deeper Self out of its prison and to let it rise up into the light." This is one of many mythopoeic moments in the drama, and the myth that is created here is a gateway myth. As with all myths, be they a gateway myth or a mythical being, this myth enables the will to power because it leads to the actor's deeper Self, his supra-Self.

There will also arise within the mind of the actor, upon having this experience, another instinct with an accompanying "voice" that tells him to not go forward because doing so will mean his destruction.

> 'Look!' said the old helmsman, 'Zarathustra is going to Hell!' [221]

The dithyrambist names this instinct the "fire hound." And then he teaches the actor how to overcome it, though it will be a long time before he finally learns to overcome the "fire hound" that dissuades him from entering the subconscious.

> And this is the story of Zarathustra's conversation with the fire-dog:
>
> The earth, he said, has a skin; and this skin has diseases. One of these diseases, for example, is called 'man.'

And another of these diseases is called 'the fire-dog': men have greatly deceived themselves about *him* and let themselves be deceived.

To fathom this mystery, I went over the sea the sea: and I have seen the truth naked, truly! barefoot up to the neck.

Now I know what the fire-dog is all about; and similarly about all the ejection and overthrowing devils which not only old women fear.[222]

Continuing,

'Up with you, fire-dog, up from your depth!' I cried, 'and confess how deep that depth is! Whence comes that which you snort up?

'You drink abundantly from the sea: your bitter eloquence betrays that! Indeed, for a dog of the depth you take your food too much from the surface!

'At most, I think you are the ventriloquist of the earth ...[223]

If you move beyond the instinctual fear of the subconscious that this dithyramb depicts, you will discover that the fear has no depth and quickly dissipates. There is no need to take a great leap into the subconscious. Life is always easier when you take small steps, even very small steps, because it is the nature of life that it proceeds only gradually and incrementally. This particular fear seems to exist only on the surface.

In fact, contrary to what fear of the fire-dog anticipates, a communion with your most difficult and subconscious emotions is a wondrous experience, per the following idioms:

... hear the story of another fire-dog, he really speaks from the heart of the earth.

'His breath exhales gold and golden rain: so will his heart have it. What are ashes and smoke and hot mud to him now!

'Laughter flutters from him like a motley cloud; he is adverse to your gurgling and spitting and grimacing of the belly of being!

'But the gold and laughter, — he takes it from the heart of the earth: for, that you may know it - *the heart of the earth is of gold.*'[224]

Then, moving beyond the instinctual fear of the subconscious, the dithyrambist goes on to speak generally about the instinctual warnings and celebrations that speak up around any supposedly significant event that arises out of the effort to find one's Self. Going forward in his journey to Self-discovery, the actor may think that success is marked by conscious, exclamatory thought and that his mind should become filled with such exclamations. But actually, every successful step forward in discovery is a silent step that is accompanied by no exclamations.

> 'And believe me, my friend from hell! The greatest events – they are not our loudest but our most quiet hours.
>
> 'Not around the inventors of new noise: the world revolves around the inventors of new values; it revolves *inaudibly*.[225]

At the close of the dithyramb, the discussion returns to the "fire hound" with a very effective resolution. The dithyrambist tells the actor to compare the exclamations and warnings uttered by the fire hound to those uttered when the actor first began to discover his Self, which we discussed previously in the dithyramb entitled Of the New Idol, which proclaimed that there was no greater good than the discovery of Self at the very early, initial stages of life. But when the actor continued into the next supra-Self, there were no similar exclamations because, at that point, the actor had learned about the supra-Self and knew that every apprehension of Self would be followed with an even deeper apprehension of Self. Most importantly, in that lesson, the actor learned to discredit celebrated exclamations in general. Thus, by comparison, the actor should try to understand that the warnings and exclamations that erupt from this instinct that the dithyrambist calls the "fire hound" should also be discredited.

'This counsel, however, do I counsel to kings and churches and to all that is weak with age and virtue –let yourselves be overthrown! That you may again come to life, and that virtue – may come to you!'

Thus I spoke before the fire-dog: then he interrupted me sullenly and asked: 'Church? What is that?'

'The church?' I replied. 'that is a kind of state, and the most mendacious kind. But be silent, you hypocrite dog! You surely know your own kind best!

'Like you, the state is a hypocrite dog; like you, it likes to talk with smoke and roars – to make people believe, like you, that it speaks from the belly of being.

'For it absolutely wants to be the most important animal on earth, the state; and people believe it, too!'

When I said that, the fire-dog acted foolish with envy. 'How?' he screamed, 'the most important animal on earth? And people believe it, too?' And so much steam and horrible voices came out of his throat that I thought he would choke with anger and envy.[226]

Lastly, notice the very last sentences of this dithyramb.

> 'Why, then, did the ghost cry: "It istime! It is
> the highest time!"'?
>
> 'For *what*, then, is it – the highest time?'[227]

The approach to the gateway that leads to the subconscious, as depicted in this dithyramb, is a mythopoeic moment. It is a mystical experience that will be difficult to understand, but the actor will experience the rushing, self-absorbing sensation as if into a deep hole and he will experience the instinctual articulation "It is time," and he must try to answer the question *"For what*, then, is it — high time?" And rumination plays an important role in the process of answering that question, as it does in every dithyramb. The actor may have to mull that question and the experience for a long time before an answer comes to him. And remember also that, as you pursue your supra-Self, you will enter even deeper into the subconscious so that you will have the same mystical experience of rushing into the subconscious again. Therefore, if you find no answer the first few times, there will be other opportunities later in which you can mull the question again and seek an answer. But, eventually, you must find an answer.

Finally, notice how there is nothing in the text about the myth that is created out of this experience, specifically the myth that arises out of finding an answer to the question "For what is it high time?" In the dithyramb, everything that is Apollonian, specifically myth and idea, are totally absent, hidden. All that is depicted is the inner turmoil of emotion out of which the myth and idea rises. All the text is strictly Dionysian, depicting emotion only. And notice also that the experience is rooted in instinct. That is the level at which the dithyrambist endeavors to teach you. He wishes to teach you instinct — because it is instinct that will successfully teach you a new way of thinking.

> If he succeeded in transforming his instincts into terms of knowledge, it was always with the hope that the reverse process might take place in the souls of his readers—it was with this intention that he wrote.[228]

The Soothsayer

On Triggering the Mythopoeic Instinct and the Creation of the Supra-Self

— And I saw a great sadness come over mankind. The best turned weary of their works.

A teaching went forth, a belief ran beside it: Everything is empty, everything is the same, everything is in the past!

And from every hill it re-echoed: Everything is empty, everything is the same, everything is in the past!

To be sure, we have harvested: but why have all our fruits become rotten and brown? What fell last night from the evil moon?

All our work has been in vain, our wine has become poison, an evil eye has singed yellow our fields and hearts.

> We have all become dry; and if fire fell upon
> us, we would we turn to dust like ashes —
> yes, we have made the fire itself weary.
>
> All our fountains have dried up, even the sea
> has receded. The ground wants to break open,
> but the depths will not swallow!
>
> Oh, where is there still a sea in which one
> could drown: this is the sound of our lament -
> across shallow swamps.[229]

Without a doubt, as I have said repeatedly, the most difficult task you will undertake during the course of this drama is integration of the subconscious with the conscious, which comprises the tragic part of this drama. And as mightily as you try and fail, so too will you become very weary of trying. Instead of rejoicing in your successes at restoring your feeling, you will lament in your failures.

> Everything is empty, everything is the same,
> everything is in the past!

My soul is empty of feeling. There is no individuation within me. Everything that exists within me exists only in my subconscious, which I cannot reach.

> To be sure, we have harvested: but why have
> all our fruits become rotten and brown? What
> fell last night from the evil moon?
>
> All our work has been in vain, our wine has
> become poison, an evil eye has singed yellow
> our fields and hearts.

The actor will think that he has spent all this time and hard work delineating his Self and he has done it well, but nothing good has come of it.

> All our fountains have dried up, even the sea has receded. The ground wants to break open, but the depths will not swallow!

The actor has reached deeply into his subconscious, but there are no longer any places into which he might look deeply. He has found them all and plumbed them all. And it is clear to him that his subconscious wishes to break open. But no matter how long he waits or how hard he tries, it will not break open.

Out of this malaise, Zarathustra has a riddling dream which the actor is asked to unriddle.

> I dreamed I had renounced all life. I had become a night-watchman and grave-guardian there upon the lonely mountain-fortress of death.
>
> Up there I guarded his coffins: the musty vaults stood full of those trophies of victory. Life that had been overcome looked at me from glass coffins.[230]

By life, he means the will to power or the pursuit of the supra-Self via the integration of the subconscious into the conscious. Just as the actor was unable to continue his pursuit of Self until he learned about the subconscious in the dithyramb Of the Tree on the Mountainside, so too will he be unable to integrate the subconscious into the conscious until he solves this riddle. Even though he can see the demons within his subconscious (as if through glass coffins), there is a possibility, given his great weariness from this malaise, that he will renounce his efforts to reach them and raise them.

So did time pass with me and creep by, if there was still time: what did I know of it! But what finally happened is what woke me up.

Three times the gate was struck, like thunder, the vault echoed and howled three times again: then I went to the gate.

Alpa! I cried, who carries his ashes to the mountain? Alpa! Alpa! Who carries his ashes to the mountain?

And I pressed the key and pulled at the door and exerted myself. But it did not open by a finger's breadth:

Then a roaring wind tore the folds apart: whistling, whizzing, and piercing, it threw me a black coffin:

And in the roaring and whistling and whizzing, the coffin burst asunder and spat out a thousand peals of laughter.

And out of a thousand grimaces from children, angels, owls, fools and child-sized butterflies, it laughed and sneered and roared at me.[231]

Many, many times, I myself tugged at my demons while trying to raise them into the light. But it was all to no avail. But finally, I solved this riddle. The solution is to be found in the idiom, "Alpa! I cried, who is bearing his ashes to the mountain? Alpa! Alpa! Who is bearing his ashes to the mountain?"

Again, this is a question that the actor must ask himself. Specifically, he must ask from whence do these demons arise? And it will likely take you a long time to find an answer. And you must plumb your depths for a good answer. If you do, and you do it long enough and deeply enough, the mythopoeic instinct will kick in and you will realize your demons arise from a much deeper Self, which, up until now, has been oblivious to you. With that realization, you will take ownership of your demons and they will become a dimension of your being, well within reach. And, again, refer back to the idiom that introduced this dithyramb,

Everything is empty, everything is the same, everything is in the past!

The truth represented in that idiom will become reversed. Your soul will no longer be empty of feeling. And you will become individuated within your inner world by a clearly defined Self. And everything that exists within you will no longer be from the past but will become reality, today. You will have overcome dismemberment, which is the fundament of sub-individuation. Only now, with this particular overcoming of dismemberment, does supra-individuation become a possibility.

The revelations in this dithyramb are profoundly transformative. Keep in mind that this is not a one-time event. The entire subconscious does not leap forward into consciousness with this revelation, only the part that you sensed and then thought through. But there is far more of the subconscious that you will not have sensed the first time you have this mystical experience, and you will incorporate that later, through a repetition of this experience.

But with this experience, you will have discovered the supra-Self, that there is always a deeper Self beyond the currently perceived Self, which you will find if only you look beyond the horizon of the current Self — and more deeply into the subconscious.

Unfortunately, though I have presented you here with an explicative concept of mythopoeia and the Übermensch, it will not come as easily to you in your own experience of the drama. Consider the explanation of one of Zarathustra's disciples of the riddle in the dream.

> Your life itself interprets for us this dream, oh Zarathustra!
>
> Are you yourself not the wind with shrill whistling that bursts open the gates of the fortress of death?
>
> Are you yourself not the coffin full of motley wickedness and angelic faces of life?
>
> Truly, Zarathustra comes into all sepulchers like a thousand peals of children's laughter, laughing at those night-watchmen and grave-

guardians, and whoever else rattles with sinister keys.

You will terrify and prostrate them with your laughter; fainting and recovering will demonstrate your power over them.

And when the long twilight comes and the fatigue of death, even then you will not perish in our heaven, you advocate of life!

You have made us see new stars and new glories at night; truly, you have stretched out laughter itself like a motley canopy over us.

Now the laughter of children will always spring from coffins; now there will always be a strong wind, victorious against the fatigue that death brings; you yourself are our guarantee and soothsayer!

Truly, you *dreamed your enemies themselves*: that was your most difficult dream!

But as you awoke from them and came to yourself, so shall they awake from themselves - and come to you![232]

Pay close attention to the last idiom, "But as you awoke from them [dreaming about your demons] and came to yourself, so shall they awake from themselves - and come to you!"

For the longest time, this, too, is what I understood. I struggled for a very long time trying to raise my demons. I truly believed that, if I could delineate my Self amidst the chaos of thought and passion within me to a sufficient extent, then, eventually, my demons would rise voluntarily or involuntarily into my consciousness. That did not happen. But when I read this dithyramb more deeply and realized that, when the dithyramb asks a question (in this instance, "who is bearing his ashes to the mountain?"), I am supposed to ask myself the same question, thus triggering the mythopoeic instinct, which is what happened. Then I solved the riddle and my supra-Self came to me.

The Stillest Hour

At the Tragic Moment When the Ground of Being Afforded by the Existing Self Collapses into the Supra-Self

Yesterday towards evening *my stillest hour* spoke to me: that is the name of my terrible mistress.

And thus it happened, for I must tell you everything, that your hearts may not harden against the suddenly departing!

Do you know the terror of him him who is falling asleep?

He is terrified to very his toes, because the ground gives way under him, and the dream begins.

I tell you this in a parable. Yesterday, at the stillest hour, the ground gave way under me: the dream began.

> The hour-hand moved, the clock of my life
> took a breath - I had never heard such silence
> around me: so that my heart was terrified.
>
> Then it said to me without a voice: *'You know
> it, Zarathustra?'*[233]

It is one thing to approach the gateway to the subconscious, quite another to reach in and plumb it. But to release the demons within and take ownership of them through mythopoeia, that is an even bigger step forward in the advancement of the will to power. But even bigger than all three of those steps is to *become* the supra-Self you sense in those depths so that the Self you once were lies behind you like a shadow (see the dithyramb entitled Of the Shadow). It is also the most frightening of all the steps involved in the tragic rite of passage. In this dithyramb, the actor is brought to the point wherein he must admit he now finally knows who he is. He can no longer hide from his Self or his bad conscience. He knows who he is. And he knows that all those very deep emotions from which he has stubbornly hidden for what seems like an eternity *are true and real*. And that realization constitutes a very frightening moment in which the ground seems to give way to a much brighter and much more sober reality.

In the above idioms, what exactly does Zarathustra know? He knows that, up until now, reality has been a sham, a false flooring, and the time has arrived for that false flooring to give way. But the actor will be too frightened to allow it to happen.

> And I cried out in terror at this whispering,
> and the blood drained from my face: but I
> was silent.

> Then it spoke to me again without a voice: 'You know it, Zarathustra, but you do not speak!'
>
> And I answered at last, defiantly: 'Yes, I know, but I will not speak it!'[234]

And what does Zarathustra know? That is a question the actor must ask himself upon acting out this particular dithyramb. The answer that came to me was "You know who you really are." But I resisted admitting it. This dithyramb teaches you to nullify that frightened defiance simply by confessing it outright — *consciously*.

> At last, however, I said what I had said at first: 'I will not.'
>
> Then a laughing happened all around me. Woe, how this laughing tore the belly of my being and cut into my heart![235]

The metaphor "laughter" requires an extensive explanation, which will come in the exegesis of the dithyramb entitled Of the Vision and the Riddle. Suffice it to say that it is a metaphor for the sensation and the experience that results from overcoming an obstacle, from rising above it.

The Wanderer

If you have any doubts that *Thus Spoke Zarathustra* is a journey toward a reclamation of Self, the following aphorism, which appears in this dithyramb near the end of the drama, should put those doubts to rest, once and for all.

> The time is now passed when accidents could befall me; and what *could* fall to me that was not already my own?
>
> It is returning, it is coming home to me at last – my own Self and those parts of it that have long been abroad and scattered among things and accidents.[236]

And by "accidents," the dithyrambist means the inability to resist a reaction to random and haphazard stimuli that may rise up or strike subindividuated man, thereby distracting him from his vision of Self. In the Will to Power, while speaking of decadence, of which there are many forms, Nietzsche says of one type:

> The *power of resisting* stimuli is on the wane—chance rules supreme [accidents are

> frequent]: events are inflated and drawn out until they appear monstrous
>
> ... a suppression of the "personality," a disintegration of the will....[237]

In this dithyramb, the actor has reached a height of power, a magnificent accumulation of power. And out of this height of power there now follows — quite naturally and *instinctively* — a grand moment of dissonance that leads directly to the deepest tragedy the actor has yet experienced. In other words, the actor has spent a long time looking for his Self in all the most distant points of his inner world and he has brought those parts into a cohesive whole. But he has not yet plumbed his deepest parts; the subconscious remains a separated part of his inner world.

According to Nietzsche's theory that proto-tragedy arises as a dissonant moment — but certainly not an unmelodious moment — out of an ascending accumulation of power (*The Birth of Tragedy out of the Spirit of Music*), now, in this dithyramb, comes the moment when the actor consciously decides — or wills — his absolute downfall. The deepest pain and horror await him. Why would he want this? Because he wants power, and power finds its greatest manifestation in the mythopoeia of Self, the imposition of being onto a world that is entirely one of becoming. There is no greater work of art than this imposition, this creation of Self via mythopoeia. This last and final downfall, which will be absolute, will lead to the greatest accumulation of even more power than he has ever attained. All growth is driven by a desire for power. Life, as an extension of the limits of Self, is driven by the need and the desire for power.

> And I know one thing more: I now stand before my last summit and before that which has been reserved for me the longest. Alas, I must ascend my most difficult path! Alas, I have begun my most lonesome wandering!
>
> But whoever is of my kind does not avoid such an hour: the hour that says to him: 'Only now do you go your way to greatness! Summit and abyss – they are now decided in one!'[238]

When the dithyrambist says summit and abyss are now united in one, he means the highest sense of Self and the deepest abyss within the subconscious now come together in one moment.

> Ah, this black, sad sea below me! Ah, this pregnant nighttime waeriness! Ah, fate and the sea! Now I have to *go under* to you!
>
> I stand before my highest mountain and before my longest wandering: therefore I must first go under deeper than I have ever ascended,
>
> — deeper down into pain from which I have ever ascended, into its blackest tide! So will my fate have it. Well then! I am ready.[239]

The "sea" he mentions is the vast sea of emotions. And the "mountains" are the elevations of spirit he has attained by raising his Self out of chaotic oblivion. But he has not plumbed the greatest depths of his subconscious, and that is what awaits him in this moment. Thus, Zarathustra says that he must descend deeper,

However, notice that he says he must descend deeper than he has ever *ascended.* That is a typical example of Nietzsche writing in a form that is clearly contradictory, which, I believe, is his way of forcing the reader to think. The more typical expectation of someone writing that he must descend deeper than he has done previously, which is what the dithyrambist is saying, is to say "I must descend more deeply than I have ever *descended* before." And that is what both Hollingdale and Kaufmann translated. But Haussmann and Adrian Del Caro translated it differently as "I must descend deeper than I have ever *climbed before*" (Del Caro) and "therefore must I go deeper than I have *ever ascended*" (Haussmann). The original German reads "darum muss ich erst tiefer hinab als ich jemals stieg." Thus, the correct translation is to say I must descend deeper than I have ever ascended or climbed. But that is not what Hollingdale and Kaufmann translated.

In this instance, the dithyrambist is referencing the springboard that suffering provides. And, in order to exact the best spring from that springboard, it is necessary to achieve the greatest stretching of the bow, the greatest tension, which means plumbing the true depth of the suffering. And that requires looking beyond the limits of percipience that are defined by the Self, looking beyond the existing Self into the supra-Self. That is the only way to *apprehend* the true depth of the suffering. In doing so, and then properly redeeming it by mounting the extraordinary spring that it will invoke and lifting the spirit to that respective height, then it would make sense to say "I must descend deeper than I have ascended."

I note this error is translation to highlight the importance of keeping a keen eye on *each and every* word in which each and every dithyramb is composed. Overlook nothing because there is meaning, if not gold, in the simplest and most typical use of words and especially phrases. What is most important in the art of the dithyramb is learning to *hear* the music, not reading the apparent but specious story.

> Whence arise the highest mountains? so I once asked. Then I learned that they come out of the sea.
>
> This testimony is written on their stones and on the walls of their peaks. From the deepest, the highest must come to its height[240]

When the dithyrambist says that "the highest mountains" arise from "the deepest" parts of "the sea," he means the greatest elevation of spirit and the clearest vision of Self arise from the deepest depth of the subconscious wherein reside the most titanic subliminal emotions.

The Vision and the Enigma

On the Discovery of the Dead Self and the Meaning of Its Resurrection

> Then, suddenly, I heard a dog howl near me.[241]

The metaphor "dog" is used to indicate pain. It is an example of a gesture that cannot be guessed. Instead, the actor must look for its use in one of Nietzsche's other writings, which, in this case, can be found in *Gay Science*.

> *My Dog.*—I have given a name to my pain, and call it "a dog,"—it is just as faithful, just as importunate and shameless, just as entertaining, just as wise, as any other dog— and I can domineer over it, and vent my bad humour on it, as others do with their dogs, servants, and wives.[242]

Continuing with this dithyramb,

> Had I ever heard a dog howl that way? My thoughts ran back. Yes! When I was a child, in my most distant childhood: ...[243]

Throughout the entire drama, I have never found an instance in which a word is used literally instead of metaphorically except here with the word "child." The word is used very extensively to indicate the supra-Self as a new beginning, which makes sense, and it is used to indicate that which is begotten or created through willful hard work. But neither of those make sense in the context of the particular conflict indicated here in this dithyramb. All that makes sense in this dithyramb is a literal reference to a time in life when one was a child. Of course, that also indicates a state of mind that exists within the actor: a time when he was a child.

> *But there was a man lying there*! And there! The dog, jumping, balking, whimpering; now it saw me coming - then it howled again, then it *cry* - had I ever heard a dog cry so for help?
>
> And truly, I had never seen the like of what I saw. I saw a young shepherd writhing, choking, quivering, his face distorted; and a heavy, black serpent was hanging out of his mouth.
>
> Had I ever seen so much disgust and pale horror on a face before? Had he perhaps gone to sleep? Then the serpent crawled into his throat - and there it had taken a strong hold with its bite.[244]

To my mind, this is the moment when the actor reaches his deepest, truest, and most original suffering Self after having dug his way through a long series of supra-Selves. At every step, within every supra-Self that the actor has grown through, this demon appears but it appears out of reach — until the actor reaches the deepest supra-Self, where the "head" of the "snake" is within reach. The metaphor of the "snake" is used to indicate this long history because it is a demon that has permeated the actor's being throughout a long lineage of devolved egos and selves. This is the moment when the actor has reached back along the long devolution that initiated his descent from whole individuation into dismembered sub-individuation. This is the moment that initiated that long trail of disintegration of mind. The actor has travelled back in time and is now in real-time with a life-changing moment. And what does the dithyramb instruct him to do?

> My hands pulled at the serpent, and pulled:
> — in vain! I could not pull the serpent out of
> his throat. Then I shouted: 'Bite! Bite!
>
> 'Take its head off! Bite!' — so it screamed
> out of me, my horror, my hatred, my disgust,
> my compassion, all my good and bad
> screamed out of me with a single scream.[245]

"Its head off! Bite!" reflects an instinct that will come to you only in that moment. In my own experience, the instinct that came to me what not "Bite" but rather "Jump." Later, while in the moment, when I pondered and looked for another instinct that might be a better match for the gesture "Bite," I did find something deeper inside me that was more ruthless and final, but "Jump" also worked well for me. Whatever instinct comes to you, the resultant action should constitute a denial of this *primordial* demonic moment within your being. You must find a way to contradict the existence of this demon. If you succeed, it will exit your being. Notice also that "tugging" at the snake will not raise it into consciousness. Instead, you should try either to "bite" its head off or "jump" over the abyss.

> But the shepherd bit as my cry had urged
> him; he bit with a good bite! He spat far away
> the head of the serpent — and sprang up.[246]

Specifically, what you will feel is something like a regurgitation as the titanic and afflictive emotion literally exits your being as if through your throat. That, in any case, has been my experience. And it is nothing less than an exorcism.

The other event that will result from this very fundamental contradiction will be like an ascension as you are raised up above the principium individuationis into supra-individuation because suffering provides a springboard, and very deep suffering provides a very powerful springboard that will raise you even higher.

In order to understand the event represented in this dithyramb, it is necessary to form a concept of what is happening.

I have written previously that Nietzsche's Übermensch is both an idea that enables becoming within a world of being (supra-Self) and a place within your heart and mind that exists high above the principium individuations (supra-individuation). This dithyramb speaks to that place.

There are two instances in Nietzsche's writings that help to form a concept of it. I have already written about one in the hermeneutics. It is Schopenhauer's concept of man sitting in a rowboat atop a sea of emotion and relying on that boat to keep him afloat atop that sea, to keep him individuated from it. And this paradigm will translate into an easily intuitable personal experience if you just imagine what happens when you approach some terrific fear within yourself and then allow yourself to momentarily be overcome by that fear. What happens is you fall from the boat, no longer protected by it, no longer sitting atop the sea of emotion but rather falling into it, into the abyss in which there is no light, no consciousness. This is that moment which is represented in this dithyramb, the moment *after which* the fall has occurred. And you have spent all this time pursuing your supra-Self and descending deeper and deeper into the subconscious to reach it. Now you've reached it. And it is a critical moment. An eternity of suffering follows from one point of the moment (entering the abyss) and another eternity of not suffering, free from the grip of our demons, follows from another point (transcending the abyss).

> 'This long lane backwards: it continues for an eternity. And that long lane forward — that is another eternity.
>
> 'They contradict each other, these paths; they directly abut on one another: and it is here, at this gateway that they come together. The name of the gateway is written above': "Moment".
>
> 'But if one followed them further — and ever further and further on: do you think, dwarf, that these paths would be in eternally contradictory?'[247]

The other instance in which Nietzsche writes about the Übermensch *as a place within your heart and mind* is in *The Genealogy of Morals*, as I cited previously, where he writes about the bad conscience. He viewed the bad conscience as a terrible illness but in the sense that pregnancy is an illness.

> Undoubtedly the bad conscience is an illness, but an illness like pregnancy is an illness.[248]

He regarded the bad conscience as a profound and historic malady that also presented a condition out of which something good will arise, provided a cure could be found. And the cure he found was in his discovery of the Übermensch.

I am not going to quote the entire passage he wrote about the origin of the bad conscience as I have already done so in the hermeneutics. But, because I consider it vital to understanding his idea of the Übermensch *as a place within the heart and mind of man* that cures the bad conscience, I will cite again the important single paragraph. Afterward, we will come back to an explanation of this place in the heart and mind of man.

> Let us immediately add that this fact of an animal ego turning against itself, taking part against itself, produced in the world so novel, profound, unheard-of, problematic, inconsistent, and *pregnant* a phenomenon, that the aspect of the world was radically altered thereby. In sooth, only divine spectators could have appreciated the drama that then began, and whose end baffles conjecture as yet—a drama too subtle, too wonderful, too paradoxical to warrant its undergoing a non-sensical and unheeded

performance on some random grotesque planet! Henceforth man is to be counted as one of the most unexpected and sensational lucky shots in the game of the "big baby" ["great child," per Kaufmann] of Heracleitus, whether he be called Zeus or Chance— he awakens on his behalf the interest, excitement, hope, almost the confidence, of his being the harbinger and forerunner of something, of man being no end, but only a stage, an interlude, a bridge, a great promise.[249]

I would direct the reader's attention to the last statement he wrote above, "he gives rise to an interest, a tension, a hope, almost a certainty, as if with him something were announcing and preparing itself, as if man were not a goal but only a way, an episode, a bridge, a great promise."

Anyone who is familiar with a reading of *Thus Spoke Zarathustra* will recognize the words man "is not a goal but only a way, an episode, a bridge, a great promise . . ." as a direct reference to Nietzsche's Übermensch.

But how is something good made to come from the bad conscience? To answer that, first, we need to clarify exactly what is meant by the bad conscience. He does not mean guilty conscience *only*. I think the clarification is best achieved by going back to Schopenhauer's paradigm of man sitting in a rowboat and relying on it to protect him from falling into the sea of emotion on which the boat keeps man afloat. When some horrific and titanic emotion comes along and shakes him out of the boat, the principium individuationis is destroyed and man becomes sub-individuated, which means tormented, among many other conditions. If such an individual who experiences such a shattering could have discharged the emotion instead of allowing to turn inward, there would have been no shattering. And this is what happens when people shout out at the instance of fear, or cry out at the instance of pain, and so on. But when the discharge is blocked, and the torment is turned inward upon oneself, that is the bad conscience from which something good can come, and I mean specifically Nietzsche's Übermensch.

But the bad conscience must be *redeemed* if something good is to come from it. And how is it redeemed? Through laughter!

Laughter is a metaphor that is used to indicate the sensation and the elevation that results from mounting and executing the springboard that inheres in suffering, once you find it. It is the moment you rise above the abyss into which your suffering pulls you so that you are no longer pulled into that abyss. On the contrary, every time you approach the same abyss afterward, you will rise up above the principium individuationis, by which I mean the fine line between individuation and sub-individuation, Schopenhauer's boat in which man sits safely and reliably atop a sea of emotion.

According to Newton's Third Law of Motion, every action has an equal and opposite reaction. Apparently, within human nature, the same is true. The action within man that has an equal and opposite action is the action that pulls him into the abyss of suffering after the principium individuationis is shattered. No amount of explanation by me of "laughter" will sufficiently induce the phenomenon within you. For that, you must spend some time at the precipice of the abyss, which is within your own subconscious. And as you become more courageous and learn to incorporate the subconscious into your consciousness so that you experience the abyss head-on and actually plumb it, it will come to you, hopefully. It is an instinct, and, if you are human, you should be able to find it. I should also like to point out that the extent of the ascension that results from this flight out of the abyss is directly equal to the extent of your ability to plumb that abyss. But this is not an instinct that will come to you without working at it. As I said, you must travel within yourself via your will to the precipice of the abyss out of which the wings of the Phoenix *become necessary*. You must create the need. And even after you create the need and the bird shows its head, you must lift it up out of yourself and you must mount it. You must develop it. If you do, the effect is to raise you up above the principium individuationis. That place within yourself is what Nietzsche calls Übermensch.

The discovery within the subconscious of the gateway into the supra-conscious, via the springboard that is to be found in suffering, renders all suffering meaningful. And it is this gateway that makes proto-tragedy meaningful as well because tragedy enables the difficult passage to the precipice where the springboard appears. Finding the springboard that inheres in suffering is the reason that the actor has spent all this time trying to incorporate the subconscious into his consciousness. And the ascension unto supra-individuated being is the *meaning* of his efforts. It is the meaning of life as a willful process of growth by which the limits of individuation are extended. In other words, the reason you want to extend the limits of Self via creation of the supra-Self, specifically the limits of Self to incorporate difficult sensation, is to create the need out of which the springboard that inheres in suffering is brought into play with the instincts and then using that springboard to ascend into supra-individuation, which is a place within the heart and mind wherein the limits of Self have been categorically transcended. And that categorical transcendence is the very definition of genius.

After you spend years practicing how to redeem human suffering in this way and succeeding in different measures, you will begin to change. Pursuing your supra-Self, you will become more and more of who you really are, as if being reborn, resurrected. And with that resurrection as proof, you will understand this process of incorporating the subconscious into the conscious and struggling to free yourself from the grip of your demons *as life itself.* How could there be a resurrection if there was no life to make it happen? And we are very fortunate to have found our way in this again and to have this map, this drama. And more and more, you will ascend incrementally into the supra-conscious, high above the principium individuationis (PI), into supra-individuation, until one day, you will find yourself spending more time above the PI than below it — or on it, as wholesome individuation. Then, you will read the following idioms (from the dithyramb *Of Manly Prudence*) and see a poetic reflection of your innermost being.

> Not the ascension into the heights; the fall into the abyss is the terrible thing!
>
> The abyss where the look shoots *downward* and the hand grasps *upward*. There the heart grows giddy through its two-way will.
>
> Ah, friends, do you also divine my heart's two-way will?
>
> This, this is *my* abyss and my danger, that my look shoots into the heights and my hand

> wants to hold on to the depths and rely thereon.
>
> My will clings to man, with chains I bind myself to man (the principium individuationis), because I am pulled upwards to the Supra-man (above the principium-individuation): for my other will wants to take me there.[250]

To ascend entirely unto supra-individuation is the love and ardor of all your work. That is the meaning of all your struggles in life. So that when you go back one day and read the dithyramb Of the Thousand and One Goals, you will see this one goal in all human struggle: finding the springboard in all human suffering, alighting on the wings of the Phoenix that arise from within that "volcano," that is depicted in the dithyramb Of Great Events, and ascension into supra-individuation.

Returning to the idioms of the dithyramb we are discussing here, which is Of the Vision and the Riddle, after the actor "bites off the head of the snake," he springs up from a previously "dead" state, and then he has a vision.

> 'Take off its head! Bite!' — so it screamed out of me, my horror, my hatred, my disgust, my compassion, all my good and bad screamed out of me with a single scream.
>
> You daring ones around me! You venturers and adventurers, and those of you who have embarked with cunning sails on undiscovered seas! You who enjoy riddles!

> Solve for me the riddle that I beheld, interpret to me the vision of the most lonesome man!
>
> For it was a vision and a foresight: *what* did I behold in parable? And *who* is it that must come one day?
>
> *Who* is the shepherd into whose throat the serpent thus crawled? *Who* is the man into whose throat all that is heaviest, blackest will thus crawl?
>
> The shepherd, however, bit as my cry had urged him; he bit with a strong bite! He spat far away the serpent's head — and sprang up.
>
> No longer a shepherd, no longer man — a transformed being, a being surrounded with light, *that laughed*! Never yet on earth had a man laughed as *he* laughed!
>
> O, my brothers, I heard a laughter that was no human laughter — and now a thirst gnaws at me, a longing that is never allayed.
>
> My longing for this laughter gnaws me: oh how can I still endure to live! And how could I endure to die now![251]

You will achieve this redemption incrementally, not all at once. When you do, you will see a vision of your Self beyond all suffering, high above the principium individuationis.

And please note accurately that I am speaking of an apprehension of Self, not a concept of Self, beyond all suffering. In those many moments, it is important that you ask yourself "what is this vision?" That vision of your Self beyond all suffering, beyond good and evil, is the meaning, the goal, the purpose, of all life within you, all struggling, all loving. And you need to grasp that.

> The shepherd, however, bit as my cry had urged him; he bit with a strong bite! He spat far away the serpent's head — and sprang up.
>
> No longer a shepherd, no longer man — a transformed being, a being surrounded with light, *that laughed*! Never yet on earth had a man laughed as *he* laughed![252]

This is another mythopoeic moment, which you yourself must answer.

> Solve for me the riddle that I beheld, interpret to me the vision of the most lonesome man!
>
> For it was a vision and a foresight: *what* did I behold in parable? And *who* is it that must come one day?
>
> *Who* is the shepherd into whose throat the serpent thus crawled? *Who* is the man into whose throat all that is heaviest, blackest will thus crawl?[253]

Lastly, notice the last line of the last idiom above: "oh how do I endure still to live! And how could I endure to die now!" This is yet another riddling trick by Nietzsche. When he says "how do I endure still to live," he means how do I allow my Ego to go on living after this because, with this event, you have seen how suffering, which is hidden away by your Ego, leads directly to the ascension you so mightily desire. And when he says "how could I endure to die now," he means, with this discovery of this gateway unto the ascension, there is nothing that you could want more in life than to enter this gateway and traverse this ascension. And now that you know the way, the worst thing that could happen now would be to die (literally, for the body to expire) and lose this opportunity.

And finally, this dithyramb also teaches something about the idea of an eternally recurring world, but I choose to explain this idea to you via a different dithyramb, Of the Convalescent. Afterward, then we will come back to this dithyramb, Of the Vision and the Riddle, and explain how the idea of an eternally recurring world plays out within it.

The Spirit of Gravity

On the Tendency to Revert to the View Afforded by the Existing Self After Discovery of the Supra-Self

> He who teaches men to fly will defy all boundary stones; he will see all boundaries themselves fly into the air; he will rename the earth – "the light one."
>
> The ostrich runs faster than the fastest horse, but when he grows heavy with burden, he plunges his head into the burdensome earth: that is how it is with the man who cannot yet fly.
>
> Earth and life are heavy to him: and so *wills* the Spirit of Gravity! But he who would become light and a bird must love himself - thus do *I* teach.[254]

The metaphor "to fly" indicates a state of ascension above the principium individuationis (PI). To fly means to rise above the PI.

Often, what will happen when you succeed in redeeming this or that subliminal torment and raising yourself up above it, you will then fall back down to the lowly state out of which you rose wherein the image of Self is less vivid, less delineated, and the sense of Self less pronounced. That penchant of human nature, which is directly related to the abyss into which you have fallen and is therefore indigenous to a sub-individuated nature, is something you will fight endlessly. It will even permeate your way of thinking. Interactions with the Spirit of Gravity, which is called a spirit because its pervasiveness will drag you down regardless of how far from the abyss you have risen, appear throughout the drama in numerous dithyrambs, like the last one we just examined.

I have found that the most effective way to fight it, as this dithyramb instructs, is to learn to love your Self. And by love, I mean a strong desire for one's Self because the desire will literally draw you toward your Self. All loving is a strong component of the will to power. "Amor fati," or love of fate, is another example.

> And truly, to *learn* to love oneself is no commandment for today or for tomorrow. Rather, of all the arts, this is the finest, subtlest, final, and most patient.[255]

Since it is the supra-Self that the actor is pursuing, and since the supra-Self appears to him as a series of unfolding images and apprehensions, one after the other, it is not possible to vow to learn to love oneself, if, as soon as the actor makes his vow, then he discovers a deeper and higher supra-Self. When that happens, he must learn a new vow to love the new supra-Self that he has recently uncovered. Therefore, the actor is constantly relearning love of Self. And let me say this, as you delve deeper and deeper into the subconscious and your vision and *sense* of the Self becomes more intense, it becomes easier to learn to love Self. The tendency to fall back down into chaos and away from Self diminishes significantly — to a point of no return.

Another dithyramb, Of Reading and Writing, says the following:

> And when I saw my devil, I found him serious, thorough, profound, solemn: it was the Spirit of Gravity - through him all things fall.
>
> One does not slay by anger but by laughter. Come, let us slay the Spirit of Gravity![256]

I have already explained what is meant by the metaphors "laughter" and "flying." When you approach the precipice of any abyss within you, find the springboard that inheres in all suffering, raise up the bird of Phoenix, mount its wings, and rise up above the principium individuations, that, too, will nullify the Spirit of Gravity — in an immediate way. And in the long run, repeated ascensions unto supra-individuation will also degrade the Spirit of Gravity. But "flying" and "laughter" will not battle the Spirit of Gravity as effectively as love of Self does.

The Convalescent

At the Moment of Raising Long-Repressed Suffering from the Subconscious into Consciousness

As difficult as it will be for you to believe me, I assure you there will come a day when you will literally summon up from the depths of your subconscious that which has caused you the deepest, gravest, and most enduring suffering — willfully, just like that.

> Up, my most abysmal thought, up from my depth! I am your rooster and morning dawn, you sleeping snake that has slept too long: Up! Up! My voice shall soon crow you awake!
>
> Unchain the fetters on your ears and listen to my command because I want to hear you! Up! Up! I have enough thunder to make the very graves listen!
>
> And rub the sleep from your eyes and all that makes you dumb and blind! Hear me with your eyes, too: my voice is a cure even for those born blind.

And once you are awake you will stay awake forever. It is not *my* way to awaken great-grandmothers from sleep and then tell them to — go back to sleep!

You move, you stretch, you wheeze? Up! Up! You will not gasp, you will speak to me! Zarathustra calls you, Zarathustra the godless!

I, Zarathustra, the advocate of life, the advocate of suffering, the advocate of the idea that everything that goes away also comes back — I call you, my most abysmal thought!

Glory is mine! You are coming — I hear you! My abyss *speaks*, I have brought my deepest depth into the light!

Glory is mine! Come here! Give me your hand — ha! Leave me be! Ha, ha! — Disgust, disgust, disgust — woe is mine![257]

And the reason it will be difficult for you to believe me that this will happen is because you will spend years trying to reach your deepest suffering and you will employ many methods to raise it. But none of your methods will work — until you learn the methods that are taught in these dithyrambs: creation of the supra-Self via mythopoeia and extensive rumination and proto-tragedy.

And remember that raising yourself up out of the chaos of thought and passion that exists within you will empower you.

And empowerment *creates a need* for more empowerment, *instinctively*, which will precipitate the phenomenon of dissonance. The dissonance that results from extreme empowerment will enable you to look more deeply into the subconscious to the point wherein one day you will literally summon up your demons. And they will come! And when they do, you will experience that day as salvation.

When you do finally embrace and incorporate into your consciousness that which has tormented you the longest while hiding within your subconscious, something extraordinary will happen. First, in addition to achieving the deepest and most extreme proximity with your truest Self than you have ever before achieved, you will also experience a profoundly transformative state of relief. This should not be difficult to understand. It is an experience similar to the relief you feel when you cry; you always feel better *because* you cried. It is the same in this instance, except that the pain you experience runs so extreme and so deep that the resulting relief will be equally extreme and deep.

Indeed, the relief you will experience will make it seem like suddenly your soul has begun singing to you.

> 'Do not speak further, convalescent" answered his animals, 'but go out to where the world awaits you like a garden.
>
> 'Go out to the roses, the bees, and the flocks of doves! But go out especially to the song birds, to learn *singing* from them!
>
> 'For singing is for the convalescent; the healthy ones like to talk. And when the healthy one wants songs, he wants songs

> different from what the convalescent
> wants.'[258]

What is referenced in the above aphorisms is the re-emergence of the fourth dimension, its resurrection. There was a time, you may remember, when you sought comfort in a metaphysical solace, when you imagined the existence of Self as a concept that was something into which you could find passage through an extreme form of contemplation and focus, as was represented in the first dithyramb, Zarathustra's Prologue. But now you have found a much more powerful comfort, as represented in this dithyramb. Indeed, you have created your own world, a real world, via mythopoeia and the supra-Self. And now you sense a great impending freedom, which you will learn about in the next dithyramb, Of the Great Longing, as you sense a final, definitive escape from the bad conscience.

Regarding the idea that the world recurs eternally, there is more than one instance within the drama when it is referenced and taught, but this instance, in this dithyramb, is a major teaching moment.

What you need to understand is that you are creating a world within yourself. Every step you take toward that creation *is lasting*. The demon you summon at will is now and forever retrievable.

> And once you are awake you will stay awake
> forever. It is not my way to awaken great-
> grandmothers from sleep and then tell them
> to — go back to sleep![259]

And when you find the springboard in that demon, that suffering, and use it to rise above the principium individuationis, that ascension, too, will be retrievable. Everything that you have worked toward and achieved is retrievable, repeatable. Indeed, everything in the world *that you have created* will recur again and again, just as the past recurred within you again and again, as unending torment. And no amount of explanation that I provide here is going to impart that idea to you. It must come to you through your own doing, through your own willing, through your own experience. When it does, you will know that this moment in which you summoned your demons into consciousness may fade but then it will recur, at will. You may return to this moment again and again, through your own willing.

> 'For your animals know well, O Zarathustra, who you are and must become: take heed, *you are the teacher of the eternal recurrence,* that is now *your* fate!
>
> 'That you must be the first to teach this doctrine - how could this great fate not also be your greatest danger and illness!
>
> 'Behold, we know what you teach: that all things eternally return and ourselves with them, and that we have already existed an infinite number of times before and all things with us.
>
> 'You teach that there is a great year of becoming, a prodigy of a year: it must, like an hour-glass, turn over again and again, so that it runs and runs out anew:

'so that all those years are like one another in the greatest and also in the smallest, so that we ourselves, every great year, are like ourselves in the greatest and also in the smallest.

'And if you would die now, O Zarathustra: behold, we know also know how you would then speak to yourself - but your animals beseech you not to die yet!

'You would say, and without trembling, but rather buoyant with bliss: for a great weight and worry would be taken from you, you most patient one!

'"Now I die and disappear," you would say, "and in an moment I am nothing. Souls are as mortal as bodies.

'"But the knot of causes in which I am entwined returns — it will create me again! I myself belong to the causes of the eternal return.

'"I will return, with this sun, with this earth, with this eagle, with this serpent — *not* to a new life or a better life or a similar life:

'"I will return eternally to this identical and self-same life, in the greatest and also in the smallest, to teach once more the eternal return of all things,

> "'to speak again the word of the great noontide of earth and man, to again proclaim to men the Supra-man.[260]

Also, you will understand that, though your demons, your subliminal suffering, have escaped you (or you them) in any one moment, your demons are, in fact, not gone — not until you have redeemed them. Consequently, it will become difficult to avoid them. Eventually, knowing what you now know from this dithyrambic experience, your demons will rise to the surface more easily, which will cause your Ego, which has previously protected you from the subconscious, to collapse more easily.

> "'I spoke my word, I broke by my word: so will my eternal fate have it - as preacher I perish![261]

After living through this dithyramb called The Convalescent, you will also know that bringing your demons into consciousness is a very, very good thing. And for that reason, you will also understand that proto-tragedy is a good thing, that bringing the Ego to the point of collapse so that you may reunite with your long-lost Self is a very good thing.

> The hour has now come when he who is going under shall bless himself. Thus *ends* Zarathustra's going under![262]

Lastly, when you reach the deepest point in your subconscious, as represented in the dithyramb Of the Vision and the Riddle, then, too, you will realize that the demon from which you have suffered for an eternity will remain eternally existent, forever haunting you, *unless and until* you find the springboard within it and rise above the principium individuationis via that springboard. You will know that, and you will use that knowledge to *raise* that demon and then transcend it.

From the dithyramb Of the Vision and the Riddle:

'Look at this gateway, dwarf!' I continued: 'it has two faces. Two roads come together here: no one has ever gone to their end.

'This long lane backwards: it continues for an eternity. And that long lane forward — that is another eternity.

'They contradict each other, these paths; they directly abut on one another: and it is here, at this gateway that they come together. The name of the gateway is written above': "Moment".

'But if one followed them further — and ever further and further on: do you think, dwarf, that these paths would be in eternally contradictory?'

'Everything straight lies,' murmured the dwarf contemptuously. 'All truth is crooked, time itself is a circle.'

'You Spirit of Gravity!' I said angrily, 'do not take it too lightly! Or I will leave you squatting where you squat, lame foot — and I carried you *high*!

'Observe," I continued, "This Moment!' From the gateway, This Moment, a long, eternal lane runs *backwards*: an eternity lies behind us.

'Must not all things that *can* run have already run along this lane? Must not all things that *can* happen *have* already happened, been done, passed by?

'And if everything has already existed: what do you think of this moment, dwarf? Must not this gateway, too, have already existed?

'And are not all things closely bound together that This Moment draws after it all things to come? *Consequently* —itself also?

'For all things that *can* run along this road forward — *must* also run once again.

'And this slow spider that creeps along in the moonlight, and this moonlight itself, and you and I at this gateway whispering together, whispering of eternal things — must we not have already been there?

' — and must we not return and run in that other lane out in front of us, down that long,

> gruesome lane - must we not return eternally?'[263]

Again, I cannot impart knowledge of an eternally recurring world via a concept; it is something you must apprehend yourself. And, when you *live through* this dithyramb, The Convalescent, you will apprehend the idea of an eternally recurring world.

The Great Longing

On the Emergence of the Lust for Power

This dithyramb is a representation of a passion that you will have never before experienced. This is an entirely new, undiscovered, and unchartered passion.

Toward the end of the drama, specifically after you have reached the point wherein you summon up your demons and bring them into the full light and then mount the springboard that inheres in them and rise up above the principium individuationis, there the actor discovers a state of utter freedom, specifically freedom from the limits and boundaries of individuation. That ascension will trigger a great longing, a passionate and moving yearning, for supra-individuation, a state of being in which the will and the spirit have become utterly unfettered.

Previously, I defined the will to power as any passion or instinct or inner conflict that assisted in your effort to apprehend your Self (or supra-Self). But now the will to power moves its focus beyond the numerous states of being defined by the supra-Self, beyond all individuation, where there are no limits and no boundaries.

Life reveals itself in the process, and now we see why the will to power desires Self so arduously: in order to transcend it. Freedom from the limits of individuation is a greater manifestation of the will to power than is the desire for Self. And Nietzsche himself defined the will to power as a will to freedom.

In the *Genealogy of Morals*, he speaks of the will to power as an instinct for freedom when speaking about the genealogy of the bad conscience.

> ... *instinct of freedom* (to use my own language, the will to power)....[264]

I do not want to sidetrack you from the point I am trying to make here, that Nietzsche defines his theory of the will to power as an instinct for freedom, by quoting the entire text surrounding this quote and then getting into a discussion of the bad conscience again. Suffice it to say that the development of the bad conscience constituted a profound loss of freedom within the individual who became afflicted with it. Therefore, the overcoming of this particular affliction arouses a primeval and intense anticipation of a restoral of that freedom.

As I said, with the summoning of your demons into the light, you will sense impending freedom from their grip, and that sense will instigate an intense and somewhat consuming longing for freedom. And that longing will drive you ever further on the path that has taken you through all that you have experienced through this drama. That longing will invigorate the will to power you have developed. And your journey to your deepest Self, which will culminate in the upcoming dithyramb called *The Cry of Distress*, will now become hastened. Life will move much more quickly now with this great longing.

This dithyramb is a good example of how some dithyrambs are utterly indecipherable to someone who has not undertaken the drama and experienced the mystical phenomena that are necessarily traversed on this journey that has been created via this new art form.

This dithyramb teaches that new winds are blowing, that the actor must heed those winds, learn how to capture them with his sails, and learn to move in the direction toward which they now move him. This dithyramb is also a recollection of the many achievements the actor has accomplished along the way.

One idiom recalls what the actor achieved in the last exegesis we just examined.

> O my soul, I taught you how to persuade so that you persuade the belly of being to come to you: *(as in the willful summoning of a demon; see: The Convalescent)* like the sun that persuades even the sea to its height.[265]

Other idioms reference the newfound longing itself.

> O my soul, you now stand exuberant and heavy, a vine with swelling udders and full clusters of golden-brown grapes:

> Filled and weighed down by your happiness, waiting in abundance and yet ashamed of your waiting.

> O my soul, nowhere is there a soul more loving and more comprehensive and more extensive! Where could future and past be closer together than with you?[266]

"Where could future and past be closer together than with you?" is a reference to the fact that the subconscious (the "past") and the growing supra-conscious (the "future") are both now clearly perceptible to the actor's mind and senses. And in the next aphorisms, we see that the actor's spirit has become so overfull with joy and with power that he now looks out over the "sea" of emotions toward which he no longer feels an antipathy with the hope of finding opportunities to rise higher still.

> O my soul, I understand the smile of your melancholy: your superabundance itself now stretches out longing hands!
>
> Your abundance looks out over roaring seas and seeks and waits; the longing of the superabundance looks out of your smiling heavenly eyes![267]

And lastly, with convalescence, so, too, does the fourth dimension become revitalized so that serenity and beauty themselves spring forth from within the soul of the actor, and all things around him in the outer world as well become infused with that beauty and that serenity. As I said earlier, with convalescence, it is as if the actor's soul now sings to him. And the teaching by which that restoration occurred is the greatest gift that "Zarathustra" could bestow. Indeed, with that gift, Zarathustra's cup has become empty again. Remember that the whole point of Zarathustra's "down-going" was so that his overflowing cup could become empty again. "Behold! This cup wants to be empty again, and Zarathustra wants to be man again."[268]

O my soul, now I have given you everything and even my last possession, and all my hands have become empty by you: – *that I bade you sing, (i.e., the fourth dimension is now reborn)* behold, that was my last thing to give![269]

The Cry of Distress

On the Discovery of the Compelling Voice of the Dead Self

The Cry of Distress depicts yet another mystical experience.

In the dithyramb called The Higher Man, which follows this dithyramb soon after, the actor will have reached the deepest depth of his subconscious and found his truest and most original supra-Self, the first Self from which the long history of devolution commenced. And with that encounter, he will have also discovered his truest and most original suffering. Most importantly, he will have found the *voice* of his deepest, truest Self, which is different from an idea or a sense of Self. And that voice will begin to speak to his consciousness clearly and *exigently*. In this dithyramb, which precedes the final encounter with the "higher man," *as the actor approaches his true Self*, he will experience, literally, a cry of distress. He will discover the voice of his deepest Self, which now speaks to him directly, and it speaks to him of that from which he has suffered for an eternity. Specifically, it will speak to him from deep within the pain and horror that has lay dormant but haunting within his subconscious for an eternity. Most importantly, that cry of distress will summon him to move more closely to the source of that cry. And the spirit of doom and gloom, which is the "Spirit of Gravity," will encourage him along that way, toward the cry of distress.

I have already explained who the prophet is. The prophet is the very prevalent and powerful inclination to think that all this work is meaningless and not worth its undertaking. The "prophet" is also the inclination to become drawn toward and entrenched within abyssal suffering, that place within the heart and mind that lies below the principium individuationis. That "prophet" will kick in at this encounter with the truest Self and impress upon the actor that it is incumbent upon him to move closer to it.

Keep in mind also that, in contrast to the "prophet," which is tantamount to the "spirit of gravity," is the spirit of laughter, which has taught the actor to learn to fly above all abysses, to find the springboard that inheres in all suffering and use it to rise above the principium individuations so as to redeem suffering.

Just as the tendency to become bogged down in abyssal suffering portends a future of eternal suffering, which is a possibility, the tendency to fly high above the abyss also portends a future also, but a future of eternal relief, which is also a possibility.

The prophet will also impress upon the actor that, despite compelling him to move closer to the abyss, going forward with an even closer proximity to Self is useless because any relief from suffering that might derive from overcoming that suffering has already occurred. There is no further relief, it says. This is false, but the actor will be swayed by it nonetheless.

This dithyramb teaches the actor to instead heed the "prophecy" of the inclination to fly high above the abyss.

Among Daughters of the Desert

On the Efficacy of Morale During a Period of No Growth

As the actor approaches a deeper and more percipient supra-Self, he will become frightened of the demonic reality that is coming to the fore, and that fear will slow down the process of life to the point wherein it will stop intermittently. The metaphor "desert" that is used in this dithyramb alludes to a place where nothing grows. This dithyramb addresses that conflict and teaches him to rouse his morale, which will refresh and assist his desire to resume life and continue forward, and to look for courage, which will also assist his ability to go forward against his growing fear.

This is a good time for me to point out that, though some dithyrambs appear in an order that precludes any understanding unless the conflict that is being represented has been entered into by the actor and, in some cases, already resolved by him, other dithyrambs — or some parts of some other dithyrambs — are not precluded by such conditions simply because all metaphors represent a human condition that is plausibly embodiable. They all depict reality.

This dithyramb appears near the end of the drama. Yet I was able to understand and rehearse the following idioms long before I reached the point in the drama where they appear, which is after reaching the Higher Man.

> Ha! Up now, dignity!
>
> Moral dignity! European dignity!
>
> Blow, blow again,
>
> Bellows of virtue!
>
> Ha!
>
> Roar once more,
>
> Roar morally!
>
> As a moral lion
>
> Roar before the daughters of the desert! [270]

Taking just these idioms and rehearsing them, as I did, I was able to summon something that is like morale but runs much deeper and discharges much more forcefully. It literally took my breath away because it carried me high above the principium individuationis. This is the "lion" that is mentioned so many times in the drama. Presently, I have no common name for this "lion roar." I have never heard anyone refer to it by name, and, except in Nietzsche's dithyrambic drama, I have never read about it, with one exception. The Persian prophet Zoroaster, after whom Nietzsche's drama is named, was the first person to teach righteousness. But Zoroaster was a moralist and he taught righteousness as something that deeply invigorated the moral fiber of a human being. Under

Zoroaster, righteousness became the bulwark of moral thought and living. I believe that Zoroaster taught a moral version of lion-roar. I believe the righteousness that Zoroaster taught and the lion-roar that Nietzsche teaches both come from the same place within the depths of the human soul, but I do not believe they are the same thing. Nietzsche's lion-roar is unbridled, and Zoroaster's righteousness is confined to the limits of moral thought.

Lion-roar becomes very significant when it is summoned through the supra-Self. It enlivens the supra-Self, which is always in an aborning stage of life, while, at the same time, elevating the actor to a place above the principium individuationis. In my experience, I was amazed that I could willfully summon the lion-roar. And secondly, I was amazed at the effect it had on me. I do not think I have to explain the effect of morale on human being. But consider this: inasmuch as I was able to summon lion-roar, I was also able to summon more of it and from a deeper depth. And for a dejected spirit, it was like drinking from a fountain of youth. And more specifically, it took me beyond the limits of individuated being and into supra-individuation, which was my first experience with supra-individuation as a place within my heart and mind, as opposed to an idea of a deeper Self lying beyond the horizon, as I have previously explained.

To explain further, there is nothing frightening about lion roar, just as there is nothing frightening about morale. And insofar as I had learned — from this dithyramb — the value of willfully summoning lion-roar, I summoned it deeply, like a flood. And the flood literally transported me beyond the limits of my Self. This, by the way, is why people become so enchanted with love and being in love. There is nothing frightening about feeling in love, so people willingly allow themselves to be taken away with it. And the intensity of love transports them beyond their Self, which imparts a sense of being raised above and free of the limits of Self. Therein lies the will to power in love.

The other metaphor in this dithyramb that I rendered with little effort was the metaphor "desert," especially its use in the very last idiom.

> The desert grows: woe to him who harbors deserts![271]

I knew that the "desert" was a period of no growth. For me, that did not require much thought. And so, whenever I entered a period of stalled growth, whatever the reason, I would summon up some lion-roar, and I was able to move forward due to that lion-roar. The above idiom also warns that a period of stalled growth can also lead to a deterioration of previously achieved growth, not that you would forget how to do what you had previously learned to do but that you would have to do it all over again. Therefore, it was important to quickly resolve the conflict that leads to a condition within the spirit that becomes like a "desert" and to move on quickly as well.

However, it was not until I had reached the dithyramb called the "Higher Man" that the full impact of this lesson in the dithyramb called "Among the Daughters of the Desert" came to me. When the actor reaches the Higher Man, life will become much more difficult. By life, I mean the process of growth that is driven by the will to power, the process of growth that leads to an ever more vivid and more real apprehension of Self. And when the process stops, the actor must summon lion-roar in order to move forward, *and he must summon it through the aborning supra-Self.* Doing so will invigorate that supra-Self and empower it to fight extreme adversity. And there is one more thing that will assist in going forward — courage. But it must be courage that comes from within whatever supra-Self you are working on.

The Sign

On the Lasting Triumph of the Over-Self as the Meaning of Life

In this dithyramb, the actor will realize that he has become entangled in the knot in which his conscience became mired so long ago, and he will find himself grappling with a very strong temptation to unravel the knot. And that would be the wrong course of action. What is crucial at this final juncture is to avoid the temptation to nullify or ease the tension that arose out of this primordial conflict. The actor must find the springboard within this particular monumental tension and then use it to raise himself above the principium individuationis, thereby redeeming the suffering, making it worthwhile, and ascending into the supra-conscience, the place within the heart and mind of man that Nietzsche calls the Übermensch, which, in this case, is not the supra-Self but the over-Self.

Consider what Nietzsche said about the need for suffering and the incorrectness in trying to undo it.

> *The Will to Suffering and the Compassionate.—* Is it to your advantage to be above all compassionate? And is it to the

advantage of the sufferers when you are so? But let us leave the first question for a moment without an answer.— That from which we suffer most profoundly and personally is almost incomprehensible and inaccessible to every one else: in this matter we are hidden from our neighbour even when he eats at the same table with us. Everywhere, however, where we are *noticed* as sufferers, our suffering is interpreted in a shallow way; it belongs to the nature of the emotion of pity to *divest* unfamiliar suffering of its properly personal character: — our "benefactors" lower our value and volition more than our enemies. In most benefits which are conferred on the unfortunate there is something shocking in the intellectual levity with which the compassionate person plays the rôle of fate: he knows nothing of all the inner consequences and complications which are called misfortune for *me* or for *you*! The entire economy of my soul and its adjustment by "misfortune," the uprising of new sources and needs, the closing up of old wounds, the repudiation of whole periods of the past—none of these things which may be connected with misfortune preoccupy the dear sympathiser. He wishes *to succour*, and does not reflect that there is a personal necessity for misfortune; that terror, want, impoverishment, midnight watches, adventures, hazards and mistakes are as

> necessary to me and to you as their opposites,
> yea, that, to speak mystically, the path to
> one's own heaven always leads through the
> voluptuousness of one's own hell.[272]

I call your attention particularly to two statements: "the path to one's own heaven always leads through the voluptuousness of one's own hell," and "the personal necessity of distress. although terrors, deprivations, impoverishments, midnights, adventures, risks, and blunders are as necessary for me and for you as are their opposites."

What he is saying is that there is an actual need for suffering. He is also saying that the road to heaven leads through hell. There actually is a place called heaven. But it does not exist in an afterlife but rather in this life, provided you *work* to ascend into it, to achieve it. And deep, deep suffering, as well as the springboard that inheres in that deep, deep suffering is the gateway through which one finds entrance, provided, again, that you redeem the suffering.

> Would one not be justified in reckoning all
> great men among the *wicked*? This is not so
> easy to demonstrate in the case of
> individuals. They are so frequently capable of
> masterly dissimulation that they very often
> assume the airs and forms of great virtues.
> Often, too, they seriously reverence virtues,
> and in such a way as to be passionately hard
> towards themselves; but as the result of
> cruelty. Seen from a distance such things are
> liable to deceive. Many, on the other hand,
> misunderstand themselves; not infrequently,
> too, a great mission will call forth great

> qualities, e.g. justice. The essential fact is: the greatest men may also perhaps have great virtues, but then they also have the opposites of these virtues. **I believe that it is precisely out of the presence of these opposites and of the feelings they suscitate, that the great man arises, — for the great man is the broad arch which spans two banks lying far apart** (emphasis added). [273]
>
> (Kaufmann/Hollingdale translate the above last statement as "I believe that it is precisely through the presence of opposites and the feelings they occasion that the great man, the bow with the great tension, develops.")[274]

In the above statement, he states that great men may possess great virtues, but, if they do, then they also necessarily possess great vices. This goes to the theory, which Nietzsche never explicitly enunciated but hinted at many times (Heraclitus, on the other hand, stated it explicitly), that all things originate from out of their opposite, such as pleasure out of pain, or, in the matter we are considering in this instance, supra-individuation out of sub-individuation, genius out of madness. It is not so much a cause that makes things happen. Rather, it is need that brings things into the world. And the greatest need precedes the greatest fulfillment. Suffering provides the greatest need. And genius, which is the incarnation of supra-individuation, requires the bow with the greatest tension. It is precisely the abyss into which the actor has finally plumbed, having spent perhaps his entire life acting out Nietzsche's dithyrambic drama to reach this point, that he finds the greatest tension. Undoing that tension at this moment in the drama would undo the potential for redemption that he so desperately seeks. This is the meaning of the aphorism, repeated so many times throughout the drama, that man is a bridge, not a goal, and that the Übermensch, the over-Self is the goal, the meaning of life. The goal in all this discordant growth, this life, is not the beauty of Self that inheres in individuation but rather the freedom of will that inheres in supra-individuation, beyond the limits imposed by Self, which is the very definition of genius.

And it is with this counsel, by the way, that Nietzsche's methodology of healing bifurcates very significantly with traditional psychiatry, which has always taught an untying of the knot, an eventual successful discharge of the afflictive fear or pain, and a restoration of wholesomeness. It is as if life made us a promise when it plunged us into abyssal torment. Redeem the suffering within this abyss, she says, and you will understand why I made you suffer. It was not — for naught, I promise you.

Lastly, the circumstance depicted in this dithyramb is the moment when the actor, after having found the voice of his highest Self, has heard the cry of distress emanating from the original Self that succumbed to the original pain and suffering that caused its demise. And that cry of distress represents a substantial distraction that may potentially draw the actor away from his goal of redeeming all his suffering.

'O you Higher Men, it was of *your* distress that old soothsayer foretold to me yesterday morning,

'he wanted to seduce and tempt me to your distress: O Zarathustra, he said to me, I come to seduce you to your final sin.

393

'To my final sin?' cried Zarathustra and laughed angrily at his own words. '*What* has been reserved for me as my final sin?'

And once more Zarathustra became absorbed in himself and sat down again on the big stone and meditated. Suddenly, he sprang up—

'*Pity! Compassion for the Higher Man*!' he cried out, and his countenance was turned to bronze. 'Well! *That* — has had its time!

'My suffering and my fellow-suffering — what do they matter! Do I strive after *happiness*? I strive after my *work*!

'Well! The lion has come, my children are near, Zarathustra has grown ripe, my hour has come!

'This is *my* morning, *my* day rises: up now, up, you great noontide!'[275]

It is the distraction from the will, which an encounter with one's abyssal torment presents, that must most carefully be avoided.

How is it at all possible for a person to keep to *his* path! Some cry or other is continually calling one aside: our eye then rarely lights on anything without it becoming necessary for us to leave for a moment our own affairs and rush to give assistance. I know there are hundreds of respectable and laudable methods of making me stray *from my course*, and in truth the most "moral" of methods! Indeed, the opinion of the present-day preachers of the morality of compassion goes so far as to imply that just this, and this alone is moral: — to stray from *our* course to that extent and to run to the assistance of our neighbour. I am equally certain that I need only give myself over to the sight of one case of actual distress, and I, too, *am* lost! And if a suffering friend said to me, "See, I shall soon die, only promise to die with me"—I might promise it, just as—to select for once bad examples for good reasons—the sight of a small, mountain people struggling for freedom would bring me to the point of offering them my hand and my life. Indeed, there is even a secret seduction in all this awakening of compassion, and calling for help: our "own way" is a thing too hard and insistent, and too far removed from the love and gratitude of others,—we escape from it and from our most personal conscience, not at all unwillingly, and, seeking security in the conscience of others, we take refuge in the lovely temple of the "religion of pity."[276]

In closing, the willful ascension unto supra-individuation is nothing less than an ascension unto heaven on earth. The extreme and unwavering proximity with Self, which arises actually from a transcendence of Self to the over-Self (rising above the principium individuationis so that one no longer sits atop the sea of emotion but exists high above it so that existence seems weightless), amounts to what we know of "eternal life." All compulsion is eradicated, as is all guilt and self-torment. Bliss is common (to such an extent that it must be sublimated to be made manageable) because all pleasure derives from an overcoming of pain and, in a supra-individuated state of being, all pain, by definition, has been overcome. And this is the only heaven you will ever know, if you reach it — through very hard work.

> The "kingdom of heaven" is a state of the heart—not something to come "beyond the world" or "after death." The whole idea of natural death is absent from the Gospels: death is not a bridge, not a passing; it is absent because it belongs to a quite different, a merely apparent world, useful only as a symbol. The "hour of death" is not a Christian idea — "hours," time, the physical life and its crises have no existence for the bearer of "glad tidings." ... The "kingdom of God" is not something that men wait for: it had no yesterday and no day after tomorrow, it is not going to come at a "millennium"—it is an experience of the heart, it is everywhere *[especially in the fourth dimension, but only if you achieve it]* and it is nowhere *[if you do not.]*[277]

Bibliography

Das griechische Musikdrama; The Greek Music Drama. Translated by Paul Bishop, New York: Contra Mundum Press, 2013.

Human, All Too Human, Part II. Translated by Paul V. Cohn. New York: The MacMillan Company, 1913.

On Moods. Translated by Graham Parkes, *The Journal of Nietzsche Studies: Mood, Music, and the Subject.* Autumn ed., vol. 2, Penn State University Press, 1991, pp. 5-10. Copyright © 1991 Penn State University Press. This article is used by permission of The Pennsylvania State University Press.

The Anti-Christ. Translated by H. L. Mencken. New York: Alfred A. Knopf, 1923.

The Complete Works of Friedrich Nietzsche: The Birth of Tragedy. Edited by Oscar Levy. Translated by Wm. A. Haussmann, Ph.D. Vol. 1. Edinburgh and London: T. N. Foulis, 1910.

The Complete Works of Friedrich Nietzsche: Early Greek Philosophy & Other Essays. Edited by Oscar Levy. Translated by Maximilian A. Mügge. Vol. 2. Edinburgh and London: T. N. Foulis, 1911.

The Complete Works of Friedrich Nietzsche: Ecce Homo. Edited by Oscar Levy. Translated by Anthony M. Ludovici. Vol. 17. Edinburgh and London: T. N. Foulis, 1911.

The Complete Works of Friedrich Nietzsche: Human, All Too Human, Part I. Edited by Oscar Levy. Translated by Helen Zimmern. Vol. 6. New York: T. N. Foulis, 1909.

The Complete Works of Friedrich Nietzsche: The Genealogy of Morals. Edited by Oscar Levy. Translated by Horace B. Samuel, M.A. Vol. 8. Edinburgh London, UK: T. N. Foulis, 1913.

The Complete Works of Friedrich Nietzsche: The Joyful Wisdom. Edited by Oscar Levy. Translated by Thomas Common. Vol. 6. Edinburgh London: T. N. Foulis, 1910.

The Complete Works of Friedrich Nietzsche: The Twilight of the Idols. Edited by Oscar Levy. Translated by Anthony M. Ludovici. Vol. 16. Edinburgh London, UK: T. N. Foulis, 1911.

The Complete Works of Friedrich Nietzsche: The Will To Power, Books I and II. Edited by Oscar Levy. Translated by Anthony M. Ludovici. Vol. 14. Edinburgh and London: T. N. Foulis, 1914.

The Complete Works of Friedrich Nietzsche: The Will To Power, Books III and IV. Edited by Oscar Levy. Translated by Anthony M. Ludovici. Vol. 17. Edinburgh and London: T. N. Foulis, 1913.

The Complete Works of Friedrich Nietzsche: Thoughts out of Season, Part 1: Richard Wagner in Bayreuth. Edited by Oscar Levy. Translated by Anthony M. Ludovici. Vol. 4. Edinburgh and London: T. N. Foulis, 1910.

The Complete Works of Friedrich Nietzsche: Thoughts out of Season, Part II: The Use and Abuse of History for Life. Edited by Oscar Levy. Translated by Adrian Collins, M.A. Vol. 5. Edinburgh and London: T. N. Foulis, 1909.

The Dawn of Day. Translated by John M. Kennedy, London: George Allen & Unwin LTD, 1911.

The Will To Power. Translated by Walter Kaufmann and R. J. Hollingdale, New York: Random House, 1989.

Thus Spoke Zarathustra. Translated by Adrian Del Caro, Cambridge New York: Cambridge University Press, 2006.

Thus Spoke Zarathustra. Translated by R J. Hollingdale, Harmondsworth, England; New York: Penguin Books, 1969.

Thus Spake Zarathustra, Translated by Thomas Common. Edinburgh and London: T. N. Foulis, 1909.

Unpublished Writings from the Period of Unfashionable Observations. Translated by Richard T. Gray, Stanford, California: Stanford University Press, 1999.

Notes

[1] Nietzsche, Friedrich. *The Complete Works of Friedrich Nietzsche: Ecce Homo*. Edited by Oscar Levy. Translated by Anthony M. Ludovici. Vol. 17. Edinburgh London, UK: T. N. Foulis, 1911, p. 56.

[2] Nietzsche, Friedrich. *The Complete Works of Friedrich Nietzsche: The Genealogy of Morals*. Edited by Oscar Levy. Translated by Horace B. Samuel, M.A. Vol. 8. Edinburgh London, UK: T. N. Foulis, 1913, p. 12.

[3] Nietzsche, Friedrich. *Human, All-Too-Human, Part II*. Translated by Paul V. Cohn. New York: The MacMillan Company, 1913, p. 9.

[4] Nietzsche, Friedrich. *Thus Spoke Zarathustra*. Translated by Adrian Del Caro, Cambridge New York: Cambridge University Press, 2006, p. 127.

[5] Nietzsche, Friedrich. *The Complete Works of Friedrich Nietzsche: Early Greek Philosophy*. Vol. 2. Translated by Maximilian A. Mugge, New York: The MacMillan Company, 1911, p. 75.

[6] Nietzsche, Friedrich. *The Complete Works of Friedrich Nietzsche: The Joyful Wisdom*. Edited by Oscar Levy. Translated by Thomas Common. Vol. 6. Edinburgh London: T. N. Foulis, 1910, pp. 5-6.

[7] Nietzsche, Friedrich. *The Dawn of Day*. Translated by John McFarland Kennedy. New York: The MacMillan Company, 1911, pp. 394-395.

[8] Nietzsche, Friedrich. *The Complete Works of Friedrich Nietzsche: Ecce Homo*. Edited by Oscar Levy. Translated by

Anthony M. Ludovici. Vol. 17. Edinburgh and London: T. N. Foulis, 1911, pp. 119-120.

[9] Nietzsche, Friedrich. *The Complete Works of Friedrich Nietzsche: The Will To Power, Books III and IV*. Edited by Oscar Levy. Translated by Anthony M. Ludovici. Vol. 17. Edinburgh and London: T. N. Foulis, 1913, p. 422.

[10] Ibid., p. 423.

[11] Nietzsche, Friedrich. *The Complete Works of Friedrich Nietzsche: Thoughts out of Season, Part 1: Richard Wagner in Bayreuth*. Edited by Oscar Levy. Translated by Anthony M. Ludovici. Vol. 4. Edinburgh and London: T. N. Foulis, 1910, pp. 172-173.

[12] Nietzsche, Friedrich. *The Complete Works of Friedrich Nietzsche: Ecce Homo*. Edited by Oscar Levy. Translated by Anthony M. Ludovici. Vol. 17. Edinburgh London, UK: T. N. Foulis, 1911, p. 74.

[13] Nietzsche, Friedrich. *The Complete Works of Friedrich Nietzsche: Thoughts out of Season, Part 1: Richard Wagner in Bayreuth*. Edited by Oscar Levy. Translated by Anthony M. Ludovici. Vol. 4. Edinburgh and London: T. N. Foulis, 1910, p. 173.

[14] Nietzsche, Friedrich. *The Complete Works of Friedrich Nietzsche: The Genealogy of Morals*. Edited by Oscar Levy. Translated by Horace B. Samuel, M.A. Vol. 8. Edinburgh London, UK: T. N. Foulis, 1913, pp. 99-102.

[15] Nietzsche, Friedrich. *The Complete Works of Friedrich Nietzsche: Ecce Homo*. Edited by Oscar Levy. Translated by Anthony M. Ludovici. Vol. 17. Edinburgh and London: T. N. Foulis, 1911, p. 93.

[16] Ibid., p. 117.

[17] Nietzsche, Friedrich. *The Complete Works of Friedrich Nietzsche: The Will To Power, Books III and IV*. Edited by Oscar Levy. Translated by Anthony M. Ludovici. Vol. 17. Edinburgh and London: T. N. Foulis, 1913, p. 428.

[18] Nietzsche, Friedrich. *The Complete Works of Friedrich Nietzsche: The Genealogy of Morals*. Edited by Oscar Levy. Translated by Horace B. Samuel, M.A. Vol. 8. Edinburgh London, UK: T. N. Foulis, 1913, p. 106.

[19] Ibid., p. 102.

[20] Nietzsche, Friedrich. *The Dawn of Day*. Translated by John

M. Kennedy, London: George Allen & Unwin LTD, 1911, p. 2.

[21] Ibid.

[22] Ibid., pp. 1-2.Nietzsche, Friedrich Wilhelm and Thomas Common. *Thus Spake Zarathustra: Zarathustra's Prologue, §2.* New York: Modern Library, 1917, p. 6. Revised.

[23] Nietzsche, Friedrich. *The Dawn of Day.* Translated by John M. Kennedy, London: George Allen & Unwin LTD, 1911, p. 2.

[24] Nietzsche, Friedrich. *The Complete Works of Friedrich Nietzsche: The Will To Power, Books I and II.* Edited by Oscar Levy. Translated by Anthony M. Ludovici. Vol. 14. Edinburgh and London: T. N. Foulis, 1914, p. 162.

[25] Nietzsche, Friedrich. *The Complete Works of Friedrich Nietzsche: The Will To Power, Books III and IV.* Edited by Oscar Levy. Translated by Anthony M. Ludovici. Vol. 17. Edinburgh and London: T. N. Foulis, 1913, p. 386.

[26] Nietzsche, Friedrich. *The Anti-Christ.* Translated by H. L. Mencken, New York: Alfred A. Knopf, Inc, 1923, pp. 43-44.

[27] Ibid. p. 44.

[28] Nietzsche, Friedrich. *The Complete Works of Friedrich Nietzsche: The Will to Power, Book III and IV.* Translated by Anthony M. Ludovici, Edinburgh and London: T. N. Foulis, 1913, p. 153.

[29] Ibid. p. 215.

[30] Ibid. p. 386.

[31] Nietzsche, Friedrich. *The Complete Works of Friedrich Nietzsche: Ecce Homo.* Edited by Oscar Levy. Translated by Anthony M. Ludovici. Vol. 17. Edinburgh London, UK: T. N. Foulis, 1911, p. 4.

[32]Nietzsche, Friedrich. *The Complete Works of Friedrich Nietzsche: Thoughts out of Season, Part 1: Richard Wagner in Bayreuth.* Edited by Oscar Levy. Translated by Anthony M. Ludovici. Vol. 4. Edinburgh and London: T. N. Foulis, 1910, pp. 167-168.

[33] Nietzsche, Friedrich Wilhelm and Thomas Common. Thus Spake Zarathustra. New York: Modern Library, 1917, pp. 41-42. Revised.

[34] Nietzsche, Friedrich. *The Complete Works of Friedrich*

Nietzsche: Thoughts out of Season, Part 1: Richard Wagner in Bayreuth. Edited by Oscar Levy. Translated by Anthony M. Ludovici. Vol. 4. Edinburgh and London: T. N. Foulis, 1910, pp. 61-62.

[35] Ibid., p. 168.

[36] Nietzsche, Friedrich. *The Complete Works of Friedrich Nietzsche: The Will To Power, Books III and IV.* Edited by Oscar Levy. Translated by Anthony M. Ludovici. Vol. 17. Edinburgh and London: T. N. Foulis, 1913, p. 107.

[37] Nietzsche, Friedrich. *The Complete Works of Friedrich Nietzsche: The Birth of Tragedy.* Edited by Oscar Levy. Translated by Wm. A. Haussmann, Ph.D. Vol. 1. Edinburgh and London: T. N. Foulis, 1910, p. 25.

[38] Ibid., p. 73.

[39] Nietzsche, Friedrich. *Human, All-Too-Human, Part II.* Translated by Paul V. Cohn. New York: The MacMillan Company, 1913, p. 9.

[40]Nietzsche, Friedrich, and Graham Parkes. *The Journal of Nietzsche Studies: Mood, Music, and the Subject.* Autumn ed., vol. 2, Penn State University Press, 1991, pp. 5-10. Copyright © 1991 Penn State University Press. This article is used by permission of The Pennsylvania State University Press.

[41] Nietzsche, Friedrich. *The Complete Works of Friedrich Nietzsche: Early Greek Philosophy.* Vol. 2. Translated by Maximilian A. Mugge. New York: The MacMillan Company, 1911, pp. 29-30.

[42] Nietzsche, Friedrich. *The Complete Works of Friedrich Nietzsche: Ecce Homo.* Edited by Oscar Levy. Translated by Anthony M. Ludovici. Vol. 17. Edinburgh London, UK: T. N. Foulis, 1911, p. 97.

[43] Nietzsche, Friedrich. *The Complete Works of Friedrich Nietzsche: Thoughts out of Season, Part 1: Richard Wagner in Bayreuth.* Edited by Oscar Levy. Translated by Anthony M. Ludovici. Vol. 4. Edinburgh and London: T. N. Foulis, 1910, p. 181.

[44] Ibid., p. 132.

[45] Nietzsche, Friedrich. *The Complete Works of Friedrich Nietzsche: Early Greek Philosophy.* Vol. 2. Translated by Maximilian A. Mugge. New York: The MacMillan Company, 1911, p. 31.

⁴⁶ Nietzsche, Friedrich. *The Complete Works of Friedrich Nietzsche: Early Greek Philosophy*. Vol. 2. Translated by Maximilian A. Mugge. New York: The MacMillan Company, 1911, p. 32.

⁴⁷ Nietzsche, Friedrich. *The Complete Works of Friedrich Nietzsche: Ecce Homo*. Edited by Oscar Levy. Translated by Anthony M. Ludovici. Vol. 17. Edinburgh London, UK: T. N. Foulis, 1911, p. 108.

⁴⁸ Nietzsche, Friedrich. *Das griechische Musikdrama; The Greek Music Drama*. Translated by Paul Bishop, New York: Contra Mundum Press, 2013, p. 32.

⁴⁹ Nietzsche, Friedrich. *The Complete Works of Friedrich Nietzsche: Ecce Homo*. Edited by Oscar Levy. Translated by Anthony M. Ludovici. Vol. 17. Edinburgh London, UK: T. N. Foulis, 1911, pp. 63-64.

⁵⁰Nietzsche, Friedrich. *The Complete Works of Friedrich Nietzsche: Thoughts out of Season, Part 1: Richard Wagner in Bayreuth.* Edited by Oscar Levy. Translated by Anthony M. Ludovici. Vol. 4. Edinburgh and London: T. N. Foulis, 1910, pp. 181-182.

⁵² Ibid., pp. 183-184.

⁵³ Nietzsche, Friedrich. *The Complete Works of Friedrich Nietzsche: Ecce Homo*. Edited by Oscar Levy. Translated by Anthony M. Ludovici. Vol. 17. Edinburgh London, UK: T. N. Foulis, 1911, p. 57.

⁵⁴ Nietzsche, Friedrich. *The Complete Works of Friedrich Nietzsche: Early Greek Philosophy*. Vol. 2. Translated by Maximilian A. Mugge, New York: The MacMillan Company, 1911, pp. 87-88.

⁵⁵ Ibid., pp. 110-111.

⁵⁶ Nietzsche, Friedrich. *The Complete Works of Friedrich Nietzsche: The Will To Power, Books I and II*. Edited by Oscar Levy. Translated by Anthony M. Ludovici. Vol. 14. Edinburgh and London: T. N. Foulis, 1914, p. 162.

⁵⁷ Nietzsche, Friedrich. *The Complete Works of Friedrich Nietzsche: Human, All-Too-Human, Part I*. Edited by Oscar Levy. Translated by Helen Zimmern. Vol. 6. New York: T. N. Foulis, 1909, p. 177.

⁵⁸ Nietzsche, Friedrich. *The Complete Works of Friedrich*

Nietzsche: Ecce Homo. Edited by Oscar Levy. Translated by
Anthony M. Ludovici. Vol. 17. Edinburgh London, UK: T. N.
Foulis, 1911, p. 57.

[59] Nietzsche, Friedrich. *The Complete Works of Friedrich
Nietzsche: The Joyful Wisdom*. Edited by Oscar Levy. Translated by
Thomas Common. Vol. 6. Edinburgh London: T. N. Foulis, 1910, p.
336.

[60] Ibid., pp. 348-349.

[61] Ibid., pp. 258-259.

[62] Nietzsche, Friedrich. *Unpublished Writings from the Period
of* Unfashionable Observations. Translated by Richard T. Gray,
Stanford, California: Stanford University Press, 1999, p. 45.

[63] Nietzsche, Friedrich. *The Complete Works of Friedrich
Nietzsche: The Genealogy of Morals*. Edited by Oscar Levy.
Translated by Horace B. Samuel, M.A. Vol. 8. Edinburgh London,
UK: T. N. Foulis, 1913, pp. 12-13.

[64] Nietzsche, Friedrich. *Human, All-Too-Human, Part II*.
Translated by Paul V. Cohn. New York: The MacMillan
Company, 1913, p. 243.

[65] Nietzsche, Friedrich. *The Complete Works of Friedrich
Nietzsche: The Birth of Tragedy*. Edited by Oscar Levy. Translated
by Wm. A. Haussmann, Ph.D. Vol. 1. Edinburgh and London: T. N.
Foulis, 1910, p. 45.

[66] Ibid., p. 46.

[67] Ibid., pp. 44-45.

[68] Ibid., pp. 46-47.

[69] Ibid., p. 2.

[70] Ibid.

[71] Ibid., pp. 6-7.

[72] Nietzsche, Friedrich Wilhelm and Thomas Common. *Thus
Spake Zarathustra: The New Idol*. New York: Modern Library,
1917, p. 52. Revised.

[73] Ibid., *Of Self-Overcoming*, p. 125.

[74] Nietzsche, Friedrich. *The Complete Works of Friedrich
Nietzsche: The Will To Power, Books III and IV*. Edited by Oscar
Levy. Translated by Anthony M. Ludovici. Vol. 17. Edinburgh and
London: T. N. Foulis, 1913, p. 18.

[75] Nietzsche, Friedrich Wilhelm and Thomas Common. *Thus
Spake Zarathustra: The Convalescent*. New York: Modern

Library, 1917, p. 248. Revised.

[76] Ibid., pp. 241-242. Revised.

[77] "In place of 'metaphysics' and religion, the doctrine of *Eternal Recurrence* (being regarded as a means to the breeding and selection of men)." Nietzsche, Friedrich. *The Complete Works of Friedrich Nietzsche: The Will To Power, Books I and II*. Edited by Oscar Levy. Translated by Anthony M. Ludovici. Vol. 14. Edinburgh and London: T. N. Foulis, 1914, p. 381.

[78] *Nietzsche, Friedrich. The Complete Works of Friedrich Nietzsche: The Will To Power, Books III and IV. Edited by Oscar Levy. Translated by Anthony M. Ludovici. Vol. 17. Edinburgh and London: T. N. Foulis, 1913, p. 423.*

[79] Ibid., p. 428.

[80] Nietzsche, Friedrich. *The Complete Works of Friedrich Nietzsche: Thoughts out of Season, Part 1: Richard Wagner in Bayreuth.* Edited by Oscar Levy. Translated by Anthony M. Ludovici. Vol. 4. Edinburgh and London: T. N. Foulis, 1910, p. 193.

[81] Ibid., pp. 172-173.

[82] Nietzsche, Friedrich. *The Complete Works of Friedrich Nietzsche: The Twilight of the Idols*. Edited by Oscar Levy. Translated by Anthony M. Ludovici. Vol. 16. Edinburgh London, UK: T. N. Foulis, 1911, p. 108.

[83] Nietzsche, Friedrich Wilhelm and Thomas Common. *Thus Spake Zarathustra: Of the Vision and the Riddle*. New York: Modern Library, 1917, p. 175-176. Revised.

[84] Ibid., *Of Manly Prudence*, p. 156. Revised.

[85] Ibid., *Of the Spirit of Gravity*, p. 214. Revised.

[86] Nietzsche, Friedrich. *The Complete Works of Friedrich Nietzsche: The Birth of Tragedy.* Edited by Oscar Levy. Translated by Wm. A. Haussmann, Ph.D. Vol. 1. Edinburgh and London: T. N. Foulis, 1910, p. 25.

[87] Ibid., p. 157..

[88] Ibid., p. 116.

[89] Ibid., p. 105.

[90] Ibid., p. 98.

[91] Nietzsche, Friedrich Wilhelm and Thomas Common. *Thus Spake Zarathustra: Of Joys and Passions*. New York: Modern Library, 1917, p. 34. Revised.

[92] Nietzsche, Friedrich. *The Complete Works of Friedrich Nietzsche: Early Greek Philosophy & Other Essays.* Edited by Oscar Levy. Translated by Maximilian A. Mügge. Vol. 2. Edinburgh and London: T. N. Foulis, 1911, p. 90.

[93] Nietzsche, Friedrich. *The Complete Works of Friedrich Nietzsche: Thoughts out of Season, Part II: The Use and Abuse of History for Life.* Edited by Oscar Levy. Translated by Adrian Collins, M.A. Vol. 5. Edinburgh and London: T. N. Foulis, 1909, p. 9.

[94] "The stronger the roots of a human being's innermost nature, the more of the past he will assimilate or forcibly appropriate; and the most powerful, most mighty nature would be characterized by the fact that there would be no limit at which its historical sensibility would have a stifling and harmful effect; it would appropriate and incorporate into itself all that is past, what is its own as well as what is alien, transforming it, as it were, into its own blood." Nietzsche, Friedrich. *Unfashionable Observations: On the Utility and Liability of History for Life.* Translated by Richard T. Gray, Stanford, California: Stanford University Press, 1995, p. 90.

[95] Nietzsche, Friedrich Wilhelm and Thomas Common. *Thus Spake Zarathustra: Before Sunrise.* New York: Modern Library, 1917, p. 184. Revised.

[96] Nietzsche, Friedrich. *The Complete Works of Friedrich Nietzsche: The Will To Power, Books III and IV.* Edited by Oscar Levy. Translated by Anthony M. Ludovici. Vol. 17. Edinburgh and London: T. N. Foulis, 1913, p. 371.

[97] Ibid., p. 386.

[98] Nietzsche, Friedrich. *The Anti-Christ.* Translated by H. L. Mencken, New York: Alfred A. Knopf, 1923, p. 43.

[99] Ibid., p. 44.

[100] Nietzsche, Friedrich. *The Complete Works of Friedrich Nietzsche: The Will To Power, Books III and IV.* Edited by Oscar Levy. Translated by Anthony M. Ludovici. Vol. 17. Edinburgh and London: T. N. Foulis, 1913, p. 153.

[101] Ibid., p. 215.

[102] Ibid., p. 386.

[103] Nietzsche, Friedrich. *The Complete Works of Friedrich Nietzsche: Early Greek Philosophy & Other Essays.* Edited by Oscar Levy. Translated by Maximilian A. Mügge. Vol. 2.

Edinburgh and London: T. N. Foulis, 1911, p. 126.

[104] Ibid., pp. 98-100.

[105] Ibid., pp. 130-132.

[106] Ibid., p. 132.

[107] Ibid., pp. 132-133.

[108] Nietzsche, Friedrich Wilhelm and Thomas Common. *Thus Spake Zarathustra: Zarathustra's Prologue, §1*. New York: Modern Library, 1917, p. 3. Revised.

[109] Ibid., *The Convalescent*, pp. 241-242. Revised.

[110] Ibid., p. 248. Revised.

[111] Ibid., *Zarathustra's Prologue, §1*, p. 20. Revised.

[112] Nietzsche, Friedrich. *The Complete Works of Friedrich Nietzsche: Thoughts out of Season, Part II: The Use and Abuse of History*. Edited by Oscar Levy. Translated by Adrian Collins, M.A. Vol. 5. Edinburgh and London: T. N. Foulis, 1909, pp. 6-7.

[113] Nietzsche, Friedrich Wilhelm and Thomas Common. *Thus Spake Zarathustra: Zarathustra's Prologue, §3*. New York: Modern Library, 1917, pp. 7-8. Revised.

[114] Ibid., p. 9. Revised.

[115] Ibid., p. 11. Revised.

[116] Ibid., Revised.

[117] Ibid., p. 12. Revised

[118] Nietzsche, Friedrich. *The Complete Works of Friedrich Nietzsche: The Birth of Tragedy*. Edited by Oscar Levy. Translated by Wm. A. Haussmann, Ph.D. Vol. 1. Edinburgh and London: T. N. Foulis, 1910, p. 14.

[119] Nietzsche, Friedrich. *The Complete Works of Friedrich Nietzsche: Thoughts out of Season, Part 1: Richard Wagner in Bayreuth*. Edited by Oscar Levy. Translated by Anthony M. Ludovici. Vol. 4. Edinburgh and London: T. N. Foulis, 1910, p. 173.

[120] Nietzsche, Friedrich Wilhelm and Thomas Common. *Thus Spake Zarathustra: Zarathustra's Prologue, §6*. New York: Modern Library, 1917, pp. 13. Revised.

[121] Nietzsche, Friedrich. *The Complete Works of Friedrich Nietzsche: The Twilight of the Idols*. Edited by Oscar Levy. Translated by Anthony M. Ludovici. Vol. 16. Edinburgh London, UK: T. N. Foulis, 1911, pp. 24-25.

[122] Nietzsche, Friedrich Wilhelm and Thomas Common.

Thus Spake Zarathustra: Zarathustra's Prologue, §9. New York: Modern Library, 1917, pp. 17. Revised.

[123] Ibid., Revised.

[124] Ibid., *§10*, p. 18. Revised.

[125] Ibid., p. 19. Revised.

[126] Ibid., Revised.

[127] Nietzsche, Friedrich. *The Complete Works of Friedrich Nietzsche: Human, All-Too-Human, Part I.* Edited by Oscar Levy. Translated by Helen Zimmern. Vol. 6. New York: T. N. Foulis, 1909, pp. 393-394.

[128] Nietzsche, Friedrich Wilhelm and Thomas Common. *Thus Spake Zarathustra: Of the Presiding Teachers of Virtue,* New York: Modern Library, 1917, p. 26. Revised.

[129] Nietzsche, Friedrich. *The Complete Works of Friedrich Nietzsche: Human, All-Too-Human, Part I.* Edited by Oscar Levy. Translated by Helen Zimmern. Vol. 6. New York: T. N. Foulis, 1909, pp. 392-393.

[130] Nietzsche, Friedrich Wilhelm and Thomas Common. *Thus Spake Zarathustra: Of the Spirit of Gravity,* New York: Modern Library, 1917, p. 216. Revised.

[131] Ibid., *Zarathustra's Prologue, §3,* p. 6. Revised

[132] Ibid., *Of the Three Metamorphoses,* p. 23. Revised.

[133] Ibid., *Of Those Who Seek the Metaphysical Worlds,* p. 29. Revised.

[134] Ibid. Revised.

[135] Ibid. Revised.

[136] Ibid., p. 30. Revised.

[137] Ibid., p. 32. Revised.

[138] Ibid., pp. 33-34. Revised.

[139] Ibid., *Of Joys and Passions,* p. 34. Revised.

[140] Ibid., p. 35. Revised

[141] Ibid. Revised.

[142] Ibid. Revised.

[143] Ibid., p. 36. Revised.

[144] Nietzsche, Friedrich. *The Complete Works of Friedrich Nietzsche: The Twilight of the Idols.* Edited by Oscar Levy. Translated by Anthony M. Ludovici. Vol. 16. Edinburgh London, UK: T. N. Foulis, 1911, pp. 103-106.

[145] Nietzsche, Friedrich Wilhelm and Thomas Common. *Thus*

Spake Zarathustra: Of the Pale Criminal, New York: Modern Library, 1917, p. 36. Revised.

[146] Ibid., p. 37. Revised.

[147] Ibid., *Of Reading and Writing*, p. 39. Revised.

[148] Ibid.

[149] Ibid., *Of the Tree on the Mountainside*, p. 41. Revised.

[150] Ibid., p. 42. Revised

[151] Ibid., p. 42. Revised.

[152] Ibid., *Of the Preachers of Death*, p. 44. Revised

[153] Ibid., pp. 44-45. Revised.

[154] Ibid.. p.45. Revised.

[155] Ibid.

[156] Ibid., p. 46. Revised.

[157] Ibid.

[158] Ibid., *Of the New Idol*, p. 49. Revised.

[159] Ibid., p. 52. Revised.

[160] Ibid., p. 52. Revised.

[161] Ibid., p. 50. Revised.

[162] Ibid., *Of the Flies of the Marketplace*, p. 52. Revised.

[163] Ibid.

[164] Ibid., *Of Chastity*, p. 56. Revised.

[165] Ibid.

[166] Ibid., p. 57. Revised.

[167] Ibid., *Of the Thousand and One Goals*, p. 60. Revised.

[168] Ibid.

[169] Ibid.

[170] Ibid.

[171] Ibid.

[172] Ibid.

[173] Ibid.

[174] Ibid.

[175] Ibid., pp. 60-61. Revised.

[176] Ibid.

[177] Ibid.

[178] Ibid.

[179] Ibid.

[180] Ibid.

[181] Ibid.

[182] Ibid.

[183] Ibid., pp. 61-62. Revised.
[184] Ibid.
[185] Ibid.
[186] Ibid.
[187] Ibid.
[188] Ibid.
[189] Ibid.
[190] Ibid.
[191] Ibid., *Of Love of One's Neighbor*, p. 63. Revised.
[192] Ibid., p. 64. Revised.
[193] Ibid.
[194] Ibid., *Of the Adder's Bite*, p. 71. Revised.
[195] Ibid.
[196] Ibid., p. 72. Revised.
[197] Ibid., *Of Marriage and Children*, p. 72. Revised.
[198] Ibid., p. 74. Revised.
[199] Ibid., *Of Voluntary Death*, p. 75. Revised.
[200] Ibid.
[201] Ibid.
[202] Ibid., p. 76. Revised.
[203] Ibid., *Of the Bestowing Virtue*, p. 80. Revised.
[204] Ibid.
[205] Ibid.
[206] Ibid.
[207] Ibid.
[208] Ibid.
[209] Ibid., p. 82. Revised.
[210] Ibid., pp. 82-83. Revised.
[211] Ibid., p. 83. Revised.
[212] Ibid.
[213] Ibid., *Of the Sublime Men*, p. 126. Revised.
[214] Ibid., pp. 126-127. Revised.
[215] Ibid., p. 128. Revised.
[216] Ibid., p. 129. Revised.
[217] Ibid., *Of Immaculate Perception*, p. 133. Revised.
[218] Ibid., p. 135. Revised.
[219] Ibid., *Of Great Events*, p. 142. Revised.
[220] Ibid.
[221] Ibid.

[222] Ibid., p. 143. Revised.

[223] Ibid.

[224] Ibid., p. 145. Revised.

[225] Ibid., p. 144. Revised.

[226] Ibid., pp. 144-145. Revised.

[227] Ibid., p. 146. Revised.

[228] Nietzsche, Friedrich. *The Complete Works of Friedrich Nietzsche: Thoughts out of Season, Part 1: Richard Wagner in Bayreuth.* Edited by Oscar Levy. Translated by Anthony M. Ludovici. Vol. 4. Edinburgh and London: T. N. Foulis, 1910, p. 193.

[229] Nietzsche, Friedrich Wilhelm and Thomas Common. *Thus Spake Zarathustra: Of the Soothsayer*, New York: Modern Library, 1917, p. 146. Revised.

[230] Ibid., pp. 147. Revised.

[231] Ibid., p. 148. Revised.

[232] Ibid., p. 149. Revised.

[233] Ibid., *The Stillest Hour*, p. 160. Revised.

[234] Ibid.

[235] Ibid., p. 162. Revised.

[236] Ibid., *The Wanderer*, p. 167. Revised.

[237] Nietzsche, Friedrich. *The Complete Works of Friedrich Nietzsche: The Will To Power, Books I and II.* Edited by Oscar Levy. Translated by Anthony M. Ludovici. Vol. 14. Edinburgh and London: T. N. Foulis, 1914, p. 36.

[238] Nietzsche, Friedrich Wilhelm and Thomas Common. *Thus Spake Zarathustra: The Wanderer*, New York: Modern Library, 1917, pp. 167-168. Revised.

[239] Ibid., pp. 169. Revised.

[240] Ibid.

[241] Ibid., *Of the Vision and the Riddle*, p. 175. Revised.

[242] Nietzsche, Friedrich. *The Complete Works of Friedrich Nietzsche: The Joyful Wisdom.* Edited by Oscar Levy. Translated by Thomas Common. Vol. 6. Edinburgh London: T. N. Foulis, 1910, p. 244.

[243] Nietzsche, Friedrich Wilhelm and Thomas Common. *Thus Spake Zarathustra: Of the Vision and the Riddle*, New York: Modern Library, 1917, p. 175. Revised.

[244] Ibid.

[245] Ibid., pp. 175-176. Revised.

[246] Ibid.

[247] Ibid., pp. 173-174. Revised.

[248] Nietzsche, Friedrich. *The Complete Works of Friedrich Nietzsche: The Genealogy of Morals*. Edited by Oscar Levy. Translated by Horace B. Samuel, M.A. Vol. 8. Edinburgh London, UK: T. N. Foulis, 1913, p.106.

[249] Ibid., pp. 101-102.

[250] Nietzsche, Friedrich Wilhelm and Thomas Common. *Thus Spake Zarathustra: Of Manly Prudence*, New York: Modern Library, 1917, p. 156.

[251] Ibid., *Of the Vision and the Riddle,* pp. 175-176. Revised.

[252] Ibid., p. 176. Revised.

[253] Ibid.

[254] Ibid., *Of the Spirit of Gravity*, p. 214. Revised.

[255] Ibid,

[256] Ibid., *Of Reading and Writing*, pp. 40-41. Revised.

[257] Ibid., *Of the Convalescent*, pp.241-242. Revised.

[258] Ibid., p. 246. Revised.

[259] Ibid., p. 242. Revised.

[260] Ibid., pp. 247-248. Revised.

[261] Ibid., p. 248.

[262] Ibid.

[263] Ibid., *Of the Vision and the Riddle*, pp. 173. Revised.

[264] Nietzsche, Friedrich. *The Complete Works of Friedrich Nietzsche: The Genealogy of Morals*. Edited by Oscar Levy. Translated by Horace B. Samuel, M.A. Vol. 8. Edinburgh London, UK: T. N. Foulis, 1913, p. 104.

[265] Nietzsche, Friedrich Wilhelm and Thomas Common. *Thus Spake Zarathustra: Of the Great Longing*, New York: Modern Library, 1917, p. 249. Revised.

[266] Ibid., pp. 249-250. Revised.

[267] Ibid., p. 250. Revised.

[268] Ibid., *Zarathustra's Prologue, 1*, p. 39.

[269] Ibid., p. 251. Revised.

[270] Ibid., p. 347. Revised.

[271] Ibid.

[272] Nietzsche, Friedrich. *The Complete Works of Friedrich Nietzsche: The Joyful Wisdom*. Edited by Oscar Levy. Translated by

Thomas Common. Vol. 6. Edinburgh London: T. N. Foulis, 1910, pp. 265-266.

[273] Nietzsche, Friedrich. *The Will To Power*. Translated by Walter Kaufmann and R J. Hollingdale, New York: Random House, 1989, p. 507.

[274] Nietzsche, Friedrich. *The Complete Works of Friedrich Nietzsche: The Will To Power, Books III and IV*. Edited by Oscar Levy. Translated by Anthony M. Ludovici. Vol. 17. Edinburgh and London: T. N. Foulis, 1913, p. 370.

[275] Nietzsche, Friedrich Wilhelm and Thomas Common. *Thus Spake Zarathustra: The Sign*, New York: Modern Library, 1917, p.p. 368. Revised.

[276] Nietzsche, Friedrich. *The Complete Works of Friedrich Nietzsche: The Joyful Wisdom*. Edited by Oscar Levy. Translated by Thomas Common. Vol. 6. Edinburgh London: T. N. Foulis, 1910, pp. 267-268.

[277] Nietzsche, Friedrich. *The Anti-Christ*. Translated by H. L. Mencken. New York: Alfred A. Knopf, 1923. p. 105.

Afterword

Thanks to a certain children's charity in Boston, whose name I omit here (but not elsewhere) for no other reason than to spare my printer any liability. Their people did everything they could to destroy me, with their vast and mighty power — continuously, throughout my *entire* life, beginning in 1963 when I was a small boy, age 11, when they inflicted horrific indecencies upon my body, and left my soul dismembered, with its parts scattered hopelessly far and wide. Confident that they had destroyed me (which they verified, if you can imagine that) and that I would never be able to speak about what they had done to me, they simply walked away, condemning me to suffer, day in and day out, with unrelenting demons — *eternally*.

However, neither one of us knew back then what I know now.

> "[A Dionysian] cut into pieces is a promise of Life: [because he] will be forever born anew, and rise afresh from destruction."*

And sure enough, I willed the scattered pieces back together, overcame dismemberment, and rose afresh from the eternal condemnation they wrought upon me. And when I set out to make them accountable for what they had done, they set out to finish what they had started — and proved themselves as evil as Evil will ever achieve on this good Earth.

And then, continuing well into my old age, when I set out to teach others what I had learned about the redemption of human suffering and this place within the heart and mind of man that is called heaven on earth, they recruited corporate America and the City of London to stop me. And they succeeded. Thus, I am my own publisher.

In all my life, I never faced a more formidable, enduring, or resourceful foe. Indeed, they were the best enemy that a robust Dionysian could have hoped for.

My thanks to them for providing the hardship that my teacher wished upon me for his success and mine.

> "To those human beings who are of any concern to me I wish suffering, desolation, sickness, ill-treatment, indignities — I wish that they should not remain unfamiliar with profound self-contempt, the torture of self-mistrust, **the wretchedness of the vanquished**: I have no pity for them, because I wish them the only thing that can prove today whether one is worth anything or not — that one endures."
>
> *Friedrich Nietzsche

They proved me very worthy. And for that I will

always be grateful. And not just me.